RETHINKING SORROW

Michigan Monograph Series in Japanese Studies
Number 6

Center for Japanese Studies
The University of Michigan

RETHINKING SORROW

SORROW

REVELATORY TALES OF LATE MEDIEVAL JAPAN

by

MARGARET HELEN CHILDS

Ann Arbor
Center for Japanese Studies
The University of Michigan
1991

© 1991

by

Center for Japanese Studies
The University of Michigan
108 Lane Hall
Ann Arbor, MI 48109–1290

Library of Congress Cataloging-in-Publication Data

Childs, Margaret Helen.
  Rethinking sorrow : revelatory tales of late medieval Japan / by
Margaret Helen Childs.
      p. cm.—(Michigan monograph series in Japanese studies :
no. 6).
    Includes bibliographical references (p.)
    ISBN 0–939512–42–4
    1. Japanese fiction—1185–1600—Translations into English.
    2. English fiction—Translations from Japanese. I. Title.
    II. Series.
    PL782.E8C45 1990
    895.6'32408—dc20   89–25394
                                                                          CIP

A Note on the Type

This book is set in Goudy Old Style. Frederic W. Goudy (1865–1947)
designed the family of Old Style fonts to recapture the feeling of Vene-
tian and French Renaissance typography. His work was a link between
the ideals of the Arts and Crafts Movement and everyday printers.
Goudy's 122 typeface designs made him the most prolific American type
designer.

Composed by Typographic Insight, Ltd., Ann Arbor, Michigan
Index by AEIOU, Inc., Pleasantville, New York
Printed and bound by BookCrafters, Chelsea, Michigan
Book design by Lisa Jacobs

∞

The paper used in this publication meets the requirements of the ANSI
Standard Z39.48–1984 (Permanence of Paper).

Printed in the United States of America

for Barbara Ruch

Contents

Preface

When applied to Japanese history, the term "medieval" has traditionally referred to the Kamakura (1185–1333) and Muromachi (1333–1573) periods. This periodization, however, is based on political events that can be pinpointed precisely. Cultural developments, on the other hand, evolve gradually. Religious beliefs, for example, are not often immediately influenced by changes in political leadership. In considering literary phenomena, periodization usually refers to the date when a text was written, compiled, or published. The times during which that text was widely read, however, may differ from when it first came into being and in certain ways may be the more relevant question.

Two of the tales treated here are Muromachi-period products, while the only extant texts of the other two tales date to the first decades of the Tokugawa or Edo (1600–1868) period. The designation "late medieval" in the title of this book is intentionally vague, being an attempt to refer to the Muromachi period plus the early years of the Edo period before the political and economic developments of that time stimulated very much cultural change.

Religious terms also present something of a problem. A wide variety of Japanese religious ranks are usually subsumed under the English "priest." Worse than the merging of categories that this practice causes, however, is the misleading connotation of the word "priest." Leaving the problem of finer distinctions aside, I have chosen to translate such terms as *hōshi*, *nyūdō*, and *hōin* as "monk" in order to emphasize the aspect of Buddhist *saṃgha*, or clerical community, membership in which, however tenuous, was central to the consciousness of those who entered its ranks in one form or another. This choice of terminology has the disadvantage of obscuring the fact that many monks also fulfilled priestly duties by performing rituals for the benefit of the laity. Nonetheless, such functions were usually not primary ones. The advantage of my choice of "monk" is its convenient parallel with "nun." Although women were traditionally considered unable to attain Buddhahood in their present existence, men and women were equally encouraged to seek it, and they followed much the same practices in cultivating it. The monks and nuns depicted in the revelatory tales

ix

translated here lived essentially the same kinds of religious lives. I have also used the word "clergy" quite loosely to refer to anyone who had made a religious commitment, whether self-ordained or officially and ceremoniously ordained.

I have often quoted the translations of Japanese texts accomplished by others. Occasionally, however, I have preferred my own translations, in which case I have cited the original text and also directed the reader to see for comparison previously published complete translated versions. In translating the four tales I sometimes added explanatory elements to the texts, sometimes omitted minor obscure details. I retained some metaphors as similes and abandoned some poetic diction as unwieldy. When I felt I was forced to choose between accuracy and readability, I tended toward the latter because it seemed that readability had been a priority in the original texts.

Japanese names have been given in Japanese style, family name first, unless a work has been published in English and the authors themselves use Western name order.

I have not attempted to calculate ages according to the Western system. The Japanese approach to this question is explained when relevant in a note.

This book is an extension of my dissertation, "Religious Awakening Stories in Late Medieval Japan: The Dynamics of Didacticism," submitted and approved at the University of Pennsylvania in 1983. Two stories, *The Tale of Genmu* and *The Seven Nuns*, are found in both, and certain other elements of the dissertation have been retained, but *Rethinking Sorrow* has quite a different focus and purpose. Nevertheless, thanks are due again to the Japan Foundation, which supported my research in Japan, and the University of Pennsylvania, which provided support for a final academic year of writing. Southern Illinois University, where I taught for four years, granted me funds for summer research that allowed me to complete the translation of *Tales Told on Mount Kōya*.

The photos that appear with *The Tale of Genmu* are courtesy of the Geijutsu Shiryōkan of Tōkyō Geijutsu Daigaku and are used with permission. The illustrations for *The Seven Nuns* are from the book *Kinsei bungaku shiryō ruijū, Kanazōshi hen*, volume 10, edited by Kinsei Bungaku Shoshi Kenkyū (Tokyo: Benseisha, 1973).

I would also like to express my gratitude to Barbara Ruch for her wise guidance and warm encouragement over many years. Satake Akihiro first drew my attention to revelatory tales and Okami Masao, Gorai Shigeru, and Tokuda Kazuo all kindly aided me with their expertise. Innumerable discussions with Komei Rikiya helped shape both my interpretations and translations of these tales. Robert Morrell, Susan

Matisoff, Edward Kamens, Fumiko Yamamoto, and Beth Schultz all carefully read and offered important suggestions for improving the manuscript. A great many friends and my family gave crucial moral support. Credit is due to a great many people, but for any deficiencies I reserve personal responsibility.

Abbreviations

C	Chinese
J	Japanese
NKBT	*Nihon koten bungaku taikei.* 100 vols. Tokyo: Iwanami Shoten, 1958–68.
NKD	Nihon Daijiten Kankōkai, ed. *Nihon kokugo daijiten.* 20 vols. Tokyo: Shōgakukan, 1972–76.
Skt	Sanskrit
T	Takakusu Junjirō et al., eds. *Taishō shinshū daizōkyō.* 100 vols. Tokyo: Taishō Issaikyō Kankōkai, 1924–32.

Introduction

"All living things must perish; all that flourishes will wither. This is the way of the world." These opening lines from *The Tale of Genmu* allude to the Buddhist teaching that human suffering is the result of our failure to accept the inevitability of change. By forming attachments to mutable things we virtually invite sorrow into our lives. Neither power, wealth, fame, love, happiness, nor life itself lasts for long. Our very first step on the path to enlightenment is to grasp the fundamental truth that all existence is ephemeral.

This simple lesson was the essential component of the Buddhist world view in medieval Japan (thirteenth through sixteenth centuries). Revelatory tales (*zangemono*), a type of late medieval short story, seek to give this teaching concrete meaning by offering specific examples of painful experiences that inspired religious commitment. Most commonly described is the happiness of love once enjoyed and the tragic events that led to separation from, or death of, a beloved. Religious awakenings also arise from other kinds of emotional loss: from humiliation, betrayal, and from witnessing grossly malicious behavior. Whatever the inspiration, each character in a revelatory tale realizes how mistaken he or she was to trust complacently in continuity, and thus discovers personal meaning in the abstract tenets of Buddhism.

There are many medieval short stories that describe religious awakenings (*hosshindan*), but revelatory tales form a small and specific subgroup of this genre. There are only four extant examples: *The Tale of Genmu*, *Tales Told on Mount Kōya*, *The Three Monks*, and *The Seven Nuns*. While stories of religious awakenings are recounted in the voice of an omniscient third person and focus on one main character, revelatory tales consist of first-hand accounts offered by a group of several monks or nuns who tell their tales in turn. The public sharing of these stories of private realizations is, in fact, a religious ritual by which means the storytellers hope to confirm their beliefs and strengthen their religious resolve. Although "confessional tale" might be an adequate colloquial translation for *zangemono* (also *zange monogatari*), "revelatory tale" seems more appropriate as a literary term insofar as it highlights the fact that the stories represent dual revelations, first private and then public.

1

Revelatory tales reflect the political and social turmoil of Japan's later medieval period, the fifteenth and sixteenth centuries. During most of this time members of the Ashikaga family occupied the highest military/political post, but the control of the Ashikaga shogunate (1338–1573) over upstart regional warlords was only tenuous at best. The turbulence that followed the Ōnin War (1467–77), when fighting raged even in the streets of the capital, was only quieted in the latter part of the sixteenth century with Toyotomi Hideyoshi's (1536–98) sudden rise to national power. Famines and epidemics also caused vast misery during this period. Although revelatory tales were certainly still read in the Tokugawa period (1600–1867) when relative peace and prosperity finally returned to Japan, by the late seventeenth century the new dominant cultural motif was a cheerful indulgence in the pleasures of the moment rather than pessimism about matters of this world and obsessive concern for salvation in the next.

The prestige of political ties with the Ashikaga military government gave Zen Buddhism the highest profile on the religious scene in medieval Japan. Although the great individual figures of the Kamakura period (1185–1333) who proselytized among the masses—Hōnen (1133–1212), Shinran (1173–1262), Nichiren (1222–82), and Ippen (1239–89)—were long dead, the beliefs that they had espoused, especially hope for rebirth in Amida's Pure Land paradise, had spread nationwide. Yet the older Tendai and Shingon schools of Buddhism, founded early in the Heian period, also continued to flourish, competing for adherents by adopting aspects of Pure Land teachings or introducing other timely modifications. While Amidism pervades revelatory tales, the religious authorities most frequently quoted are Kūkai (Kōbō Daishi, 774–835), Saichō (Dengyō Daishi, 767–822), Genshin (942–1017), and the *Lotus Sutra*. Thus the tales reflect a wide-ranging eclecticism comprised of the teachings of Amidism and the doctrine of the traditional Tendai and Shingon schools, plus elements of Zen and folk belief.

The prominent new literary arts in medieval Japan, the Nō drama and *renga* (linked verse), shared with revelatory tales a basic premise, the sad truth of transience. Ironically though, poets and dramatists who celebrated evanescence achieved immortality of a sort by gaining entry to the elite literary canon, while the authors of revelatory tales remained anonymous. Although the Nō drama of Zeami (1363–1443), for example, and the linked verse of Sōgi (1421–1502) have touched generations of readers and scholars, their laments are founded on highly stylized conventions and are couched in well-wrought phrases that bespeak the luxury of patronage. Revelatory tales, on the other hand, are a popular literature written with a frankness and naivete that more compellingly evokes the harsh and troubled times of Japan's medieval period.

Religious Background

While there are various stages in clerical life and varying degrees of clerical status, revelatory tales depict the experiences of men and women who have made only the most basic religious commitment: they have abandoned family ties (*shukke*) and renounced the mundane world (*tonsei*). Their religious awakenings led them to forsake lay life, even though Pure Land teachings encouraged lay practice. However, none of the revelatory tale characters embarked upon any orderly program of religious study, nor were they properly ordained. They did not become officially recognized members of any established institutional hierarchy. Rather, they seem to have acted quite freely and autonomously. Some lived in loosely organized monastic communities such as that on Mount Kōya; others became itinerant pilgrims. Much of their religious activity was directed toward gaining salvation for their deceased loved ones.[1] Their devotional practices earned religious merit that could be dedicated to the benefit of another through prayer. Given the materials and talent, they might also have copied sutras, painted or sculpted sacred images, or constructed shrines. Most, however, apparently simply recited the *nenbutsu*, an invocation of Amida Buddha indicative of one's faith in Amida's vow to grant rebirth in his Western Paradise, a Pure Land, to all believers. The *nenbutsu* originally had been a meditative ritual of philosophical import rather than a literal, oral expression of faith. It undoubtedly retained a meditative effect insofar as continual repetition of the *nenbutsu* thousands of times daily was a common practice.

The prominent mention of *nenbutsu* practice in revelatory tales seems to suggest the influence of Pure Land Buddhism. Although this practice was already one facet of religious ritual in the earlier schools, Pure Land doctrine rejected other practices and advocated sole reliance on Amida through *nenbutsu* invocation. This exclusivity is not to be found in the characters of revelatory tales: they are engaged both in asceticism and in good works. Moreover, the teachings propounded by a former imperial princess in The Seven Nuns are specifically Tendai concepts, and Mount Kōya, the center of the Shingon school, plays an important role in The Tale of Genmu, Tales Told on Mount Kōya and The Three Monks. In all three of these tales the characters are said to be

---

1. See Ichirō Hori, *Folk Religion in Japan* (Chicago: University of Chicago Press, 1968), 83–139, esp. 96–98. See Oliver Statler, *Japanese Pilgrimage* (New York: William Morrow and Company, Inc., 1983) for a partly fictionalized account of the lives of such holy men.

practicing the *nenbutsu* on Mount Kōya and longing for rebirth in Amida's Western Paradise. This may have been Amidist *nenbutsu* practice that had simply infiltrated the Shingon headquarters, or it may have been Shingon *nenbutsu*: Kakuban (1095–1143, founder of Shingi Shingon) asserted that Vairocana (Japanese [hereafter J] *Dainichi*, the central object of Shingon worship) was equivalent to Amida, that his Pure Land Mitsugon was the same as Amida's Western Paradise, and that Shingon mantra should be uttered, especially on one's deathbed, to insure rebirth into the Western Paradise.[2]

In revelatory tales two characters are depicted as spending considerable time on a pilgrimage without specific destination. Their only stated objective was to gain religious instruction. Historically, itinerant monks traveled in order to proselytize, but they also worked as community organizers and civil engineers, doing good deeds by mobilizing people and resources to build needed public works and facilities such as irrigation ponds, bridges, orphanages, and hospitals.[3] In other cases itinerant monks simply offered prayers and performed religious rituals for health and prosperity as they wandered, proselytizing. Some preached sermons and told stories of the origins of temples or of the miraculous benefits of faith as part of their fund-raising appeals.[4] Perhaps more important than the social contribution and interaction afforded by pilgrimaging, however, is the inner journey made by the pilgrim as he or she traverses the countryside. For the seventh of the seven nuns, for example, continuous pilgrimage is in part an ascetic challenge. The goal of this asceticism is to tame the ego that craves physical comfort for the self. A pilgrimage is also an effort to experience Buddhist philosophy directly and concretely: what better reminder that all is transient than a daily change of one's own physical environment?[5]

The sedentary religious vocation of managing a bathhouse as seen in *The Seven Nuns* is another example of compassionate public

2. See Gorai Shigeru, *Kōya hijiri* (Tokyo: Kadokawa Shoten, 1975), 113; Daigan and Alicia Matsunaga, *The Foundation of Japanese Buddhism 2* (Los Angeles: Buddhist Books International, 1976), 297. Orthodox Shingon identified Mitsugon with this world, not Amida's Western Paradise.

3. See Hori, *Folk Religion*, 87 and Janet R. Goodwin, "Building Bridges and Saving Souls: The Fruits of Evangelism in Medieval Japan," *Monumenta Nipponica* 44.2 (Summer 1989):137–49.

4. See Gorai, *Kōya hijiri*, 59–64, 123–34 and Barbara Ruch, "Medieval Jongleurs and the Making of a National Literature," in John Whitney Hall and Toyoda Takeshi, eds., *Japan in the Muromachi Age* (Berkeley: University of California Press, 1977), 279–309.

5. See Mezaki Tokue, *Hyōhaku* (Tokyo: Kadokawa Shoten, 1975), esp. 224–40.

service. This practical undertaking also had a symbolic function: as bathers physically washed away surface dirt and grime, they might have reflected on the fact that inner impurities could be cleansed by religious devotion.

The religious site most often mentioned in revelatory tales is Mount Kōya, an important center of the Shingon sect founded by Kūkai in 816. It is located on the flat top of a small mountain in northeastern Wakayama Prefecture, some fifty-five miles from the capital. Mount Kōya flourished when it began to attract pilgrims to Kūkai's shrine after he was posthumously granted the title Kōbō Daishi in 921. His tomb was opened at this time, and those who entered it reported that Kūkai was not dead but in a perpetual state of deep meditation. Kūkai's death thus came to be interpreted as his achievement of enlightenment and eternal life. It was said that to set foot in the sacred precincts of Kōbō Daishi's shrine was to nullify all transgressions and to banish all troubles, that anyone who died on Mount Kōya was assured of rebirth in a Pure Land. Those who were thus inspired to make this considerable journey from the capital included the most powerful figure in late Heian court politics, Fujiwara no Michinaga (966–1027), and the politically active emperors of the age of cloister government— Shirakawa (1053–1129), Toba (1103–56), and Goshirakawa (1127–92). In later centuries it attracted pilgrims from every level of society and from every part of the country.

The religious community on Mount Kōya was dependent upon the aristocracy for financial support and was forced to turn elsewhere as this resource proved insufficient: fire repeatedly ravaged shrines and other buildings, and a growing number of monks presented increasing needs. While fund raising among the aristocracy continued as the responsibility of eminent priests such as Jōyo (957–1047) and Kakuban, considerable numbers of Kōya holy men (hijiri), traveled widely to solicit funds among the general populace.[6] These holy men grew in number and in influence as the power and wealth of the aristocracy gradually waned in the late Heian period. There is evidence that there were some two thousand holy men affiliated with Mount Kōya in 1173.[7] They preached and collected offerings as they wandered the provinces, and they accepted cremated remains for transport and burial on Mount Kōya. The result of this latter endeavor is a graveyard that stretches for two kilometers along the path leading to Kōbō Daishi's shrine, in which are crowded the grave markers of over 200,000 persons.

6. Gorai, Kōya hijiri, 88–91, 108.

7. Ibid., 123.

Since women were prohibited from ascending Mount Kōya, nuns sought alternative religious sites. One such site is Zenkōji, an important pilgrimage center and base for itinerant clergy in the modern city of Nagano, which figures in *The Seven Nuns*. The statue of Amida Buddha enshrined in Zenkōji is said to have been the gift of the king of a Korean state in 551, an act associated with the official introduction of Buddhism to Japan. The statue was supposedly brought to the Shinano region in 601 by order of Empress Suiko (554–628) and then moved to its current site in 642. It is known for certain only that the temple was in existence by the latter half of the seventh century. Zenkōji now belongs to both the Tendai and Jōdo sects of Buddhism and is administered jointly. The Jōdo superintendent is a nunnery originally affiliated with the Sanron sect, which flourished in the Nara period (710–94). Legend has it that this nunnery was founded by the daughter of Soga no Umako (?–626), an influential minister in the Yamato court and an early proponent of Buddhism.

The popularity of Zenkōji was based on faith in Amida Buddha, whose compassionate promise of salvation for all was advertised by fundraisers who proselytized and solicited throughout Japan. Money and supplies were always needed to rebuild Zenkōji, which, according to records, burned down more than ten times. The itinerant fundraisers, who persuaded the likes of shogun Minamoto no Yoritomo (1147–99) and Toyotomi Hideyoshi to make donations, suggested that Zenkōji was the Pure Land of the living Amida and encouraged burial at Zenkōji as a way to insure rebirth in the Pure Land. Like the Kōya holy men, these itinerant clerics served the faithful by transporting cremated remains back to Zenkōji. Thousands of graves in the area testify to this practice.

Literary Context

The basic tenet of revelatory tales is that the human condition is suffering and that our sorrows are caused by our ignorant refusal to accept the inevitability of change. In Buddhist thought transience (*mujō*) is a metaphysical concept. All material things are considered to have come into existence through some cause and are subject to the process of creation, abiding, transformation, and extinction. This painful process, moreover, is cyclical: all things are born and die over and over again. The cycle of rebirth can be escaped only by eliminating all desire and thus attaining Nirvana, or enlightenment, the only stable, nontransient state. According to certain Buddhist schools this goal is achieved by one's own efforts through scriptural study, meditation, self-discipline, and charitable works. In popular Mahāyāna Buddhism, which flourished in Japan especially after the twelfth century, the believer, having despaired of his own abilities,[8] put his trust in a deity such as the compassionate Amida Buddha, as did adherents of Pure Land Buddhism, or in the *Lotus Sutra*, as encouraged by Nichiren. Instead of enlightenment, then, the goal was salvation in the form of rebirth in the Pure Land.

As a fundamental Buddhist concept, transience became a pervasive motif in Japanese literature of the Heian period, and its expression subsequently underwent various developments.[9] What especially shifts over time is the literary response to death, that most painful and traumatic manifestation of transience. At first the most common images used to express an awareness of evanescence were the passing of the beauties of the natural world and of love. Falling blossoms, dew evaporating in the morning sun, and the fading calls of crickets are ubiquitous examples of the former. Brief spring nights, when dawn forces a lover's departure, and lonely sleepless hours spent remembering a lost love are common motifs used to lament the sorrows that accompany passion. Dreams, which in medieval literature came to stand as metaphors for illusion, were appreciated as opportunities to meet a lover who no longer visited in reality, although even these fantasized visits were by definition frustratingly brief.

In some early Heian court literature, an acceptance of transience led to a bittersweet carpe diem attitude. Poem 82 in *The Tales of Ise*, a tenth-century text, reads:

It is because they fall that we admire the cherry blossoms.
Nothing lasts for long
In this sad world.[10]

To love something beautiful is also to mourn its passing. The kind of emotional sensitivity reflected in this poem was a positive value in aristocratic society[11] to the extent that sorrow itself became beautiful. It

---

8. Such despair became prevalent with the development of the concept of *mappō*, the "Latter Days of the Teachings." Thought to begin in 1052, this was a period in which the human capacity to achieve enlightenment was expected to fail.

9. See William R. LaFleur, *The Karma of Words: Buddhism and the Literary Arts in Medieval Japan* (Berkeley: University of California Press, 1983), 60–79, and *Mirror for the Moon* (New York: New Directions Books, 1977), xvii-xix.

10. See also Helen Craig McCullough, trans., *Tales of Ise: Lyrical Episodes from Tenth-Century Japan* (Tokyo: University of Tokyo Press, 1968), 125.

11. See Ivan Morris, *The World of the Shining Prince: Court Life in Ancient Japan* (Harmondsworth, England: Peregrine Books, 1969), 209.

is also true, however, that one's sorrow over the imminent loss of the cherry blossoms is mitigated by their beauty. This attitude of elegant resignation is even found in poetic expressions of grief at the illness or death of a loved one. In *The Tale of Genji* (Murasaki Shikibu, early eleventh century), Murasaki, her health slightly improved after a serious illness, philosophically composes this poem:

> It is a life in which we cannot be sure
> Of lasting as long as the dew upon the lotus.[12]

The implication of this delicate metaphor is that death is part of nature. Presented in these terms, death is neither frightening nor terrible, only unfortunate or lamentable. Such an understanding of transience leaves one with an ache of sadness, not the searing pangs of grief. The tone is one of resignation in the face of the inevitability of transience, but it reflects an acceptance of the sorrow brought by change rather than an acceptance of change itself.

From the thirteenth century onward, transience is a much more prominent and pressing theme in literary works. The opening paragraph of the well-known hermitic journal, *Hōjōki* (An Account of My Hut), written by Kamo no Chōmei (1153–1216) in 1212, begins with a powerful image of the inexorability of change: "The river's current is ceaseless and its waters are ever changing."[13] However, no elegant imagery mitigates Chōmei's despair at the death and destruction wreaked by several recent natural disasters that he describes: a great fire, a whirlwind, a famine, and an earthquake. In defense against such hazards, he chooses to live simply as a hermit in the mountains. There he tries to come to terms with impermanence but instead discovers the beauty of the passing seasons and the serenity of self-sufficiency.

In his miscellany, *Tsurezuregusa* (Essays in Idleness), Yoshida Kenkō (1283–1350) considers the unpredictability of death: "It does not matter how young or strong you may be, the hour of death comes sooner than you expect."[14] Although Kenkō advises that peace of mind can only be found as Chōmei sought it—by abandoning all ambitions

---

12. Edward Seidensticker, trans., *The Tale of Genji* (New York: Alfred A. Knopf, 1978), 621.

13. See Miki Sumito, ed., *Hōjōki*, in *Shinchō Nihon koten shūsei* (Tokyo: Shinchōsha, 1979), 15. See also *An Account of My Hut* in Donald Keene, ed., *Anthology of Japanese Literature* (Rutland, Vermont: Charles E. Tuttle Company, 1963), 197–212.

14. Donald Keene, trans., *Essays in Idleness* (New York: Columbia University Press, 1967), 120. See *Tsurezuregusa* 137 in Tashio Minoru, ed., *NKBT* 30, 205.

and devoting oneself exclusively to Buddhist practices—overall, Kenkō is more concerned with making the most of life. He echoes the Heian period attitude that evanescence heightens our appreciation of beauty: "If man were never to fade away . . . how things would lose their power to move us!"[15] Thus, both Chōmei and Kenkō confront the harsh reality of death but turn away from it to seek peace and pleasure in the present, physical world. In facing the question of the meaning of death, they reflect the temper of medieval Japan, but their answers evoke the aristocratic aesthetic of the Heian period.

There is no such aesthetic relief, however, in the bleak world depicted in the epic fourteenth-century narrative, *The Tale of the Heike*, which recounts the events of decades of armed conflict between the Taira and Minamoto clans (1156–85). The opening line establishes impermanence as the theme of this work: "The sound of the bell of Gion Temple echoes [the truth] that all things are transient."[16] In contrast to Chōmei's essentially impersonal account of regional disasters and to Kenkō's generalized laments about death, *The Tale of the Heike* describes the bitter defeat of the men of the Taira clan in vivid, concrete detail. Although the fall of the Taira clan is seen in part as retribution for Taira no Kiyomori's abuse of power, the larger lesson is that the clan members were merely victims of the natural law that all things are transient. The survivors' only solace is in tears and religious devotions. Insofar as *The Tale of the Heike* concludes by describing the religious life of Kenreimon'in, once an empress and now a lonely nun, this narrative can be taken as the story of her religious awakening. A scene in this section actually prefigures the revelatory tale: in conversation with the former emperor, Kenreimon'in recounts her experience of the fall of her clan and interprets this in religious terms.[17]

While the members of the Taira clan were known for adopting aristocratic pastimes, their background was fundamentally different from that of the Heian courtier. The rise of the Heike in society was achieved through military might, not through inherited status and artistic skills. Nevertheless, there is a certain similarity in the view of transience reflected in the literature of these two groups. For the aristocrat the beauty of the natural world was some compensation for its

15. Keene, *Essays in Idleness*, 7. See *Tsurezuregusa* 7 in Tashio, NKBT 30, 151.

16. *Heike monogatari* in NKBT 32, 83. See also Hiroshi Kitagawa and Bruce T. Tsuchida, trans., *The Tale of the Heike* (Tokyo: Tokyo University Press, 1977), 5 and Helen Craig McCullough, trans., *The Tale of the Heike* (Stanford: Stanford University Press, 1988), 23.

17. See Kitagawa and Tsuchida, *Heike*, 775–78 and McCullough, *Heike*, 433–36. See also McCullough, *Heike*, 469–71.

impermanence. In the war tale, the honor that accrued to Taira warriors for courageously facing their foes was their highest virtue and
ambition. There is, moreover, an acquiescence among the characters in
The Tale of the Heike to the belief that they were born to their fate of
violent death, an attitude not unlike the Heian aristocrats' acceptance
of impermanence and death as part of the natural order.

In contrast to the delicacy of the Heian courtiers' response to
mortality and the valor with which Taira warriors face their deaths,
setsuwa (legend or anecdote) collections can be gruesome and morbid.
There is, for example, a graphic description of posthumous decay in the
late Heian *setsuwa* collection, *Konjaku monogatarishū* (Tales of Times
Now Past). "The Conversion of Munemasa, Officer of the Crown
Prince's Bureau" (19.10) explains that Munemasa's wife has died and her
body is being kept in a coffin in his house until the funeral. Over ten
days have passed when Munemasa opens the coffin for a last look at her
body:

> Her long hair had come loose and fallen down over the
> pillow, and her eyes, which had been so charming, had
> fallen out, leaving a place not unlike the scar which is left
> on a tree after a knot has been dug out of it. Her body had
> turned to a yellowish color and was quite frightening. The
> bridge of her nose had caved in, causing her nostrils to flare
> out. Because her lips had become wrinkled up like thin
> paper her upper and lower teeth seemed to be biting sharply
> into one another. When he looked at that face he felt both
> disgust and fear, and covered it up and fled the room. The
> odor entered his mouth and nose and the stench was with-
> out limit; he felt as though he had a lump in his throat.
>
> From that time on he could think only of the remains of
> that face, and a religious faith arose from deep in his
> heart.[18]

This vivid account of the physical decay of the corpse of a loved
one reflects the concept of *kusō* (nine phases or nine thoughts), which
refers to the practice of meditating on the process of bodily decay in
order to quell one's physical desires. Genshin included an account of
this concept in his widely influential *Ōjōyōshū* (Teachings Essential for

---

18. Michael William Kelsey, "Didactics in Art: The Literary Structure of the *Konjaku
Monogatari-shū*," (Ph.D dissertation, Indiana University, 1976), 346–47.

Rebirth, 985), which aimed to both frighten and entice its readers into practicing the *nenbutsu*:

> After death, when a day or two or a week has passed, the corpse will swell and turn the blue-black color of old blood. A stench will rise, the skin will rupture and blood will ooze out. Hawks, eagles, kites, owls, foxes, and dogs will peck at it and chew on it. When they have finished, innumerable insects will swarm over the putrid remains. . . . When it has been reduced to bare white bone the limbs will be scattered about. Hands, feet, and skull will lie askew. The wind will blow, the sun will beat down, rain will fall . . . and the bones will turn to dust and mingle indistinguishably in the dirt. [19]

There is certainly no mitigating beauty or honor here. Such a focus on the grotesque side of transience was intended to disturb the reader, to inspire disgust and discourage desires of the flesh. This Buddhist literary art implies a total rejection of this impermanent world and an all-consuming concern for salvation in the next.

Late medieval revelatory tales share with such Buddhist teachings both this brutal view of transience and obvious didactic intent. In these stories we find death by murder, by suicide, and by accident. Here death is neither natural nor honorable. The dark sides of human nature—greed, lust, and especially jealousy—motivate many of the characters and drive innocent victims to despair. The world depicted in revelatory tales is a harsh place, and death is very cruel indeed.

19. From *Ōjōyōshū*, chapter one, "Despising This Polluted World," section five, "Human Life"; see Ishida Mizumaro, trans. mod. Japanese, *Ōjōyōshū* 1 (Tokyo: Heibonsha, 1976), 46–47. See also A. K. Reischauer, "Genshin's Ojo Yoshu: Collected Essays on Birth Into Paradise," *The Transactions of the Asiatic Society of Japan* second series, 7 (1930):53–54. The itemized version of the nine-step process included (1) swelling, (2) changes of color due to exposure, (3) collapse of the body cavity, (4) blood of the decaying corpse staining the earth, (5) festering and decomposition of the corpse, (6) birds and animals eating the corpse, (7) scattering of the body parts by birds and animals, (8) reduction of the body to bare white bone, and (9) burning of the bones and mingling of the ashes with the earth.

A series of poems describing these nine phases of decay by the Chinese scholar-statesman Su Shih (1036–1101) were known in Japan and perhaps inspired the attribution in the thirteenth century of similar poems on this subject to Kūkai. Illustrations of this phenomenon were also executed: Emperor Enyū (959–91, r. 969–84) ordered illustrations of the *Ōjōyōshū*, and the nine phases were personally illustrated by the influential Zen monk Musō Sōseki (1275–1351). See Komatsu Shigemi, ed., *Gaki sōshi, Jigoku sōshi, Yamai no sōshi, Kusōshi emaki*, in *Nihon emaki taisei* 7 (Tokyo: Chūō Kōronsha, 1977), 110–19, 165–70.

There is also a tendency in revelatory tales, as in the *setsuwa* cited above, to dwell on the ugly aspects of transience. In an incident in *The Seven Nuns* a man is forced to make a gruesome comparison between his wife's face and a skull that she had put by his pillow during the night. This is obviously inspired by the line of thinking reflected in the concept of nine phases of bodily decay. A religious essay by the Zen monk Ikkyū (1394–1481) may have been a more direct inspiration. *Gaikotsu* (Skeletons, 1457) makes the same point:

> Who among us is more than a skeleton? So we should see ourselves—as skeletons wrapped in a skin of five elements and patterned into two sexes. When breath goes out, the skin will rupture, even sex will be lost, and superior and inferior will be indistinguishable. Beneath the skin of the person we fondle today, there, too, is a skeleton propping the flesh up.[20]

Also in *The Seven Nuns* jealousy causes the horrifying metamorphosis of a woman into a dragon. There is nothing in secular medieval experience to mitigate the emotional toll that transience exacts.

Theologically speaking, the only escape from this harsh reality is the hope for salvation in a future lifetime. The characters in revelatory tales cope with their losses by taking the tonsure. However, when their despair has been caused by the death of a loved one, they devote themselves to praying for their beloved's salvation. Thus they do not actually sever their worldly attachments, except superficially; only the means of expressing their love is changed. This religious irony is resolved insofar as a concern for the salvation of another motivates a commitment to religious practices, which itself should ultimately lead to enlightenment. Kenreimon'in, for example, expressed the hope that her prayers for her son's salvation might become the seed of her own future enlightenment.[21] The seventh nun in *The Seven Nuns* actually achieves enlightenment by this means. In order to gain religious merit on behalf of the two men who died on her account, the seventh nun took up a life of pilgrimage and mendicancy. Through these religious practices she learned to see her personal loss in the wider perspective of the transience of all things, and thus gained enlightenment.

20. James H. Sanford, *Zen-man Ikkyū* (Chico, California: Scholars Press, 1981), 203–4.

21. See Kitagawa and Tsuchida, *Heike*, 775 and McCullough, *Heike*, 434.

Other than the ultimate solution of enlightenment, another form of consolation is subtly suggested in revelatory tales—membership in a religious community. Only the seventh nun, who has reached the supreme goal, is seen to abandon her bathhouse colleague and her group of storytellers to resume the solitary life of a pilgrim. Every other character in all four tales *gained* enduring companionship after his or her religious awakening. The monk Genmu and his colleague Ono are said to live out the rest of their days in close harmony, and the three monks in the story of that name vow to do so. Thus, the clerical community is depicted as a stable and emotionally rewarding environment, a haven offering what the secular world lacked. In revelatory tales, then, the attachments that were the cause of grief in lay life become a source of solace and support in a religious context, and the cold, hard teachings of Buddhism are made palatable, if not enticing.

Medieval Short Stories

Revelatory tales are among the medieval tales commonly known as *otogi zōshi* (literally, companion stories), an anachronistic term that refers to a wide range of short, anonymous works of prose fiction from the late medieval period. The term *otogi zōshi* comes from the title of a collection of twenty-three late medieval stories entitled *Otogi bunko* (The Companion Library), collected and published around 1700 by Shibukawa Seiemon, an Osaka publisher. Shibukawa's anthology of "old tales" was described in contemporary book catalogs under the alternate title, *Otogi zōshi.* It was this title that in the nineteenth and twentieth centuries became a general name for all short, prose fiction of the late medieval period and that now refers to over four hundred titles.[22] However, since the term *otogi zōshi* has contributed to the misunderstanding that these were fairy tales for children, the purely descriptive phrase, "medieval short story," is perhaps a preferable way to refer to this diverse body of literature from the fourteenth through early seventeenth centuries.

The content of medieval fiction varies widely, but much of it speaks in some way of love, conflict, human ingenuity, or miracles wrought by faith or poetic skill. The characters include a wide range of living beings: gods, aristocrats, clergy, warriors, commoners, and animals. The tone is sometimes tragic and heroic, sometimes comic and trivial. Though much of this material presents Buddhist ideology, the faith reflected here is general and eclectic, not specifically illustrative of

---

22. See Barbara Ann Ruch, "'*Otogi bunko*' and Short Stories of the Muromachi Period" (Ph.D. dissertation, Columbia University, 1965), 7, 29–33.

the orthodox doctrines of any particular sect. Other tales, in contrast, reflect a very secular orientation, and a few even ridicule the clergy.[23]

While little is known about the authorship of medieval short stories, apparently there was a wide audience. Barbara Ruch considers these texts part of a "national literature" that was "well known and held dear by a majority of people across all class and professional lines, a literature that is a reflection of a national outlook."[24] Written literature in previous periods had been the province of aristocrats and clergy. As the military classes gradually gained complete control of the land and the wealth it produced, and as improved transportation encouraged commercial development, literacy and leisure were available to greater numbers of people in places more widespread. Probably even the illiterate participated in this literary culture insofar as itinerant monks and nuns certainly recited some types of these tales to the public.[25]

For all their importance in the daily cultural life of medieval Japan, however, these tales have not attracted the same intensity of scholarly attention that poetry and Nō, the "high" literary arts, have received. Although sometimes awkwardly expressed or logically flawed, these tales are interesting precisely because their occasional naivete and directness reflect the hearts and minds of ordinary people and make them easily accessible to contemporary readers. If some tales seem to fit a predictable pattern, perhaps it is because familiarity can be comfortable and pleasing. The tales embody long-held cultural values such as courage, initiative, honesty, loyalty, and religious devotion. They describe people confronting such timeless dilemmas as frustrated ambition, unrequited love, jealousy, betrayal, and death. In any case, originality and variety, wit, and the effective use of imagery are by no means lacking.

Genre

Recent scholarship treats the four-hundred-odd medieval short stories essentially as one large group, distinguishing subcategories on the basis

---

23. See James T. Araki, "Otogi-zōshi and Nara-ehon: A Field of Study in Flux," *Monumenta Nipponica* 36.1 (Spring 1981):1–20; Margaret H. Childs, "Didacticism in Medieval Short Stories: *Hatsuse monogatari* and *Akimichi*," *Monumenta Nipponica* 42.3 (Autumn 1987):253–88; Frederick Kavanagh, "Twenty Representative Muromachi Period Prose Narratives: An Analytic Study" (Ph.D. dissertation, University of Hawaii, 1985); and Virginia Skord, "The Comic Consciousness in Medieval Japanese Narrative: *Otogi-zōshi* of Commoners" (Ph.D. dissertation, Cornell University, 1987) and "Monogusa Tarō: From Rags to Riches and Beyond," *Monumenta Nipponica* 44.2 (Summer 1989):171–98.

24. Barbara Ruch, "Medieval Jongleurs," 290–92.

25. Ibid., 294–304. See also Hayashi Masahiko, *Nihon no etoki* (Tokyo: Miyai Shoten, 1982); and Hayashi Masahiko and Tokuda Kazuo, eds., *Etoki daihonshū* (Tokyo: Miyai Shoten, 1983).

of superficial differences. In Japanese scholarship distinctions among medieval short stories have been made on the basis of the social class or some other identifying aspect of the characters,[26] or on the basis of some general theme.[27] Such simplistic approaches have led to vague and overlapping categories. There are classifications labeled, for example, stories of nonhumans, of stepchildren, and of miracles; there are felicitous stories,[28] tales of commoners who rose in the world, of monks who broke their vows, and poets' biographies. The labels mislead by oversimplifying the nature of particular tales. Referring to *Komachi sōshi* (The Tale of Komachi) as the biography of a poet obscures its deeply religious content. Labeling *Saiki* as a story of religious awakening highlights its conclusion at the expense of its main focus, an ironic reversal of the common motif of the jealous wife. Another example of the unfortunate results of traditional approaches to classification is the whole category of *chigo monogatari*, stories of young acolytes. While some of these tales, such as *The Tale of Genmu*, describe homosexual relationships that led to a monk's religious awakening, others have little to do with either homosexuality or faith.[29] *Hanamitsu*, for example, concerns a stepmother who slanders her stepson.

It has been proposed that stories be distinguished on the basis of generic origins in one of four traditions (courtly prose, military epic, religious tale, or folk tale).[30] While this could produce useful and interesting results, it is impractical to apply in more than a few instances due to a paucity of evidence. Moreover, this approach would also leave us with still overly broad groupings.

Meaningful genre distinctions may be made, however, if a variety of *multiple* differences are taken into account. Formal features such as narratological types and substantive qualities such as content, tone, and purpose are all elements crucial to the creation of varying genres.[31] Minor variations of literary conventions are also vital to the appreciation of creativity and meaning. Instead of trying to impose on this large body of over four hundred tales some cursory, superficial order, I propose

---

26. See Ichiko Teiji, *Chūsei shōsetsu no kenkyū* (Tokyo: Tokyo Daigaku Shuppankai, 1978), 70.

27. See Fujimura Saku, ed., *Nihon bungaku daijiten* 1 (Tokyo: Shinchōsha, 1950), 407–8.

28. Ibid.

29. Margaret H. Childs, "*Chigo monogatari*: Love Stories or Buddhist Sermons?" *Monumenta Nipponica* 35.2 (Summer 1980):127–31.

30. See Ruch, "'*Otogi bunko*' and Short Stories," 122.

31. See Alastair Fowler, *Kinds of Literature: An Introduction to the Theory of Genres and Modes* (Cambridge: Harvard University Press, 1982), 55.

to analyze in detail a few comparable stories to see just what they share and exactly how they differ. Such an approach, if applied in additional cases, is eventually more likely than any other so far to produce a useful understanding of genre as it functioned in the medieval period.

One of my purposes in choosing to analyze revelatory tales is to demonstrate this possible alternative approach to the problem of the subcategorization of medieval short stories. The other is to present a genre that was historically significant. The *zange* motif appears in other tales than these four revelatory tales. For example, while its primary theme is the power of poetry, *Komachi sōshi* includes an element of mutual revelation: a portion of the story depicts both Ono no Komachi (dates unknown, Heian period) and Ariwara no Narihira (825–80), now in their old age and facing death, reviewing and revealing their romantic histories to each other.[32] Insofar as Nō plays frequently depict ghosts looking back on their lives and reliving bitter experiences, the concept of *zange* underlies their dramatic structure. This is explicit in *Atsumori* (Zeami): The fallen young warrior is called upon to "tell with us the tale of your confession."[33] Atsumori proceeds to tell of the fall of the Taira clan and of his own defeat and beheading on the battlefield. The *zange* phenomenon is parodied in Ihara Saikaku's (1642–93) *The Life of an Amorous Woman*: The protagonist offers her licentious life story to two young men eager to learn the "mysteries of love" and then refers to it as a "confession of sins" by which she claims to "have cleared away the clouds of my own delusion."[34]

Revelatory tales are also intrinsically interesting. I do not suggest that these are unsung treasures: the meaning and literary qualities of these tales are not especially profound or subtle. They are, however, engaging and informative, and our readings of them are enhanced by dint of the effort of literary analysis. Only after a fairly close examination can we attest with any certainty to the essential meanings, functions, and worth of these tales.

Revelatory tales are a convenient object for this study because they comprise one particularly coherent and limited genre of medieval short stories. They share many important features of form, content, tone, and function. As already mentioned, they all present accounts of religious inspiration. To this extent they are like the two or three dozen

32. See *Komachi sōshi* in NKBT 38, 91–94.

33. Keene, *Anthology of Japanese Literature*, 290. See *Atsumori* in NKBT 40, 238.

34. Ihara Saikaku, *The Life of an Amorous Woman and Other Writings*, Ivan Morris ed. and trans. (Norfolk, Connecticut: New Directions Books, 1963), 123, 208.

medieval short stories called *hosshindan*, religious awakening stories.[35] The basic component of religious awakening stories is that they conclude with an attestation of religious inspiration. Usually this takes the form of cutting one's hair and leaving the family home. Occasionally, a lax monk will describe experiences that led him to resolve to follow both the letter and spirit of the precepts.

What distinguishes revelatory tales from religious awakening stories is the narratological situation, that is, all the conditions associated with the telling of the story: the storyteller, audience, time, and place as depicted within the story itself. In religious awakening stories a traditionally omniscient, third-person narrator tells the tale to an only vaguely identified audience. Each revelatory tale, however, is introduced by a primary narrator who provides the framework for the set of tales that comprises the whole. Within that framework are first-person accounts told in group settings in which each narrator serves as audience for the others. This is the crucial requirement of a revelatory tale: it must depict group storytelling in which each member of the group tells his or her own story to the other members.[36]

While the study of other features may yield more insight in the case of other genres, the strong and clear identification of both narrators and narratees in revelatory tales is crucial to their didactic effect, an essential feature of the genre. Since readers are inclined to identify authors with narrators and themselves with narratees, their interpretations can be molded by manipulation of the narrator and narratee. Because of the uniquely prominent role of narrators in revelatory tales, this genre provides an excellent opportunity to study the dynamics of didactic readings. A text may have didactic potential, but it cannot have didactic effect without a reader's cooperation. Only when a reader follows the cues in a text, only when there is docile acceptance of the interpretation offered by the narrator or characters in the text rather

35. See Margaret H. Childs, "Religious Awakening Stories in Late Medieval Japan: The Dynamics of Didacticism" (Ph.D. dissertation, University of Pennsylvania, 1983), 90–103. Prototypes include *The Tale of the Heike* 1.6, "Giō" (Kitagawa and Tsuchida, *Heike*, 21–32; McCullough, *Heike*, 30–37) and 3.8, "Ariō" (Kitagawa and Tsuchida, *Heike*, 185–88; McCullough, *Heike*, 110–13); *Tales of Times Now Past* 19.8 (Marian Ury, trans., *Tales of Times Now Past: Sixty-two Stories from a Medieval Japanese Collection* [Berkeley: University of California Press, 1979], 121–24); *Konjaku monogatarishū*, esp. 19.5 (Kelsey, "Didactics in Art," 323–29); *Otogi sōshishū*, "Otogi sōshi mokuroku" (Matsumoto Ryūshin, ed., *Otogi sōshishū* in *Shinchō Nihon koten shūsei* [Tokyo: Shinchōsha, 1980], 394–410).

36. This setting is fairly common in Japanese literature and is used for other kinds of storytelling. For example, anecdotes of romantic affairs are shared by some members of a group of young men in the "rainy night scene" in *The Tale of Genji* (Seidensticker, *Genji*, 21–38).

than free and independent interpretation, only then is a didactic reading achieved.[37] Revelatory tales make excellent use of the didactic potential of manipulative narrators and narratees.

There are many approaches to narratological analysis, but Susan Sniader Lanser's is particularly useful in this context. She describes three main categories of narratorial possibilities: status—the relationship between narrator and speech act, especially in terms of authority, competence, and credibility; contact—the relationship between narrator and audience or narratee; and stance—a speaker's relationship to the discourse content or message being uttered.[38]

In revelatory tales there is the status, contact, and stance of both the primary and the embedded narrators to be considered. The primary narrator introduces the site and situation and then pretends, at great length, to quote the several embedded narrators. Primary narrators are quite self-effacing; their overt presence is limited to opening and closing statements. *The Seven Nuns*, for example, presents a *pair* of framing narrators, a person who has returned from a trip to Nagano and an innkeeper he or she met there. The traveler quotes the innkeeper, who had quoted the seven nuns. For most of the tale the reader forgets both of them, but to the extent that the identity and attitudes of these framing narrators are known, they influence the reader. In status both are credible narrators. The traveler speaks as a reporter who has visited the scene of the events, while the innkeeper is a local authority. The traveler's intentions are clearly revealed in a concluding remark: "I have stained my writing brush with these many words hoping to inspire piety in my worthy readers. If anyone who might learn from this tale has the opportunity to read it, I shall certainly accrue religious merit for having spread the faith." While this kind of remark may have degenerated into a meaningless convention later, it seems sincere here and is, indeed, consonant with its context. In the category of contact, the traveler shows both self-interest and concern for the religious well-being of the audience. Stance is also apparent in this final comment: the hope of earning religious merit attests to the traveler's own confidence in the reliability of the story. Thus, the framing narrators' status, contact, and stance all enhance the didactic effect of *The Seven Nuns*. The same is true, in varying degrees, for the other revelatory tales.

We learn much more about the embedded narrators, the monks and nuns who tell their personal histories in detail. Although the

37. See Childs, "Didacticism in Medieval Short Stories," 253–57.

38. See Susan Sniader Lanser, *The Narrative Act: Point of View in Prose Fiction* (Princeton, Princeton University Press, 1981), 9, 86, 92.

secondary or internally embedded narrators must be clergy, their lay backgrounds vary considerably. For the most part they are not described as having specific clerical rank, but simply as people who have committed themselves to lives of religious practice, whether officially sanctioned by ordination or not. Naturally these character/narrators are competent and credible in speaking of their own experiences and feelings. Their commitment to the religious life grants them authority and further credibility. Since they are listening to each other's stories, the narrators' relationships to their audiences are those of trusting and sympathetic peers. Finally, each is telling of the major turning point in his or her life, of events that led to a revolution in values, a radical transformation. The stories are not told for amusement, or for posterity, but as a religious ritual meant to deepen the faith of all present. The narratees are consistently deeply moved. They frequently weep and express their admiration for the religious insight reflected in the stories.

The Three Monks includes an incident that suggests the potential power of these stories: when Aragorō confesses to Kasuya that it was he who murdered the latter's beloved, Kasuya's first instinctive reaction is to think of taking revenge. Aragorō persuades Kasuya to hear him out, however, and his tale frees Kasuya of all hatred and anger. Just as Kasuya the narratee is changed by Aragorō's story, so too should we, as readers of the whole, be affected by *The Three Monks*. These particular kinds of status, contact, and stance are the basis of the characteristically didactic nature of revelatory tales.

Another crucial component of the didactic impact of these texts is redundancy.[39] Revelatory tales present a veritable parade of characters whose experiences all exemplify the Buddhist concept of transience, whose deeds all model the Buddhist monastic or pilgrim ideal, and whose beliefs all echo scripture. Narrators and narratees, moreover, repeatedly offer explicit interpretations and evaluations of the stories, all of which promote Buddhist practice and belief. Only *Tales Told on Mount Kōya* ends without an injunction to the reader to seek his or her own religious inspiration. Such an extremely high degree of redundancy of events and belief eliminates ambiguity and establishes the singular meaning of these didactic texts.

Some contemporary readers of these tales have argued that there is a paradox in the phenomenon of telling a love story for religious purposes. They suggest that this beguiling content subverts the serious message. Close reading of revelatory tales, however, reveals that this is

---

39. Susan Rubin Suleiman, "Redundancy and the 'Readable' Text," *Poetics Today* 1.3 (1980):120.

an anachronistic and recalcitrant interpretation. This attitude probably stems from the assumption that instruction is bitter medicine and must be sweetened with elements of entertainment, a Western concept that dates at least from Sir Philip Sidney's *An Apology for Poetry* (1583).[40] The tales contain accounts of romantic entanglements because these are essential to their religious purpose. In most cases, moreover, romantic encounters are described rather perfunctorily and without ironic undertones. It is always the anguish of separation and loss that receives the storytellers' closest attention. Indeed, in *The Three Monks* the misery of falling in love with a woman beyond one's station receives two to three times as many lines of text as the delights of that consummated love. The same is true of "Hanakazura's Story" in *The Seven Nuns*. She is the most eloquent of all the nuns in describing her happy marriage, but her comments are all conventional generalizations: "After our marriage we were never separated by even a hair's breadth. We spent our days oblivious to the passing of time, concerned only with admiring the moon and spring blossoms." Such briefly experienced and cursorily described relationships do not undermine the religious lesson of revelatory tales, but contribute to them. The pain of romance is the crux of the argument, but it can only arise in contrast with the preceding pleasures. Without the context of desire there is no potential for despair. Without the reality of heartfelt losses the Buddhist concept of transience is irrelevant. The inclusion of romantic elements in revelatory tales is therefore inevitable and does not necessarily create tension between the content and the message. Rather, it provides momentum and evidence for the religious message. There is tension between erotic content and didactic comment in several bawdy novels by Saikaku,[41] but there is little if anything that is titillating in revelatory tales; overall, the tone of these tales is sincerely and thoroughly devout.

There are only four known medieval short stories that either partially or fully embody the criteria for revelatory tales outlined above. While none has been dated with much precision, they are presented here in their presumed chronological order. The first tale included in this anthology may have been a forerunner of the genre: *The Tale of Genmu* is primarily a tale told by an omniscient narrator in a third-person voice, but it incorporates an important scene that, alone, would

---

40. Sir Philip Sidney, *An Apology for Poetry* in *An Apology for Poetry or the Defence of Poesy*, Geoffrey Shepherd ed. (London: Thomas Nelson and Sons, Ltd., 1965), 103, 113–14.

41. See Ihara Saikaku, *Five Women Who Loved Love*, Wm. Theodore de Bary, trans. (Rutland, Vermont: Charles E. Tuttle, 1971) as well as *The Life of an Amorous Woman*.

comprise a revelatory tale. The second story, *Tales Told on Mount Kōya*, is comprised of six tales, one of which provides comic relief (and one of which is similar to the murderer's tale in *The Three Monks*). The best known revelatory tale, *The Three Monks*, brilliantly interweaves the tales of its first two monks,[42] while the third monk makes short work of explaining why he first renounced the world and then proceeds to recount at length a painful incident in his life as an itinerant monk. *The Seven Nuns* seems a self-conscious innovation of the genre, in which the seventh nun refuses to tell her own tale of religious inspiration, denounces the others' storytelling, and gives a philosophical lecture instead. An account of her tragic elopement is appended, however (obtained from some unidentified source), and thus the value of these confessional stories is reasserted.

Excluded from this collection is a tale entitled *Inin bikuni* (The Nun Inin). Although this story is designated as a *zangemono* in an index compiled by Matsumoto Ryūshin and published in *Otogi sōshishū*,[43] it does not to any significant degree display the characteristics of the other revelatory tales. The story begins with the nun Inin, who had been wet-nurse to a woman named Otohime, telling a monk her revelation, which concerns the unhappy fate of her former charge. Otohime married a man whose stepmother harrassed her until she was driven to abandon her husband and son by becoming a nun. This wicked stepmother then was the cause of the deaths of both Otohime's son and husband, one directly and the other indirectly. It was this sad lot of Otohime's that inspired Inin to become a nun. After Inin has finished telling her sad story to the monk, Otohime emerges from the shadows for a miraculous reunion. The two women later encounter the ghost of Otohime's son and are reunited with Otohime's brother at a temple, where he is coincidentally observing memorial services for his and Otohime's mother. Learning that her late husband's stepmother is ill, Otohime, innocent of any grudge or antipathy, tries to offer condolences, but she is met with continued hatred. The tale concludes with the death of the unrepentant stepmother, from whose coffin crawls a horrifying snake. In the final lines some unidentified bystander briefly exhorts the reader to faith.[44]

The major focus of *The Nun Inin* is the evil perpetrated by the stepmother, not the religious insight it produced in Inin or even

---

42. Partially translated as *The Three Priests* by Donald Keene in *Anthology of Japanese Literature*, 322–31.

43. *Otogi sōshishū*, 397.

44. See *Inin bikuni* in Fujii Ryū, ed., *Mikan otogi zōshishū to kenkyū* 1 (Toyohashi: Mikan Kokubun Shiryō Kankōkai, 1956), 53–102.

Otohime. To the extent that there is spiritual benefit gained from this maliciousness, moreover, it is not reaped by Inin, the teller of this pseudo-revelatory tale, so much as by Otohime. Yet, Otohime's decision to become a nun was based on her hope that this would spare her family the wrath of her stepmother-in-law, not because of religious insight. The salutary effects of her clerical status are only revealed when, in asking to be allowed to pay her respects at her stepmother-in-law's sickbed, she demonstrates her forgiveness of this malevolent woman. Inin's pseudo-revelatory tale seems, after all, primarily a vehicle for conveying an account of a stepmother's maliciousness toward her daughter-in-law. It does not qualify as a revelatory tale because Inin's audience, the monk, does not recount his experience and because the outcome of her account is a secular reward, reunion with her long lost "daughter," not a deeper religious commitment. What is being demonstrated in this story is not the principle of transience, but the doctrine of karma, specifically, that rewards and retribution will come immediately, in this world, not the next.

The only extant manuscript of *The Nun Inin* has been dated to the mid-Edo period, but internal evidence suggests it may have been written between 1598 and 1618.[45] If such were the case, it was roughly contemporaneous with the latest of the true revelatory tales, *The Seven Nuns*, a chronology that allows the possibility of direct influence by the revelatory tale genre.

It is the sharing of a whole constellation of various features of both form and content that constitutes a genre. Examining several examples of one genre gives a clear idea of the degree of sophistication (or naivete) of this dimension of the medieval literary scene. While a survey of differing types of medieval short stories will also be welcome to provide the broad view, a thorough knowledge of this one group of tales affords a certain depth of understanding of popular medieval culture.

Sange

As mentioned above, revelatory tale is my translation of *zangemono* (or *zange monogatari*), which is derived from the term *sange*, a word usually defined and translated as "confession" or "repentance." Identical Chinese characters are used for both: generally, when used in its technical religious sense, the word is pronounced *sange*, and *zange* when used in a lay or literary context. Neither "confession" nor "repentance," however, captures the full sense of the term as it is used in *zangemono*, and both have misleading connotations from the Judeo-Christian tradition. To

45. Ibid., 147.

render *zangemono*, therefore, I have proposed the alternative, "revelatory tales," in which "revelation" is used in its first and most general English meaning: "the act of revealing what was previously unknown" and not in the Judeo-Christian sense of divine revelation. Further, there is both a public and private aspect to the phrase: "revealing what was previously unknown." Revelatory tales depict a revealing to others, a public announcement. *Zange* was often used in Japanese to mean simply "making public," as the word "confession" is sometimes used in English.[46] The private aspect of "revelation" intended here is the religious awakening as it has occurred in the heart of a character in a *zangemono*. Thus, it means both "exposing" and "coming to know."

The term *sange* derives from Sanskrit words: *kṣamā*, meaning "forebearance" or "forgiveness" and *āpatti-desanā*, "to point out one's transgressions or mistakes." By no means, however, does the term in the context of *zangemono* imply the feeling of guilt found in the Christian practice of confession or repentance of sins. Rather it resembles the concept of realization, as in the definition of repent: to "change one's mind with regard to past action in consequence of dissatisfaction with it or its results."[47]

To clarify the meaning of *sange* we may contrast concepts of "sin" in the Buddhist and Christian traditions. In its Christian sense sin is essentially "an indifference or opposition to the will of God,"[48] or "some deliberate and voluntary defiance . . . to a moral law which expresses the will of God, and the breach of which tends to separation from God."[49] Thus, God must grant his forgiveness for the sinner to be absolved. In Buddhism, on the other hand, there is no monotheistic god whose will determines moral law, hence there can be no opposition nor breaking of his law and alienation from him. While there is a strong ethical aspect to Mahāyāna Buddhism, and compassion is of fundamental importance, the precepts against killing, stealing, lewd behavior, and the like can be seen as reflecting self-interest in that they are ultimately intended as guidelines for conduct that will accumulate

---

46. For a discussion of the lay and other religious uses of the term prior to *zange monogatari*, see Margaret H. Childs, "The Influence of the Buddhist Practice of *Sange* on Literary Form: Revelatory Tales," in *Japanese Journal of Religious Studies* 14.1 (March 1987):58–62.

47. C. L. Barnhart, ed., *The American College Dictionary* (New York: Random House, 1969), 1027–28.

48. James Hastings, ed., *Encyclopaedia of Relgion and Ethics* 11 (New York: Charles Scribner's Sons, 1951), 541.

49. Ibid., vol. 1, 49.

positive karma and eventually lead one to enlightenment. Enlightenment is the consideration that supersedes all others. This notion is
implicit in the concept *zen'aku funi*, which means that distinctions
between right and wrong cannot be made. A radical example of this
idea is seen in *The Three Monks*, in which a murderer experiences a
religious awakening as an indirect consequence of murdering a young
woman. While not condoning the murder, this crime is viewed as
having a positive aspect insofar as it is the expedient to the man's
religious awakening. Any implication that life is cheap if expended to
this end is avoided by considering the victim to have been an incarnation of a bodhisattva whose intention and function it was to inspire the
murderer's religious awakening.

There are, of course, specific and numerous precepts to guide
monastic clerical behavior, but violations of this code are perceived as
offenses against the community. There are rituals of repentance called
keka or *sange* in which participants confess any transgressions they have
committed and express their remorse. Disclosure itself effects redemp-
tion. It was the Tendai school that broadened the concept of *sange* by
creating two categories of "repentance." *Jisange* refers to repentance of
phenomenal aspects of existence or wrong deeds. The *sange* ritual that
underlies revelatory tales is *risange*, recognition of the absolute nature of
reality, which is that all things are empty, including sin.[50] For one who
truly comprehends emptiness (*kū*), the distinction between right and
wrong becomes pointless. The meaning of emptiness is that nothing
has an individual existence, that things have no self (Sanskrit [hereafter
Skt] *ātman*); they are only a temporary coalition of parts. One therefore
ceases making distinctons between oneself and others. Self-interest is
thus transformed into selflessness or universal compassion. "Clinging
and acquisitiveness" are put to an end, and "harmony" between the
individual and his environment is established.[51] Once such comprehen-
sion has been achieved, wrongdoing is said to be extinguished (*metsu*)

50. See Heinrich Dumoulin, "The Consciousness of Guilt and the Practice of Confession
   in Japanese Buddhism," in *Studies in Mysticism and Religion* (Jerusalem: Magnes
   Press, Hebrew University, 1967), 121. See also M. W. de Visser, *Ancient Buddhism
   in Japan* 1 (Leiden: E. J. Brill, 1935), 282–86. De Visser (p. 284) cites *Daijō honjō
   shinji kangyō* (T no. 159, Mahāyāna Sutra on the Contemplation of the Processes
   of Consciousness of the Original Lives [of the Buddha]): "If one meditates . . .
   entirely concentrating his mind upon the *Dharmakāya* . . . of the Buddhas, he
   begins to understand that the real nature of all *dharma's* is Emptiness . . . which
   cannot be grasped, and that all sins are originally empty too. If one meditates day
   and night on this Wonderful Absolute Emptiness, all his sins, obstacles on the
   road to salvation, are taken away."

51. See Daigan and Alicia Matsunaga, *The Buddhist Concept of Hell* (New York: Philosophical Library, Inc., 1972), 54–55.

because when one is in this state, wrongdoing has become meta-physically impossible.

The concept of *risange* is explained in some detail in *Maka Shikan* (The Great Cessation and Insight), a manual for meditation by Chih I (Chigi, 538–97), a founder of Tendai Buddhism in China (T'ien-t'ai), and in *Ōjōyōshū*, the profoundly influential work by the Tendai scholar Genshin. The basis for these ideas is found in Mahāyāna scripture. The seventh nun herself cites the *Kanfugenbosatsugyōhōkyō* (Sutra of Meditation on the Bodhisattva Universal Vow), which outlines the *sange rokkon kan Fugen hō*, or "rite of repenting the perceptions of the six senses through meditation on Fugen."[52] This sutra teaches that the six faculties—seeing, hearing, smelling, speaking, feeling, and thinking—are the source of wrongdoing, that is, sense perceptions, words, and thoughts are so many obstacles to enlightenment. For example, our auditory sense allows us to hear random sounds that disrupt our tranquility, and by the faculty of thought one's mind constantly wanders, preventing peacefulness.[53] To achieve peace of mind despite these obstacles, we are advised to study Mahāyāna texts, to consider the ultimate truth (*daiichigi*), to meditate on emptiness (*hōkū*) and formlessness (*musō*), to think about the meaning of Nirvana (*shinjaku*), and so forth. The poetic summary of this section of the sutra concludes:

> All negative karma arises out of delusion,
> If you would "repent," seat yourself properly and contem-plate true reality [*jissō*].
> Transgressions [*zai*] are nullified through wisdom,
> As frost and dew vanish in the sunlight.[54]

To "repent" the six faculties, then, means to realize that what one perceives through the senses is illusory and that the senses are hindrances to enlightenment. Similarly, in medieval Japanese revelatory tales, to "repent" lost loves and other disappointments is to realize that emotional attachments are premised on an ignorant and deluded assumption that existence is durable. Having once experienced a private revelation of this truth, the monks and nuns in revelatory tales publicly

·52. *Kanfugenbosatsugyōhōkyō* (T no. 277) 9, 389–94. See also Bunnō Katō, Yoshiro Tamura, and Kōjirō Miyasaka, trans., *The Threefold Lotus Sutra: Innumerable Meanings, The Lotus Flower of the Wonderful Law, and Meditation on the Bodhisattva Universal Vow* (New York: Weatherhill/Kosei, 1975), 347–70; and de Visser, *Ancient Buddhism in Japan* 1, 269–72.

53. *Kanfugenbosatsugyōhōkyō* 9, 393.

54. Ibid. See also Katō, Tamura, and Miyasaka, *Threefold Lotus*, 366.

review their past attachments as a way to deepen their understanding of the essential meaning of transience.

The Texts

The Tale of Genmu, the earliest extant copy of which is dated 1497, is commonly classified as a chigo monogatari, a [homosexual] acolyte tale. As I have pointed out in "Chigo monogatari: Love Stories or Buddhist Sermons?"[55] however, that classification is the result of a modern view of homosexuality as aberrant behavior and ignores the prominence of the religious awakening aspect of the tale. As a whole The Tale of Genmu is not technically a revelatory tale, but it contains a lengthy final scene, about one-sixth of the whole, which fits the definition of the genre. This portion of the tale depicts the monk Genmu and another monk exchanging the stories of how they came to devote their lives to prayer on Mount Kōya.

The text of The Tale of Genmu chosen for translation here was originally printed in 1664 but reproduces a manuscript with a postscript dated 1486. As reprinted in Muromachi jidai monogatari taisei (A Complete Collection of monogatari from the Muromachi Period),[56] it includes a handwritten postscript of 1668. Of the other four extant copies, the earliest is dated 1497, one is dated 1689 with postscripts from 1691 and 1704, another dates from 1664 with a postscript from 1778, and one is undated.[57] The concluding postscript in the 1689 version states that The Tale of Genmu is a tale handed down through many generations on "this mountain" and that the copyist has corrected mistakes found in the text.[58] "This mountain" could be a reference to Mount Nikkō, home to one of the main characters, to Mount Kōya, where the zange scene takes place, or to Mount Hiei, site of Enryakuji, the religious headquarters of the Tendai sect and the setting of some of the events related early in the tale.[59]

Scholars assume that The Tale of Genmu owes much to Aki no yo no nagamonogatari (A Long Tale for an Autumn Night), a story that

---

55. See Childs, "Chigo monogatari: Love Stories or Buddhist Sermons?" 127–31.

56. Genmu monogatari in Yokoyama Shigeru and Matsumoto Ryūshin, eds., Muromachi jidai monogatari taisei 4 (Tokyo: Kadokawa Shoten, 1981), 398–416.

57. See Nara Ehon Kokusai Kenkyū Kaigi, ed., Otogi zōshi no sekai (Tokyo: Sanseidō, 1982), 76.

58. Genmu monogatari in Hanawa Hokinoichi, comp., Zoku gunsho ruijū 18 (Tokyo: Zoku Gunsho Ruijū Kanseikai, 1958), 411.

59. See Ichiko Teiji, Chūsei shōsetsu no kenkyū (Tokyo: Tokyo Daigaku Shuppankai, 1978), 139–40.

dates to at least as early as 1377, in which a monk experiences a religious awakening because of the suicide of an acolyte with whom he was in love.[60] *Sangoku denki* 12.15 (Legends from Three Countries, ca. 1446) was perhaps the inspiration for the scene in *Genmu* in which Genmu encounters the ghost of his beloved.

There is only one extant copy of *Tales Told on Mount Kōya*, which scholars presume dates from the Muromachi period. It is considered likely to predate and to have influenced *The Three Monks*. This text is also found in *Muromachi jidai monogatari taisei*.[61]

The setting of *The Three Monks* is the period of the northern and southern courts (1336–92). The third monk alludes to the fact that Kusunoki Masanori turned against the southern court to ally himself with Ashikaga Yoshiakira, an event that occurred in 1369. A story that may have been a source for this third monk's tale is found in *Yoshino shūi*, a *setsuwa* collection that was possibly compiled by 1384. Another source may have been *Shasekishū* 10.7 (Sand and Pebbles), a *setsuwa* collection completed in 1283 by Mujū Ichien (1226–1312), in which is found a brief version of the stories of the first and second monks, although the order of presentation is reversed. However, the earliest extant copies of *The Three Monks* date from 1624, 1646, and 1658.[62]

It is possible that the title *Sannin sō* (also meaning "three monks"), which is mentioned in a diary entry dated 1605, refers to the text now known as *Sannin hōshi*.[63] Other titles under which this tale appears include *Aragorō hosshinki*, *Sannin zange sōshi*, and *Sannin sō no monogatari*. Donald Keene translated the first two monks' accounts, about half of this tale, in his *Anthology of Japanese Literature*, but he omitted the lengthy third monk's story. The text used here is found in *Nihon koten bungaku taikei*.[64]

The earliest extant text of *The Seven Nuns* is a printed book that dates from 1635. Two subsequent reprintings occurred in 1665 and 1682. *The Seven Nuns* has traditionally been classified as a *kana zōshi*, which refers to a broad range of publications printed during the Edo period (1600–1868) in *kana* script, the Japanese phonetic *hiragana* syllabary, with very few Chinese characters. Some scholars, however, now consider *The Seven Nuns* a late medieval short story, believing that

---

60. See Childs, "*Chigo monogatari*: Love Stories or Buddhist Sermons?" 132–51.

61. Yokoyama and Matsumoto, *Muromachi jidai monogatari taisei* 4, 547–67.

62. See *Otogi zōshi* in NKBT 38, 19–20.

63. See Nishizawa Masaji, *Meihen otogizōshi* (Tokyo: Kasama Shoin, 1978), 11.

64. *Sannin hōshi* in NKBT 38, 434–59.

earlier manuscripts, now lost, must have existed.[65] The distinction between medieval short stories and *kana zōshi* has traditionally been that
the former were composed during the middle ages and circulated in
manuscript form, whereas the latter were written specifically for the
newly burgeoning printers' trade of the early seventeenth century. Both
types of works were of course a part of seventeenth-century life, and the
two terms seem at times to overlap. In either case *The Seven Nuns* is
unquestionably part of the medieval literary revelatory tale
phenomenon.

A story quite similar to that of the sixth of the seven nuns is
found in a Nō play, *Aizomegawa*, which dates from 1514. In this drama,
however, the estranged wife who commits suicide is miraculously revived. In a late Muromachi short story of the same title, *Aisomegawa*,
the tale is told as in *The Seven Nuns*: the suicide is final. These events
were also fashioned into a puppet play that was performed between 1683
and 1684, and which possibly was written by Chikamatsu Monzaemon
(1653–1724), the foremost playwright of the Edo period.

The illustrations that accompany this translation of *The Tale of
Genmu* are taken from a seventeenth-century copy of the 1497 text.
This two-scroll copy measures 28.7 centimeters in height by 1,642.5
centimeters (scroll one) and 1,501.7 centimeters (scroll two) in length.
Seven scenes are illustrated in the first scroll, and six illustrations are
found in the second. The source of the illustrations for *The Seven Nuns*
is the 1635 woodblock print edition, a set of three bound volumes
measuring 24.7 centimeters (height) by 17.4 centimeters (width) and
containing a total of thirty-four scenes. It is revealing of the breadth
and durability of interest in the revelatory tale genre that the physical
form of these tales ranges from an attractive and laboriously produced
picture scroll version of *The Tale of Genmu* to the sketchily illustrated,
mass-produced *Seven Nuns*. (The single extant copy of *Tales Told on
Mount Kōya* is not illustrated, and illustrated copies of *The Three Monks*
were not available to the author.)

The revelatory tales that follow both provide insight into the
popular religious culture of medieval Japan and represent a new approach to the study and categorization of medieval short stories. Their
interest, however, is not only historical. Dealing as they do with timeless human tragedy, modern readers may well find them moving and
instructive.

65. See Kishi Tokuzō, "*Shichinin bikuni* oboegaki—sono 'katari' to 'etoki' ni tsuite,"
    Kokugo kokubun 28.4 (April 1959):44–45. Okami Masao is also of this opinion
    (personal communication).

The Tales

The Tale of Genmu

Part One

Clouds obscure the thirty-two[1] natural features of the full moon. Brisk spring breezes scatter the blossoms of the Ten Shining Virtues.[2] All sentient beings must perish; all that flourishes will wither. This is the way of the world.

Yet we idle away our springs and summers admiring blossoms and birds. Preoccupied with the beauty of the moon and snow, we let autumns and winters slip by. These interests are the bonds that bring about our perpetual rebirth. If even the lay person should shun these ties, how much more so the Buddha's disciple.

Some time ago, there was a monk in Ōhara, near the capital, who sought to comprehend the singular truth of the Three Views of Reality[3] and whose studies ranged widely through all the many teachings of the Buddha.[4] He was called Genmu.

One quiet day when he had only the gentle sound of a drizzling rain for company, he gazed out the window of his hut and thought: "I have had the chance to study Buddhism, an opportunity as rare in all

1. This is a reference to the Thirty-two Marks of a Buddha. These include such things as long, slender fingers, hands reaching below the knees, forty teeth, and a white curl in the forehead, which emits light. The moon is said to have these thirty-two features because it is a symbol for Buddhahood, or enlightenment. The clouds that obscure the moon suggest both transience—we cannot long enjoy the beauty of the moon in a clear sky—and illusion—just as clouds conceal the moon, illusions prevent us from understanding religious truths.

2. The Ten (Shining) Virtues are abstinence from the ten "evils" or transgressions: killing, stealing, lewdness, lying, dazzling rhetoric, slander, equivocation, greed, anger, complaining.

3. *Isshin sangan* or the Three Views refer to a Tendai meditative practice in which one strives to accept that reality is empty, that reality is provisional, and that both of these viewpoints are one truth. One is thus required to accept simultaneously both a world-affirming and a world-negating attitude.

4. Literally, the Four Teachings and the Five Periods. The former refers to the division of the Buddha's teachings into four phases by content; the latter refers to a five-part classification based on when Buddha delivered the various sutras.

eternity as a one-eyed turtle poking its head through a knothole in a floating log,[5] as uncommon as the blooming of the *udumbara*[6] tree. If I let this life go by frivolously, I shall never nullify my burden of negative karma.

"The lot of humankind, the nature of the world before our eyes, the fact that time awaits no one—these are reflected in the morning glory that wilts as the sun rises and in the clouds of dawn that gather to veil the night moon. Indeed, my own body gives me evidence of this truth.

"I, Genmu, have been spending the months and years in idleness. I have let time pass without taking the opportunity to break free from that which traps me in the cycle of rebirth. Pondering the past, I remember that Eshin[7] said, 'Poverty is the seed of Buddhahood,' and that Kūya Shōnin[8] once remarked, 'Poverty is the hermit's friend.'

"Although I have not undergone the Three Modes of Training—discipline, concentration, and wisdom—I have had the chance to seek truth as a poor and humble layman. Yet, without enlightenment, it is impossible to escape the cycle of rebirth.

"Such is the condition of all things, from the thousand grasses and the ten thousand trees to mountains, rivers, and plains. There is nothing that is not involved in the cycle of rebirth. Though the clouds of illusion hang over us for the time being, deep in every heart shines the clear, bright moon of understanding.

"Thus Dengyō Daishi[9] wrote in a commmentary that to be reborn in hell is the same as to become a Buddha, and that Vairocana is no greater than a common man's single invocation of the Buddha.

"Also, there is the poem that reads:

Do not think that its light shines only after
The clouds disperse.
The morning moon has been there all along.

---

5. The source of this familiar image is the *Lotus Sutra*. See Leon Hurvitz, trans., *Scripture of the Lotus Blossom of the Fine Dharma* (New York: Columbia University Press, 1976), 328, 409.

6. The *udumbara* (J *udonge*) tree was thought to bloom only once every three thousand years.

7. Eshin (942–1017), or Genshin, was a Tendai monk, famous as the author of the *Ōjōyōshū* (Teachings Essential for Rebirth).

8. Kūya (903–72) was said to have originated the practice of *odori nenbutsu* in which one beats a drum or bell and dances while invoking the Buddha's name.

9. Dengyō Daishi (767–822), or Saichō, was founder of the Tendai sect in Japan.

"Furthermore, the commentaries on the various sutras are explicit: there is no Buddhahood, no living being in need of salvation, and no delusion other than in one's heart.

"Then, in a commentary by Kōbō Daishi,[10] it is written: 'There is a transgression greater than the Four Grievous Crimes and the Five Wicked Offenses[11]: that is to have received the rare gift of humanity, and yet to fail to study Buddhism.'

"Not to brush away the polluting dust of this world, not to polish the mirror of the mind,[12] is the most regrettable of all regrettable things. Yet it has always been the case that enlightenment is something we can attain only by praying to the gods.

"Though the gods and Buddhas show their grace in various ways, I have heard that, as a patron of the Buddhist law, the mountain god of Hiei is especially sympathetic to those who practice Mahāyāna Buddhism."

Having decided to place his trust in the mountain god, Genmu went often to the shrine at the foot of Mount Hiei and prayed for release from the cycle of birth and death.

Once when he had come to worship the mountain god, he prayed: "You are a manifestation of Śākyamuni Buddha, and your vow to save all sentient beings is greater than that of other gods. I beseech you with all my heart for the complete fulfillment of my prayers." Immediately the worship hall shook, the bejeweled blinds rustled, and a voice like that of a bird of paradise issued forth from inside the shrine: "If you want your true Buddha self to shine brightly, pray to the Yakushi Buddha[13] in the main hall of Enryakuji." This was not just a dream that he mistook for reality, but a divine revelation.

Overjoyed, Genmu decided to go to the main hall, to put his faith in the Yakushi Buddha, and to pray without respite. Since it was the occasion of the conferral of vows, he decided to ascend the mountain that very night. Leaving his thatched hut in Ōhara, he went to the main hall, where he knelt before the sacred image.

---

10. Kōbō Daishi (774–835), or Kūkai, was founder of the Shingon sect in Japan (see the introduction, p. 5).

11. The Four Grievous Crimes are killing, stealing, lewdness, and lying. The Five Wicked Offenses are, in order of increasing seriousness: matricide, patricide, killing an arhat, disturbing the harmony of the clerical community, and causing injury to a Buddha.

12. This metaphor for the mind (or heart) suggests that the mind must be kept pure in order to reflect/perceive religious truth.

13. The Yakushi Buddha was the Buddha of Medicine who vowed to heal all diseases and to lead all beings to enlightenment.

To the joy of the faithful, the statue of the Buddha there had been sculpted by Dengyō Daishi himself and was endowed with miraculous power. For all these years since Emperor Kanmu [737–806, r. 781–806] had decreed that the hall be built, ceaseless streams of worshipers had come bearing candles.

Genmu seated himself on the wide veranda and prayed, "Oh wondrous Buddha! I beseech you to grant all that I wish." Then he proceeded to the hall where the rituals for the conferral of vows were taking place, intending to go home after they had concluded. Those taking vows comprised a crowd of thousands. Young acolytes and monks of various ages and ranks[14] had come from all over Japan. They filled the temple precincts like a nebulous mist. While he watched, clouds gathered in the sky, and it began to snow heavily. He took shelter in Shiō'in Hall.[15]

There, Genmu noticed a youth of sixteen or seventeen in the company of two monks who seemed to be his colleagues. The boy probably had come from some distant province insofar as he appeared quite footsore. Having taken his vows, he had been about to set off on his return journey when the heavy snow brought him to Shiō'in Hall to wait for the storm to lift.

Perhaps it was simply that he was worn out from traveling, but the youth appeared lost in thought and dispirited. Yet the luster of his disheveled hair brought to mind cherry blossoms drooping under a spring rain on a quiet evening, or the limp branches of a willow at dawn. No word or picture could have conveyed his loveliness. Dressed in a silk kimono the color of autumn leaves, a white silk under-robe, and a jacket of Chinese brocade, the youth looked frail and delicate. He was a truly elegant sight.

When the snow did not let up after a short time, the youth remarked to his colleagues: "Are not the shores of Shiga to the east and Mount Nagara to the south? It reminds me of Tadanori's poem."[16] In poetic cadence, the boy remarked: "Today I understand what it is when the wind sweeps out of the west, down from the mountain peaks. In this

14. The text lists the following: *chigo*, youths who functioned as servants in temples; *kasshiki*, those who call the monks to meals, usually youths who have not taken the tonsure; *shami*, young monks who have taken the tonsure and accepted the Ten Vows or young lay monks, i.e., monks who are married; and *kozō*, young monks.

15. A hall where the Shitennō, the Four Guardian Kings, are enshrined. They are guardians of the four directions.

16. Taira no Tadanori (1144–84). The reference is to poem 66 in the seventh imperial anthology, the *Senzai waka shū* (Collection of a Thousand Years), completed

season of desolation the rain clouds threatened only a brief shower as they summoned the leaves from the trees. Now the rain has turned into this swirling snow that hinders our mountain crossing. If we were at Karasaki,[17] the sight of the froth on the waves beneath the pines would make us think of buds blooming in spring, and we would call them 'little pine blossoms.' In another month we will be saying: 'Spring has come before the old year is out.' This is a season when it is hard to keep still. Let's each take a turn starting a round of verse to pass the time."

One of the monks accompanying the youth observed: "Since our own first verses are never very good, please, you begin."

The boy gazed at Mount Nagara and then recited:

The snow is in bloom.
Although it is still winter on Mount Nagara, the blossoms
    are at their peak.[18]

At that one of the monks spoke to Genmu: "When the youth offers an opening verse, we usually contribute the following lines, but, traveling monk, why don't you compose them this time?"

"I was hoping to join in," replied Genmu, "but I did not want to interrupt. I was just wondering what to do when you spoke so graciously. Although I am afraid my verse will sound like the coarse call of a crow and only provoke your laughter, I would be delighted to participate. It will be a memento in this ever-changing world." He added the line:

Hiding these time-worn branches, a frost of cherry
    blossoms.[19]

about 1188: *Sazanami ya/ Shiga no miyako wa/ arenishi o/ mukashi nagara no/ yamazakura ka na.*

Froth on the waves.
The palace on the shores of Shiga is now in ruins.
Only the cherry blossoms on Mount Nagara remain as of old.

See also Kitagawa and Tsuchida, *Heike* (7.16), 439 and McCullough, *Heike*, 247.

17. Karasaki is a town on the shores of Lake Biwa.

18. *Yuki zo saku/ fuyu nagarayama/ hanazakari.* This is a *hokku*, a "beginning verse" for the linked form, a unit of 5–7–5 syllables. As in Tadanori's poem, *nagara-* is a pivot word in the phrase *fuyu nagarayama.* It functions as "still winter" and also as the proper name Mount Nagara.

19. *Furue o kakusu/ shimo no sakuragi.* Genmu suggests that the youth's presence makes him forget his age, which is thirty-seven, as we can calculate from information given later.

The youth and his colleagues were moved by his verse, and the four of them idled away the rest of the day composing poetry until, when the snow had stopped and the sun had set, the boy announced that they should be off for Sakamoto.[20]

"By the way, from what province have you come?" inquired Genmu of the monks.

"Humbly dressed as we are in these traveling clothes, we'd rather not say, but karmic affinity has brought us together and we have shared a long conversation. Why should we hide anything from you? We are monks from Mount Nikkō in Shimotsuke.[21] The youth came to take his vows and we have accompanied him. Tomorrow we have to hurry home," explained the monks in some detail.

"Just as you say," said Genmu, "our taking shelter under the same tree or drinking from the same stream is the result of karmic destiny, which originated in previous lives. If today we have met and talked, it is due to our having had some relationship in the past. I am so sorry you must leave. Please stay through tomorrow and rest your weary feet. I would like to go with you to East Sakamoto, but since I must not neglect my daily worship, I should return to my grass-thatched hut in Ōhara. Please, let us compose linked verse again early tomorrow. I shall cherish the memory of it all my life."

20. Sakamoto, north of Karasaki, is also on the shores of Lake Biwa.

21. Mount Nikkō is the site of Rin'ōji, a temple of the Tendai school, which dates from the eighth century. Shimotsuke is now Ibaragi Prefecture.

Touched by Genmu's ardent plea, the monks said: "How can we refuse so earnest a request? We'll linger just through tomorrow. By all means, come visit in the morning. We have taken lodgings near Shōgenji. Ask there where the vow-taker from Nikkō in Shimotsuke is staying." The two parties then took leave of each other.

Genmu followed the road down to West Sakamoto, heading for his humble home. Along the way he mused to himself: "I should have gone with them to East Sakamoto even if it meant missing my prayers." He did not, however, actually go so far as to turn around and retrace his steps.

On the road before him he saw nothing but the image of the youth. His love flared, red as the autumn leaves on Mount Tatsuta.[22] Thus he passed through Shizuhara and Seryō[23] as though they were cold, foreign lands. With love-stricken heart he arrived at his hut in Ōhara.

He knelt before his private altar, offered clean water, arranged fresh flowers, and worshiped for a time. Suddenly, as he prayed, the image of the boy with whom he had fallen in love displaced all his pious thoughts. The youth could have been standing by his side, it was so vivid an image.

In the frosty winter dawn, the peal of temple bells rang out sharply and the crowing of roosters announced the hour. Genmu left his hut and hurried up the mountain. From there he hiked down to East Sakamoto and at lodging houses near Shōgenji he asked for the vow-taker from Mount Nikkō, as he had been told. One innkeeper answered his query with the question, "From where have you come?"

"From Ōhara."

"Really? Someone who said he had come from Mount Nikkō to take his vows did, in fact, stay here. He left for the provinces early this morning, before dawn. He told me, though, that if someone from Ōhara were to come looking for him, I was to give him this. He left a letter for you." The innkeeper handed it to Genmu.

Genmu was dismayed. It seemed like a bad dream. He had come all this way eagerly expecting to see the one who had stolen his heart. In his anticipation the dawn had been long in coming. Now he hastened to read the letter that had been entrusted to the innkeeper. Through a flood of falling tears, he read:

> Yesterday we met by chance and exchanged words. Our
> meeting was the result of karma from previous lives. The

---

22. Mount Tatsuta is a mountain in Nara Prefecture famous for the beauty of its autumnal colors.

23. Shizuhara and Seryō are villages neighboring Ōhara.

wind blew wildly on Mount Hiei while a gentler breeze
ruffled blossoms that would not bloom on a snowy pine.[24]
We spent the day speaking but half our thoughts: tomorrow
the words we exchanged then will become a tale of old
times. Although the desire to stay here one more day burns
deep in my heart, I must be on my way. And so our
thoughts must be left half unspoken. I am sorry to go; I
falter as we set off this morning. If you ever make the
journey east, please visit me. Ask for Sotsu and Jijū of
Chikurin Cloister on Mount Nikkō.

At the end was appended a poem:

> Awake all night
> On my cold and lonely travel pillow,
> I cannot see you in dreams I do not dream.

This poem from the boy he loved created in Genmu's heart a
turmoil of tangled and unforgettable recollections.[25] Irrepressible tears
welled up and soaked his sleeves.

Since Genmu could hardly go on standing there indefinitely, he
returned tearfully to Ōhara. After that his ardor in the practice of his
faith cooled. He prayed earnestly only for an opportunity to see the
youth once again. Day and night he gazed at the letter and wept.

Genmu put aside his rosary and quit reading sutras. He forgot all
about vespers and services of repentance. The days and months slipped
by while Genmu did nothing but think endlessly of the boy.

The year finally drew to an end, and a hint of spring came with
the new year. At the beginning of the third month, when the night-
ingales came to perch in the interlaced branches of the cherry trees,
when the scattering blossoms looked like drifting snow, and when the
mountain cherries bloomed in unison, masking the hillsides, Genmu
was again moved to tears by his vision of the youth, who had likened
the winter snow to spring blossoms. Why had he so lost his heart to that
boy?

24. This is a reference to Genmu's poetic comment that the youth was, to Genmu, like a
    "frost of cherry blossoms." Here the youth remarks that he, the gentler breeze,
    gave Genmu, the pine tree, a brief rush of passionate feeling that could not come
    to fruition (blossoms that don't bloom).

25. "Recollections" is literally *wasuregusa*, a name for the miscanthus reed, which was
    thought to cause one to forget sad things if carried on one's person. In carrying the
    reed, however, one would be continually reminded of what one was trying to
    forget.

As Genmu burned with passion for the youth from whom he had parted, images of the boy rose up like smoke, engulfing him. He became as if possessed by this love. His longing deepened as the days passed, and he resolved to go to Mount Nikkō in Shimotsuke to see the youth once again. Having made this rash decision, his love burned even more strongly, and the flames of his consuming passion became beacons lighting his way. He hurried to Shimotsuke, traveling both by day and by night. It was late in the afternoon on the fifteenth day of the third month when he arrived.

From door to door he went, asking for the Chikurin Cloister, but since there were two or three thousand such cloisters on Mount Nikkō, finding it was no simple matter. He continued his search for some time, but at length the sun began to set. He needed lodgings no more elaborate than the evening blossoms on which the dew settles at twilight, but there were none. Then, while he stood forlornly in front of the main hall, a monk approached Genmu and asked him where he was from.

Genmu replied with a question of his own: "Can you tell me where on this mountain I might find the Chikurin Cloister?"

The monk replied at some length: "I know just where it is, but no one will open the gate at a traveler's request now that night has fallen. We are very strict on this mountain. If you go wandering about at night as you are, you are sure to be challenged. Put up somewhere for the night and pay your visit in the morning."

"Well then, where can I find lodgings?"

"No temple will take you in at this hour, but if you go about five hundred meters up toward the summit, there's a hall where you can spend the night. It's over there where you can see candles burning. The main hall, unfortunately, is strictly off limits. I am forbidden to have you in my own quarters, or I would give you lodgings for the night." Then the monk excused himself and walked off toward the main hall.

Feeling more and more discouraged, Genmu made his way along the unfamiliar mountain path with only his tears for company. He headed toward the candlelight, but although he had been told it was only about five hundred meters, he had gone some two thousand or so before he reached the hall.

He peered inside. Apparently no one had lived in the place for many years, but flowers, an incense burner, and candles had been set out by monks of the temple, he presumed, and the candlelight shone brightly. He approached the altar to pray to the gods enshrined there and saw Amida, flanked by Kannon and Seishi.[26] The light of a misty moon on this cloudy spring night shone in, mingling with the radiance emanating from Amida's brow.[27]

The night wind rustled through the pines and scattered the cherry blossoms. It was a lovely moment that enabled Genmu to calm himself, but he longed all the more for his beloved. As if in sympathy, the moonlight glistened on his tear-drenched sleeves while he waited for morning.

Then from the lower slopes of the mountain he heard the notes of a flute, the most beautiful in the world. "How wonderful a sound! Even in the capital I have never heard such playing. Music like this might cause heavenly beings to appear and induce even grasses and trees to lean in its direction," he thought to himself.

Wondering who the musician might be, he listened carefully and could hear the sound approaching, ascending the mountain. "How strange!" he thought. "That path didn't look well traveled. I doubt that anyone lives here. It's odd that someone playing a flute should be coming in this direction." As he listened intently, Genmu realized that the flute player had stopped in front of the hall.

The music continued for close to an hour. It was at once frightening and delightful. Genmu considered going out to see who it was, but in the end, he remained where he was, listening.

Then he caught the sound of quiet footsteps nearing the hall. The door opened with a rasping moan and someone entered. It was a

26. Amida, ruler of the Western Paradise, is usually accompanied by the compassionate Kannon and Seishi.

27. Light was thought to emanate from a white curl between the Buddha's eyebrows. It is one of the Thirty-Two Marks of a Buddha. See n. 1.

boy of sixteen or seventeen clad in robes of silk and brocade, a pale-green chest protector, thigh guards, and a white silk cape. At his waist was a sword decorated with gold.

"If some demon or devil has come to do me in, so be it. If I am going to die for my beloved, there is nothing I can do about it," Genmu thought. Looking more closely, however, he realized it was the youth to whom he had lost his heart. It was Hanamatsu![28] "How strange! How could this be?" He was stunned.

"Somehow, traveling monk, I feel as though I've met you before," said the boy, "but I don't quite remember. It's as though it happened in a forgotten dream one spring night. Who are you? How did you find your way to this unknown mountain where there aren't even any cuckoos to challenge a passerby?"

"I'm from Ōhara near the capital. I have cut my roots, and, like an unanchored waterlily, I let the wind set my course as I wander through the provinces. I know someone who lives here, and I was looking for him, but I have been unable to find him. Not having a place to stay, I thought I would pass the night in this hall."

"Whom at this temple have you come to see?"

"I am looking for Jijū of the Chikurin Cloister."

"Are you, by any chance, the monk who came to wait out the snowstorm at Shiō'in on Mount Hiei last winter and with whom, for a little while, I had a casual conversation? Are you Genmu of Ōhara?"

"Why should I hide anything from you now? In longing for you my soul has separated from my body so that I have become an empty locust shell. My only cry is the sound of my weeping. Unable to bear my yearning, I have come here to visit you. I am so happy to see you." He drew out the letter he had received from the boy and gave in to the tears that welled up in his eyes.

"I also have been very unhappy," admitted the youth. "Perhaps the blur of my tears has obscured its brilliance, or maybe it is a typical spring phenomenon, but this pale light of the midnight moon casts such a beautiful hue upon the cherry blossoms that I couldn't maintain my composure without picking up my flute. Then I heard that someone from the capital was asking for the Chikurin Cloister. Thinking it might be you, I made my way here secretly through the dew on the grasses along this mountain road. How glad I am to see you! Come along now. I'll show you the way to Chikurin Cloister," he said, tugging on Genmu's sleeve.

"I'm ashamed to have you see me in these traveling clothes. I came only to see you, so I can go back to the capital now."

28. This is the first use of the youth's given name.

"Everyone knows that no one looks his best when he's been traveling," the youth replied. "Besides, how can you care so much as to come all this way to see me and then disregard my wishes? How am I to trust you?" He looked peeved.

"Don't take it that way. I'd be delighted to do whatever you'd like." In his happiness Genmu forgot all his recent misery. When they had walked quite some way they arrived at a cloister and could hear people talking inside, but there was no one in the sleeping quarters yet.

"This is where I live, Chikurin Cloister. Wait here for a moment," the boy said before going inside. In a short time he reappeared and, at the youth's invitation, Genmu entered.

Genmu thought it strange that in a place as splendid as this neither the abbot nor the youth's colleagues had come out to greet him, that only Hanamatsu had welcomed him. He assumed the boy was feeling shy about having him visit.

Genmu found himself in a well-furnished, medium-sized room.[29] On a sandalwood table there was a funeral tablet that read "the spirit of the deceased Kakaku."[30] An ink stone and writing paper had been laid out in front of the tablet. It was a handsome reception room. Genmu could hear sounds of desultory conversation coming from another part of the building, but no one joined them.

Hanamatsu explained that the abbot would have liked to meet Genmu that night, but a brisk evening breeze threatened the blossoms, and since he was an old man, it grieved him. He would greet Genmu the following day. Sotsu and Jijū had pressing chores to do, so they too would see him the next morning.

"How wonderful that fate brought us together that day," Hanamatsu continued. "Intending only to wait out the wind-driven snow on Mount Hiei, we spoke casually, briefly, and after that—I'm embarrassed to say it, but—I could not forget you. Amid my tears I hoped that I might have word of you even though there was only the fickle wind to bring it. And here, you've come. I am very, very happy to see you. Our being able to talk together here now, so unexpectedly, must be the result of our intense longing for each other. Since you and I are both fond of linked verse, let us compose poetry for a while." Hanamatsu took up the ink stone and paper from the table. "I will record our poem myself," he said. "Please make up the opening lines."

29. The room is six *ma*, or about 216 square feet.

30. The *ka* of "Kakaku" is the Chinese pronunciation of the Japanese word *hana*, a hint that this is Hanamatsu's name in death. The text in *Muromachi jidai monogatari taisei* gives "Kakaku" in *kana*; the Chinese characters are found in *Zoku gunsho ruijū* 18.1:403.

"If you don't mind," Genmu replied firmly, "would *you* please do it, so I'll have a memento of this visit?"

"As you wish," the youth agreed. Then he recited:

With this evening squall
We will be parted from the blossoms,
Not to be seen again in the morning.

"Although it's rude of me to say so, I trust you won't mind," Genmu began, "but, beautiful though they are, those lines are rather ominous. Won't you alter them a bit?"

Part Two

"You're right," replied Hanamatsu, "but the uncertainty of life is an old truth. You may think you can rely on what is here today, but tomorrow it will have vanished. Hardest of all to love are the cherry blossoms. *Literary Selections*[31] includes the lines: 'Time passes and nothing endures; blossoms do not bloom a second time.' The blossoms in spring, the song of the nightingale in summer, the red maple leaves in autumn, and the first snow of winter are the most moving of beautiful things, but which of them lasts forever? Human life is no different. Even a northerner who lives a thousand years passes away in the end. That is the way of this fragile, transient world. Because I know we are to part, not to meet again tomorrow, I chose those lines."

Genmu was deeply touched by Hanamatsu's acute sensitivity. They composed verses on the subjects of the four seasons, love, the expression of feelings, and nostalgia for one's birthplace. A round was finished in no time at all.

Hanamatsu drew his flute from his belt, folded around it the paper on which he had written their linked verse, and handed it to Genmu. "I'll miss you so much more than words could ever convey," he said, and then he bade Genmu farewell. He picked up his sword and left abruptly, vanishing into the night.

"Am I dreaming or have I really spent the night with Hanamatsu?" Genmu wondered. He could not be sure. He thought that perhaps a demon had bewitched him. Fearful that people would be suspicious and that there might be some kind of trouble, he decided to

31. *Literary Selections* (Chinese [C] *Wen hsuan*, J *Monzen*) is a sixth-century collection of Chinese prose and poetry.

hasten on his way. When dawn broke, however, Genmu was still sitting there in a daze, with Hanamatsu's flute and their poem in his hand.

An old monk who might have been the abbot of the cloister stepped into the room. Frost tinged his eyebrows and a network of wrinkles creased his forehead. He wore a black robe and brown mantle. Having been lost in thought, he was startled to see Genmu. "Who are you? What are you doing in here?" he demanded.

"I'm from Ōhara, near the capital," replied Gemmu.

"That's no answer! What is someone from the capital doing here? You're a strange one. Monks! Hurry! There's a suspicious character in here! Throw him out!" he shouted roughly.

"Something strange has happened," said Genmu. "Listen a bit. I'll explain." He asked if this was the Chikurin Cloister.

"Indeed it is," was the answer.

"Did, by any chance, a youth called Hanamatsu go to Mount Hiei to take his vows on the eighth of the eleventh month last year, traveling with two colleagues called Sotsu and Jijū?"

The old monk admitted that was so.

"Let me tell you calmly what has happened," Genmu began. He related in detail how the winter before he had gone to Shiō'in to wait out the drifting snow and driving winds and had spoken casually with Hanamatsu; how from that day on he had loved the youth as profoundly as Lake Asaka in Michinoku is deep[32]; and how, this very dawn, his beloved blossom had been parted from him by the wind.

32. *Asaka no numa* is a lake located at the foot of Mount Asaka in Fukushima Prefecture. Partially homophonous with *asakarazu*, "not shallow," it allows for a pun in

When Genmu showed him the flute and writing paper, the old monk, choking on his tears, could say nothing. In a few minutes, he called out: "Sotsu, Jijū! Come here!" The two monks entered. "Have you ever seen this traveling monk before?"

"Yes, last year, when Hanamatsu took his vows, we met him briefly." They pressed their sleeves to their faces and wept, unable to utter another word.

After a short time the old monk spoke: "Traveling monk, listen to me. That youth was the son of a man of this province, a lieutenant in the Division of the Left, Taiko no Ieaki. When Hanamatsu was seven, his father Ieaki had an argument with the eldest Ono brother, Chikatada of the Military Guards, and was slain. Afterward Hanamatsu declared that he would grow up in a hurry, slay his father's murderer to settle the score, and dedicate the act to his father's benefit in the next world. I said he mustn't, that someone who was to enter properly into the Buddhist life as my disciple must never think of such a thing. I counseled him repeatedly to renounce the world and pray for his father's salvation. He finally agreed to follow my advice, and the months and years went by. Then on the tenth of this month he begged leave. 'The blossoms are out in my home town,' he said, 'and there are many people dear to me who are fond of linked verse, both family members and friends. I would like to spend a little time with them now.'

Japanese, which I have rendered as a metaphor. Michinoku is the old name for northeastern Japan.

"'It's been quite a long time since you first came up this mountain, so go ahead, but you are to come right back. I can allow you to leave the temple to compose a bit of poetry as long as violence is not your ulterior motive. Your goal is to master the teachings of Buddhism, even if you never attain enlightenment. You must come straight back here,' I told him. He was very glad to have received my permission and left immediately.

"About eight o'clock the next morning Hanamatsu's attendants arrived out of breath and nearly hysterical. 'Our lord killed that villain Ono last night! He slipped right past the guards and slew Ono with ease! He even escaped the mansion without getting hurt, but then someone caught up with him, and he was struck down!' They blurted out their awful news.

"I knew I wasn't dreaming, but neither could I believe my ears. I looked heavenward, remembering that in response to my lectures he had denied having any such intentions. I had believed him. Secretly, though, he had been planning this revenge. When I realized that he had known his farewell the day before would be his last, old man that I am, I could not restrain my tears.

"I went down to his village at once. My grief at the sight of his body was almost unbearable. But there were things to be done. We took charge of his corpse and arranged his funeral. Today is the seventh day[33]

33. Memorial services for the deceased were held seven times, once every seven days. During this time the deceased is in the intermediate state of *chūu*, the state of

after that blossom on a young tree fell, cruelly leaving behind this old pine. Since he had so loved his flute while he lived, we placed it in his casket. His spirit must have felt consoled by your deep love for him, and he has given you his flute as a memento. Since he loved linked verse too, we set out that writing paper yesterday in preparation for the memorial service today. You say you met him last night and composed poetry with him? That first verse speaks of transience because he was no longer of this world."

Genmu had listened intently and was now weeping. He felt as though he had lost his senses and his sanity. In anguish and sorrow he reflected: "I stupidly let myself become entangled in an attachment, in a romantic passion, and so I have encountered a spirit. It is like Chuang-tzu's having dreamed of being a butterfly.[34] If we would just stop long enough to think about it, the fact that we must all grow old and die is only too obvious. I prayed to the mountain god of Hiei and the Yakushi Buddha in the main hall on Enryakuji for faith and enlightenment, but after meeting Hanamatsu I never let the tears on my sleeves dry. I was deluded! How ashamed I am! The Lotus Sutra repudiates love for novices or youths as something to be avoided.[35] Genshin, in the Teachings Essential for Rebirth, quotes the Sutra of Meditation on the True Law, which asserts that such love is punished in the third hell.[36] Could it lead to anything but continued rebirth in this world? Hanamatsu

wandering between incarnations. Those who are reborn into the Western Paradise are reborn there immediately. Others are reborn at the end of a period of seven days, or after a second period of seven days, and so on. The longest one might wait to be reborn is forty-nine days (NKD 13:430).

34. Having dreamed that he was a butterfly, Chuang-tzu (late fourth century B.C.) awoke and wondered if perhaps he were not a butterfly dreaming that it was a man.

35. Chapter 14, "Comfortable Conduct," of the Lotus Sutra reads: "He [a Bodhisattva-Mahāsattva] has no desire to rear a young disciple or a srāmanera-boy [J shami, 'novice']" (Hurvitz, Lotus Blossom 209). Nenshō deshi, shami shōni [o] yashinau [koto] tanoshimazu (T no. 262, 9:37).

36. The text mistakenly reads Shobō nenju kyō rather than the correct Shōbō nenjō kyō (T no. 721). The Teachings Essential for Rebirth reads:

Those who have committed the transgression of male homosexuality fall into Takuno [a section within Shugo jigoku]. When they see their former lovers their whole bodies heat up as if on fire. When they approach and embrace their former lovers their bodies fall to pieces. Having died and revived, they are frightened and flee but fall over a cliff and are devoured by fire-breathing birds and foxes.

Ōjōyōshū, 1, 17–18. See also Reischauer, "Genshin's Ojo Yoshu," 33.

blossomed only briefly and was scattered in the wind, but he was, after all, the answer to the prayer I addressed to the gods and Buddhas."

The fact that the seed of Buddhahood sprouts from karmic rela-tionships was, for Genmu, cause both for rejoicing and for mourning. He took his leave of the monks on Mount Nikkō and returned home. From there he proceeded to Mount Kōya where he lived in seclusion. He spent his time reading Tendai texts, which praise Amida above all and extol his Western Paradise. All the sutras and commentaries he studied laud the Buddha and commend the Pure Land. The three syllables of Amida's name symbolize the Three Bodies of the Buddha[37] and the Three Views of Reality. This doctrine, most appropriate to the temper of the present degenerate age, is fully explained in the three most revered sutras of the Pure Land school.[38]

Many years ago Hōnen advocated the practice of invoking Amida's name, and many people were able to realize their hope for rebirth in his Pure Land. Genmu, like Shan-tao[39] long ago and Hōnen more recently, prayed for the fulfillment of his earnest desire to be reborn in the Western Paradise.

Moreover, the monks of the Chikurin Cloister on Mount Nikkō abandoned the path to Buddhahood by personal effort and converted to Zen. In order to achieve enlightenment by means of direct experience, they sought out a master who taught them without the use of written or spoken words, relying instead on unmediated spiritual communication. They devoted themselves to meditation in order to recognize their essential, inherent Buddhahood. They lived together in a mountain forest, sleeping under the trees and practicing seated meditation. Every moment of their lives was spent under the guidance of their master. How wonderful that they could hope to enter the realm of thoughtlessness, that the lotus flowers of their hearts might blossom in pure understanding!

On the tenth day of the third month of the following year, the anniversary of Hanamatsu's death, Genmu went to the inner sanctum of Mount Kōya to worship at Kōbō Daishi's shrine. There he was fer-vently reciting the *nenbutsu*, praying for the salvation of each and every being in the universe, when he noticed a young monk. This young monk was only about twenty years old and wore a tattered black

---

37. The Three Bodies of the Buddha, or *trikāya*, refer to the Buddha as absolute truth, the various Bodhisattvas, and the historical Buddha.

38. The three sutras are: *Sutra on the Buddha of Measureless Life* (Muryōjukyō, T no. 360); *Sutra on Meditating on the Buddha of Measureless Life* (Kanmuryōjukyō, T no. 365); and *Amida Sutra* (Amidakyō, T no. 366).

39. Shan-tao (J Zendō, 618–81) founded the Pure Land school in China.

hempen robe. He seemed totally intent on his salvation in the next world, as he too recited the *nenbutsu*. "How strange!" thought Genmu. "As young as he is, he seems very anxious about his fate in the next world. How wonderful!"

Just then the youth, apparently thinking he was alone, started talking to himself: "Hail Amida Budda. The way of this sad world is uncertainty. A year ago last night[40] my father was struck down and I slew his enemy. I can picture that boy in my mind even now. What torment it is!" He held his sleeves to his face, but his tears were a tide that could not be stemmed.

Genmu overheard him and his curiosity was aroused. "Excuse me, traveling monk, but where are you from and how did you come to renounce the world?"

The young monk turned to him and replied: "Although I am embarrassed to speak about myself, I have, after all, abandoned the world and have nothing to hide. I would be glad to tell you the story of my religious awakening. I am from Shimotsuke. My father was the eldest of the Ono brothers, an officer in the Military Guards. Hana-matsu, the son of a lieutenant of the Left Division of the same province, bore a long-standing grudge against my father. It must have been his destiny—my father was slain a year ago tonight, when I was eighteen. I wasn't there when it happened, but the instant I learned of it I gave chase. The murderer had a good head start, but I easily caught up with him and killed him. At that point I was very pleased with myself. I went home with a big grin on my face.

"The next day when I went to examine the corpse I discovered that I had cut down a youth no more than sixteen or seventeen years old. His beauty was that of a fresh blossom torn from the branch by a rough wind. It was a heart-rending sight. Only because he had been born the son of a samurai had his fate been thus sadly fixed. This was a lesson on the uncertainty of life, I realized. Feeling that I should both mourn my father's death and pray for the youth's salvation, I came to a firm decision. That same night I left my home. I came here to Mount Kōya and took the tonsure. Having put my faith in Amida, I have been praying for rebirth in his Western Paradise. Since it was just a year ago last night that they both were killed, I came here to pray for their salvation." The young monk had spared no details in telling his story.

"It is true," he continued, "that this fragile world is fraught with sorrow and that my tale is an unusual one. I am not surprised to see you

---

40. Apparently Genmu spent the night in prayer and noticed this youth the following morning.

moved to tears, but you seem quite overwhelmed. Why do you grieve so intensely?"

"Yours is only a story of the way of the world, but who could fail to be deeply touched?" replied Genmu. "I feel as though I can see that boy even now. It's this vision of him that brings these tears to my eyes."

"That's just it!" exclaimed the young monk. "I think it strange that you should say, 'I feel as though I can see that boy even now.' That's the kind of thing you'd say about someone you knew. Please, tell me how you came to renouce the world."

"I'm embarrassed to tell anyone," said Genmu, "but since you told me the reason for your religious awakening, I will share my revelation with you." He wept as he related how he had fallen in love with Hanamatsu that winter day and how, ever since the dawning of the night of their brief reunion, he had been practicing ritual austerities to deepen his religious understanding. When he finished his tale of this sad, ephemeral world, the young monk and Genmu had both succumbed to tears.

They could no more see their loved ones again than the fisher girls tending salt fires by the wild sea had leisure to adorn their hair with even simple combs.[41]

A certain scripture, however, says that while clinging to memories is an illness, giving them up is like taking medicine. Perpetual rebirth is the result of former actions, but when we repent and reveal past deeds we bring this cycle to an end.

From that day on Genmu and the young monk each treated the other as his mentor. They devoutly recited the *nenbutsu* and vowed that they would share the same lotus seat when they were reborn together at the very highest level of the Western Paradise.[42] As they practiced *nenbutsu* meditation, they anticipated living amid the seven-jeweled trees[43] in the Pure Land.

---

41. These lines paraphrase a poem in item 87 in *The Tales of Ise* (McCullough, *Ise*, 130):

> Tending salt-fires by the wild sea
> Fringed with reed-thatched huts,
> The fisher girls have no leisure
> Even to dress their hair
> With simple wooden combs.

42. Those who entered the Pure Land at the highest level were immediately granted an audience with the Buddha. Others had to wait periods of varying length for this and other privileges of salvation.

43. These trees had roots of gold, trunks of gold-copper alloy, white gold branches, agate streaks, leaves of coral, white jade blossoms, and pearls for fruit.

What a blessed fate they shared! One evening, having reached the ages of seventy-seven and sixty, Genmu and the monk from Shimotsuke quietly passed away together. In their last moments they knelt in prayer and invoked the name of the Buddha ten times. Thus they attained Buddhahood. Flowers rained down from the heavens and music was heard coming from the clouds.

Flanked by Kannon and Seishi, Amida appeared in order to escort them to his paradise. The deity addressed them, saying, "Like light shining into every corner, I will reach every *nenbutsu* believer in the cosmos to bring them in rebirth to my Western Paradise."

The Buddhas' reliance on expedient means and the vows of the gods are long standing. How marvelous that Genmu's fervent prayers to the mountain god of Hiei and the Yakushi Buddha in the main hall of Enryakuji caused many to awaken to the truth!

Hanamatsu was an incarnation of Mañjuśrī.[44] How wonderful that he manifests himself in human form in order to bring salvation to all sentient beings!

Anyone who has heard this tale should read one scroll of a sutra and recite once the *nenbutsu* for the sake of those whose lives have been recounted here. Tales of the past are said to be foolish talk and dazzling rhetoric, but they are expedient means useful in teaching the unenlightened. By comparing the state of this uncertain world to the fragile blossom of a youth who succumbed as though to a gust of wind, by likening his short life, his transient self, to a dream inspired by the sound of the bells that toll at dawn, this tale sweeps away the clouds of darkness and brings us face to face with the moon of ultimate reality.

It is wretched of us to idle away our days until illness suddenly overtakes us, until we are at death's door. Do we postpone digging a well until we are suffering from thirst? Young or old, we must not delay another day. We should profoundly dread the cycle of life and death and strive diligently for rebirth in the Western Paradise. We must not waste days and months in frivolity. People of earlier eras valued every moment of time as preciously as gold. Just as surely as the moon travels westward behind the clouds of a rainy night, without doubt, those who rely on Amida will reach the Western Paradise.

First Postscript

The pathos of this tale as I read it for the first time has moved me to tears.

---

44. Mañjuśrī (J Monju), the bodhisattva of wisdom, is sometimes associated with male homosexuality. See Ihara, *Five Women*, 150.

A storm in the night and we are parted from the blossoms;
They are gone in the morning.
These few words and tears alone remain.

Look at them, the blossoms that fall so quickly.
Realize that the pine too,
After a thousand years, will wither.

The brief snow
Promising to stay for the night
Turns into the tears of Genmu's dream.

1486, fourth month, second day

Second Postscript

Chinese texts convey the truth to the learned and wise in our country.
For those who are slow and unenlightened, it is revealed in our native
tongue.

Although this is only an insignificant little story, there is not a
single falsehood in it. It is an expression of truth. I sincerely hope that
those who read it will put away their doubts and pray for salvation.

1668, fifth month, third day[45]

---

45. Just as the author of the tale is anonymous, so too are the writers of these postscripts
unknown.

Tales Told on Mount Kōya

What we call Mount Kōya is 250 miles[1] from the capital, and far from any village. There are no human voices, nor do mountain breezes rustle the branches of the trees. In the shadows of the setting sun, all is quiet. This holy place is particularly sacred. Here Kōbō Daishi[2] established a retreat, and here he died in the spring of 835. The path from the main temple of Kongōbuji[3] to Kōbō Daishi's shrine is thirty-seven chō,[4] representing the thirty-seven practices [for achieving the wisdom of enlightenment].[5]

Awaiting dawn, the wind in these pines will rouse you from your dreams and awaken you to the illusory nature of this unreliable world. Thus, men of discretion come here to renounce the secular world. Hoping to attain salvation in their next lives, they follow the example set by Kōbō Daishi and practice the teachings of the Shingon sect. There are also those who seat themselves on the floor to practice *zazen* meditation. There are others who built a hall in which to practice *nenbutsu* meditation. They sit at the window [facing the western sky] in anticipation of being welcomed into Amida's Pure Land. Their methods vary but derive from one original source.[6] They pray that the deceased, faithful and faithless alike, may attain salvation in the Pure Land.

---

1. Literally, one hundred *ri*, which equals 244 miles. The distance is actually only about 50 miles. A similar description of Mount Kōya, claiming the distance is two hundred *ri*, is found in *The Tale of the Heike* 10.9, "On Mount Kōya"; see Kitagawa and Tsuchida, *Heike*, 613–14 and McCullough, *Heike*, 343–44.

2. See the introduction, p. 5.

3. Kongōbuji was founded in 816 as the head temple of the Shingon sect.

4. Thirty-seven *chō* equals 2.5 miles.

5. The text reads *tosotsu no sanjūshichibon* (thirty-seven practices of Tuṣita), but there does not seem to be any particular connection between these practices and Tuṣita, which is the fourth of the six heavens in the world of desires and is where Maitreya, the Buddha of the future, now resides.

6. Insofar as there was one original, historical Buddha, Śākyamuni, there is one source of the various Buddhist sects.

53

On Mount Kōya there is a hall called Kayadō,[7] which is used for the practice of uninterrupted *nenbutsu*. Here the six daily services[8] are meticulously carried out. The head monk of Kayadō had been lord of an estate of 3,000 chō[9] in Nanjō in Hōki Province[10] and, moreover, landlord of considerable property in other provinces. Needless to say, his was a prosperous family. Yet, perhaps because of karma from a former life, at the age of thirty-three he renounced the world to become a monk at Kayadō. He was sixty-two when he realized his cherished wish for rebirth in the Pure Land.[11]

One night in the middle of the ninth month the moon shone with incomparable clarity, unobscured by clouds of transgression despite the great height of the peak of Mount Kōya. "The moon looks just like this even in the unreliable world," thought the head monk, and he remembered past days. He wept, dampening his black sleeves. "Why do these memories linger," he wondered, feeling perturbed. He bemoaned [his failings] and was restless and uneasy.

His colleagues numbered over three hundred. Among those who were not inferior to the head monk were Shun Amidabu,[12] heir to the lord of Hōki, Ichi Amidabu of Utsunomiya, Kō Amidabu of Yūki, and Sei Amidabu of Sasaki. From the ranks of the nobility were Sai Amidabu of Fukakusa and Myō Amidabu of Tsukinowa.

These men, and others, when they had finished the early evening *nenbutsu* service, said to the head monk, "We should not waste a night when the moon is so beautiful. Let us indulge ourselves in some casual literary pastime." Those intending to take part opened the latticed

7. This cloister is associated with the religious tale *Karukaya*, which describes a man who, in becoming a monk, abandons his family and vows never to see them again. His son loses both his mother and sister while searching for the father he had never met, and then he also becomes a monk. He in fact meets and spends several years together with his father on Mount Kōya while never learning his father's identity. See *Karukaya* in Muroki Yatarō, ed., *Sekkyōshū* (*Shinchō Nihon koten shūsei*) (Tokyo: Shinchōsha, 1977), 9–77.

8. The six daily services are held in the early morning, at midday, at sunset, and in the early evening, mid-evening, and late evening.

9. In this context, one chō equals 2.45 acres. Three thousand chō is thus the equivalent of 7,350 acres, a vast estate.

10. Hōki is now the western part of Tottori Prefecture. Nanjō probably refers to the region controlled by the Nanjō family, which was a local power in eastern Hōki from early in the Muromachi period.

11. That is, he was sixty-two when he died.

12. This type of name was often taken by adherents of the Ji school, founded by Ippen, the most popular form of *nenbutsu* belief in the Muromachi period (Matsunaga and Matsunaga, *Japanese Buddhism*, vol. 2, 134).

shutters in the southern, front face of the hall and took out narrow sheets of paper or folded paper on which to jot down poems.

Someone had asked for a first line when the head monk said, "Poetry and linked verse are well valued, but as 'foolish talk and dazzling rhethoric'[13] they are distractions that create obstacles to enlightenment. As I look around at each of you I don't see anyone unworthy. The fact that we all came from different towns and provinces to gather here in one place is evidence of a bond of more than one lifetime. It is said that sharing the shade of the same tree or drinking from the same stream is the result of ancient karmic bonds from other lives. Of course, being companions in many years of religious practice, how could [our karmic bond] be any less than that of like-minded friends? Since it is said that revealing what led to our religious awakenings nullifies wrongdoing, let us do so. Leaving nothing in our hearts unsaid, let us reveal why we each renounced the world, and let us tell of our years of religious practice. Let us hear what it was that originally hindered each other's enlightenment."

The others agreed, saying, "That would be very appropriate."

Shun Amidabu of Hōki, who occupied the lowest ranking seat, was the first to tell the tale of his religious awakening.

"I don't have any special incident to relate, but my father was exceedingly wicked.[14] Naturally, he punished the guilty, but he even arrested innocent people if they crossed him in the least way and threw them into the jail he had built. He always had fifty to sixty people locked up. There was a constant stream of heads and bodies to be disposed of because executions were carried out day and night. It was awful to hear the cries of grieving husbands and wives. It did not matter to my father if he stole land that belonged to shrines or temples. It did not bother him to commit crimes against the Buddha, religious law, or the clergy. He took whatever he wanted, knowing no shame. He devoted himself solely to evil.

"Once my father bound a prisoner and tortured him. He put a large snake inside a bamboo tube and put that down the prisoner's throat. When the snake reached the pit of the prisoner's stomach, the

---

13. "Foolish talk and dazzling rhetoric" renders *kyōgen kigo*, an important literary/religious concept. See LaFleur, *Words*, 1–25 and Margaret H. Childs, "Kyōgeñ-kigo: Love Stories as Buddhist Sermons," *Japanese Journal of Religious Studies* 12.1 (March 1985):91–104.

14. Shun Amidabu's story parallels the life of Odawara Kyōkai (late 11th century), who established the first organization of Kōya holy men (*hijiri*). As the son of the Lord of Sanuki, he felt pity for the prisoners that his father tortured. When his family all died, it was thought that the vengeful spirits of the torture victims had killed them. Kyōkai, the lone survivor, became a monk (Gorai, *Kōya hijiri*, 99).

man lost consciousness. It was too awful for words. Though I often admonished my father, he never listened to a word I said.

"One day, for no special reason, I started reading an old story: 'However fresh, a fallen blossom cannot regain its branch. Human beings are born into this world, and for a time we prosper, but the days and nights pass quickly. The dreams that are our lives will shatter, and in the end our bones will be buried beneath the moss of Hokubō.'[15]

"These words struck a chord deep in my heart, moving me to tears. In this world of dream and illusion, my own father was a wicked man, but I hated this unreliable world and decided to enter the true way. In the autumn of my nineteenth year I came to this holy mountain."

Many in the group were touched and wept as he finished.

Ichi Amidabu of Utsunomiya[16] spoke next. "When I was three, my cousin murdered my father. I grew up with my heart set on getting revenge against my enemy, Officer Okuma. One day I entered my private Buddhist altar room to make an offering of flowers and incense and to pray for my father's salvation, but all I could think of, with bitter regret, was the fact that I had not yet avenged my father's death. I could not suppress the tears that flowed spontaneously.

"The man who was my teacher and mentor saw me like this, approached me, and said, 'I can well guess what is in your heart. You are thinking about your enemy, Okuma. Before I knew you I often went to his house to pray with him, so I know it very well. Because of my relationship with you, though, he and I are no longer on speaking terms. I am already over sixty, and so I can't be of much help, but be resolved! I will go with you, and we will cut him down. As your teacher our bond will extend for three lifetimes, so we will meet again in the next world.' He spoke with great earnestness.

"I was overjoyed. Apparently, my inner thoughts had shown on my face. I told him that I was moved beyond words to learn that he was willing to help me.

"There were only the two of us in our humble quarters. We left shortly after dark, just he and I. Clearly he felt that these were his last moments; he wrote a poem and left it on the double realm *mandala*[17]:

15. Mount Hokubō in Honan, China, is where kings and aristocrats were buried from the late Han to the T'ang period.

16. Utsunomiya is presently Tochigi Prefecture.

17. A double realm *mandala* represents both the Taizōkai and the Kongōkai. The Tai-zōkai (womb or matrix realm) symbolizes the Buddha as described in the *Ma-hāvairocana Sutra*. Here Mahāvairocana "appears as the Body of Principle and is represented by a lotus which stands for Principle yet unrealized, compassion,

Tonight's frost will vanish before morning.
It is the last night of an old man's life.
When I'm gone, ask for me in the shadows of the grasses.

"Next to his skin he wore a white unlined robe, and over that he had on a narrow-sleeved garment of white linen. He put on body armor, a helmet, and arm guards. He sheathed a beautiful sword at his left hip, took up a small halberd, about thirty-three inches in length, and put on a small clerical mantle. On the mantle he had jotted down the following: 'Ajari Meihan of Chōranji, Kitatani, aged sixty-one, and the youth, Rikishumaru, aged sixteen, will strike down the enemy of the latter's father, Okuma, and realize a long-cherished desire.'

"I wore a silk, narrow-sleeved undergarment, blue and yellow trousers, and body armor.[18] I carried an eight-inch dagger made by Rokumonji, a swordsmith in Sanjō. It had a red wooden haft that I had wrapped tightly with koto string. I picked up a red-tipped fan and sheathed at my side a sword thirty-two inches long, [like] Onimaru or Sakura, made by Aukuchi Kunitsuna.[19] Anxious though we were, we set out hand in hand, just the two of us.

"Having gone seven miles, we arrived at Okuma's estate well past midnight. We stealthily made our way in and found Okuma composing linked verse in a small, inner room. Never imagining [that I might dare to attack him], he was not on his guard. I wondered joyfully if the gods and Buddhas had not arranged it. Having determined that our enemy was vulnerable, my teacher made a move to go first, but I grabbed his sleeve. 'It has been my life-long dream to kill Okuma with my own hand,' I whispered, and took the lead. Brandishing my sword, I burst in on Okuma. His companions panicked. Okuma snatched up a blade lying nearby and was trying to throw open a papered door to escape into an inner room when I felled him with a slash to his right thigh. As he collapsed against the flimsy door, I cut off his head with a second stroke.

potentiality, growth, and creativity." The Kongōkai (diamond realm) depicts the state of Buddhahood as preached in the *Vajrasekhara Sutra* in which Ma-hāvairocana is the Body of Wisdom, standing "for the power of illumination, for penetrating insight that breaks through the darkness of ignorance, for infallibility, dynamic function, and actualization" (Yoshito S. Hakeda, *Kūkai, Major Works: Translated with an Account of His Life and a Study of His Thought* [New York: Columbia University Press, 1972], 85).

18. Specifically, he is wearing *nerinuki odoshi* body armor, which is made of small overlapping plates of narrowly folded silk cloth.

19. Aukuchi Kunitsuna, an unknown figure, is perhaps a mistake for Awataguchi Kunitsuna, a swordsmith of the early Kamakura period (1163–1255) who made "Onimaru" for Hōjō Tokiyori (1227–63).

"I was unutterably pleased, but then I heard young attendants and retainers shouting, 'Don't let them get away.' Whirling about, my teacher and I fought off their attack, and in moments we had killed nine of them. Not having been wounded ourselves, we picked up our enemy's severed head and withdrew. Defiantly proclaiming our names, we fought off a few more men who pursued us. Thinking it was finally all over, we were about to retreat quietly when Okuma's brother and a force of twenty men clad in full armor caught up with us, yelling, 'You won't get away with this.' We turned back and fought wildly, but we were hopelessly outnumbered and Meihan was struck down. Though I was hurt, wounded in three places, I was fighting furiously when I heard a voice say, 'I'm your father.' Suddenly there was a great bolt of lightning and a roar of thunder. The earth shook and rain began to pour down so heavily that you could not discern enemy from ally. Okuma's men shouted in confusion and ended up attacking each other.

"Since my teacher had fallen, my own life was no longer dear to me. I was about to disembowel myself when I faintly heard my teacher's voice coming from somewhere down the road: 'Your fate is here, Rikushu, come this way. Retreat.'

"'Then he hasn't been killed,' I thought, and happily followed his voice all the way to our quarters. Yet I never caught sight of him. 'How could this be?' I thought, mystified. There was no use in lamentations, though, so I retraced my steps before dawn the next morning to look for his body. It was still there at the scene of the struggle. I carried his corpse home and then brought his bones to this mountain. That was more than ten years ago," he explained.

The third to speak was Kō Amidabu of Yūki.[20] "I'm embarrassed to speak, but when I was eighteen I went to Kamakura to file a claim in a property dispute. I took as a mistress a prostitute from Tō no Tsuji[21] and lived with her for two or three years. We grew poorer and poorer as time went by, until, one New Year's Eve, we ran out of provisions to see us through the holiday. Rashly we had had not just one but two children, and, when they cried about being cold and hungry, I didn't know what to do.

"'Be a man and break into some house tonight or rob someone on a mountain road. You're not the only man who has ever had a wife and children to support. How can you bear to just abandon these children and let them die?' She complained insistently and wept loudly.

"'She's right,' I thought. I knew where a certain wealthy man lived. I broke into the place, frightening a number of women who made

20. Yūki is in what is now western Ibaraki Prefecture.

21. A neighborhood in Kamakura.

a terrible commotion. Chasing and cornering them, I stripped them of their clothes.

"I found one woman who looked about seventeen or eighteen, hiding behind a screen, clutching her nightgown. When I grabbed for it she said, 'Please, I beg you, allow me this,' and would not let go of it. I broke her grip with a stroke of my sword, took the gown, and went home.

"My wife was delighted. She said she would decide which robes to sell and which to put aside to keep and wear herself. Well, she noticed the nightgown and picked it up first. As I remembered using my sword to wrench it away from its owner, a severed hand fell out of the sleeve. The hand still clenched the gown tightly.

"'Oh, how awful! I never thought . . . ,' I said, feeling pity for the young woman.

"My wife responded, 'This is nothing. Do you think it's sad? A severed hand has a strong grip, but I'll take care of it.'

"She took out some moxa and twisted it into small clumps, which she put on each knuckle of the fingers. As the moxa burned, the fingers relaxed and the hand fell to the floor. She laughed when it was done. She seemed inhuman.

"'This is altogether too frightening and despicable; I can't bear it,' I thought. I slipped out of the house and arrived here on the eighth day of the New Year. That was eighteen years ago."

Next, Sei Amidabu of Sasaki[22] spoke. "I had two wives, and I never had any peace day or night because of their jealousy. One year early in June I went to the capital on business and remained there for some time. While I was there my first wife [whom I had left behind in Sasaki] contrived a wicked plan. She wrote letters to my second wife saying, 'Never mind how things have been till now, let's make an oath to quit being jealous and act like men.' My second wife, living with me in the capital, agreed wholeheartedly. She went to see my first wife, and they shared various intimacies. My first wife entertained her with banquets every day.

"My first wife told her, 'Since I am many years older than you, please think of me as your elder sister, and let me look upon you as my younger sister.' She spoke with such deep sincerity that my second wife, not yet twenty, naively trusted her. My first wife had persuaded a retainer of several years standing, called Sakon no Shō, to join her conspiracy. One night she had him collect a monk's various accoutrements and hide with them in my second wife's bedroom. Then, saying she wanted to enjoy the sight of the first snow of winter, my first wife

---

22. Sasaki is in what is now a part of Shiga Prefecture.

paid a visit to my second wife. She had arranged for refreshments to be served, and she encouraged my second wife to drink too much wine. She only went home after it had gotten quite late. When my second wife, tired from the wine and oblivious to her surroundings, fell asleep, Sakon no Shō put a thin cord around her neck and strangled her. He buried her deep in the graveyard of the Jizō worship hall, two-tenths of a mile to the east.

"The next morning while it was still dark, my first wife sent a letter to my second wife saying, 'I have not forgotten the beauty of your garden last night, but the snow in the dim light of early dawn this morning is also lovely. Please come and see it.' She dispatched a palanquin to fetch her. My second wife's servants accepted the letter and knocked on her door to announce the arrival of the palanquin dispatched by my first wife, but there was no answer. Concerned, they went in to find only an empty room. Quite frightened now, they informed her former wet nurse, Jijū. Jijū searched frantically for my second wife but could not find her anywhere. She was deeply distressed, but, as it was not something she could keep secret, she explained the situation to those who had brought the palanquin and sent them away. My first wife, anticipating this, immediately got into the palanquin and went to see for herself. Even before she alighted from the palanquin, she was sobbing loudly. Demanding to know what could have happened, she appealed to the heavens and then threw herself on the ground. Such grief she displayed!

"Well, she soon found the monk's things in my second wife's room. 'This is very strange indeed,' she said. 'Last night when I was here visiting, I came out to the edge of the veranda and I saw a monk standing at a gap in the brush fence. "You're a moody one! You've kept me waiting so long," he called. He came toward me and then seemed to realize that he had mistaken me for someone else and became flustered.' Then my first wife 'discovered' the monk's mantle bag and cushion and concluded that my second wife's disappearance had been his doing. Needless to say, Jijū and everyone else were extremely distraught.

"It was just then the third anniversary of the death of my second wife's father, and for the memorial service she had ordered a recitation of the *Lotus Sutra* by one thousand monks. She personally welcomed the monks and gave a garment to all those who participated. In fact twenty or thirty monks had been coming and going each day.

"Let me explain who her father was. She was the daughter of an illustrious Chūnagon, who had served the Cloistered Emperor Kazan [968–1008, r. 984–86]. As the years had gone by, the family's fortunes had waned. With her father's death she had been left like a rootless reed with no one on whom to depend. She was living in a lonely and neglected house when I heard about her and spirited her away. We had lived as husband and wife for three years.

"Well, my first wife immediately sent someone up to the capital with the message that my second wife, while arranging services for her father, had become intimate with a young monk and run off with him the night before. I dropped everything to go and see for myself. She was indeed gone.

"Having heard my first wife's story, I considered any monk my enemy. I tore down all the temples and cloisters that had been on my estate. I thought any itinerant monk who was handsome and charming might have been the culprit. I killed a great many of them until there wasn't a single monk left on my land.

"Once a monk was passing by at twilight but was afraid to ask for lodging. Having no other recourse, he decided to spend the night in the Jizō hall by the graveyard. Late that night the wind began to blow fiercely. His hair stood on end as he sensed someone coming. Since it was a lonely old graveyard, he thought there might be an evil spirit, so in wholehearted devotion he faced the altar[23] and held himself still in front of the image of Jizō. Soon he realized by the tolling of the bell of some distant mountain temple that it was about midnight. That was when he heard a tearful voice coming from the graveyard behind the hall saying, 'Oh, how painful! How painful!'

"He wasn't merely frightened. He was on the verge of fainting. At first the voice came from a hermitage behind the hall. Gradually, it approached him. He watched some kind of phantom come in through the front entrance. For a time it said nothing. Then it said, 'Ah, monk, don't be afraid of me. Please listen to what I have to say.' Finally he was able to see that it was the ghost of a woman.

"'I was raised in the capital, but after my father, the Chūnagon, died, I lived in a shabby little place. I had no prospects at all, but suddenly Toyora no Jirō of the Sasaki clan came and took me to be his wife. I was then sixteen, and I lived with him for three years. His first wife was jealous of me and conspired to have me strangled and buried behind this hall. She said I had run off with a monk like you. No one knows I am dead, and so no one is praying for my salvation. What's worse is that my husband is taking revenge by killing monks. Not only

23. The text is not clear here. "Altar" seems to be about the only thing that would make sense.

am I heavily burdened with sin as a woman because of the Five Obstacles and Three Subjugations,[24] but since it is on my account that a
considerable number of monks have been murdered, the obstacles to my
salvation are steadily mounting. Take pity on me and tell Toyora my
story. If you do he will stop despising monks and pray for me. Only then
will I be freed from all that obstructs my salvation. If he doesn't believe
you, show him this narrow-sleeved robe. It is embroidered with a design
of red plum, withered reeds, and wild ducks. Last month, on the
fifteenth of the eleventh month, he sent it to me from the capital. In
his letter he included an old poem:

> The bay is awash with white waves
> While wild ducks clamour among the reeds:
> I don't think you realize how it feels to love you as I do.[25]

"'His letter concluded, "I've had my feelings expressed in this
embroidery to give to you. I will be sending for you as soon as possible,
in the spring.""

"'When she told me [the monk] about the letter, I was overcome
with emotion and lost consciousness. In the morning I looked around
and there was the robe. I reminded myself that the basic principle by
which a monk lives is compassion. "Even though it may cost me my
life, I must go and tell Toyora," I decided.[26] I put the robe over my
shoulder and walked the short distance westward to Toyora's estate.
Everyone I met on the way said, "Oh my, how awful! Don't you know
you're heading straight for disaster? Once the lord catches sight of you,
do you think your life will last any longer than the morning dew?" All
who saw me lamented my fate.

"'I entered the front gate and looked around. Intrepid-looking
young men on guard duty were tending to some hawks. I walked over to

24. The Five Obstacles are the inability of women to become "first a Brahmā king, second
the god Sakra, third King Hāra, fourth a sage-king turning the wheel, fifth a
Buddha-body" (Hurvitz, *Lotus Blossom*, 201). The reasons for the Five Obstacles
are that women have various evil attitudes, are lewd and self-indulgent, have
contempt for others, are secretive and unclean, and are lustful (see Mochizuki
Shinko, ed., *Mochizuki Bukkyō daijiten*, vol. 2 [Tokyo: Sekai Seiten Kankō
Kyōkai, 1957], 1226–27). The Three Subjugations are that women must obey
their fathers, husbands, and sons.

25. This is poem 533 in the *Kokinshū* (905). Ducks are a conventional symbol of conjugal
love and fidelity. See Helen Craig McCullough, trans., *Kokinwakashū: The First
Imperial Anthology of Japanese Poetry* (Stanford: University of California Press,
1985), 122 and Laurel Rasplica Rodd and Mary Catherine Henkenius, trans.,
Kokinshū: A Collection of Poems Ancient and Modern (Princeton: Princeton University Press, 1984), 201.

26. Having quoted his wife speaking to the monk, Toyora is now again quoting the
monk, so the "I" here is the monk referring to himself, not to Toyora. Strangely,

them and said, "Excuse me." They looked at me as though they were thinking, "Oh, what a waste! We're going to have to get this monk's blood on our hands." No one said a word. They only clenched their sweaty fists. I repeated myself loudly several times: "Hello! Excuse me!" As I expected, the sliding doors of the main building were thrown open violently.

""Isn't there anyone on duty?" demanded the man who stormed out. I realized this was the lord himself. He looked about thirty years old and held a long sword in his left hand. When he saw me his face brightened.

""It's been a long while since I've seen a monk. How good of you to treat me to a visit just when I was in low spirits! Tie him up! Torture him until he tells us where that woman is. If you don't confess, your head will fly." He finished in anger. The young men and other attendants ran over to me, picked me up, carried me into a courtyard, and sat me down on the ground. Toyora stood on the veranda and said, "Hurry up and start the torture!"

""There is no need to torture me. I know what has happened to the lady. I came here to tell you."

"'Everyone was stunned. "How on earth . . .?" they asked me.

"'I explained just what had happened the night before. I took out the narrow-sleeved robe and gave it to Toyora. I told him everything in detail, not failing to mention the letter he had written to his second wife from the capital. Looking at the robe, Toyora said, "There is no doubt. This is the robe I sent her from the capital. My letter was exactly as you described."

"'There were two sword holes and blood stains in the front breast of the robe. There were more blood stains, which looked like writing, on the left sleeve. Looking more closely, Toyora read: "How sad and bitter I feel! We hadn't even spent three years together and now we are parted. What's worse, I'd been with child since May. Since it was my first time, I'd been embarrassed and hadn't told anyone, not even Jijū. A child who dies in the womb is heavily burdened with obstacles to salvation. Hurry and dig up my body, remove the child from my womb, and give it a funeral." There was also a poem:

> Rough wind, why do you sweep it away?
> Short lived, the ripening *susuki* grass/the fruit of my womb,
> Together with the dew, is gone.'[27]

Toyora maintains the monk's point of view when he quotes the monk's description of their meeting.

27. The original includes a word play on *harau,* "to sweep away," and *haramu,* "to conceive" and "to come into ear," which contain *hara,* "womb."

"A close look revealed that, without doubt, it was the handwriting of the woman I had loved.[28] Of course, I was shaken to the core. I had the monk lead the way to the graveyard, and when we dug up the earth, moved the stones, and retrieved the body, it was, unquestionably, my wife.

"Around her neck was a money cord, and in her chest were the marks of two sword wounds. I had to avert my eyes when I saw that her breasts were swollen. Well, my task could not be left undone. I unsheathed the sword at my side and slit open her abdomen to find a beautiful baby boy. I felt dizzy and almost fainted. Needless to say, I was grief stricken.

"Nothing was to be gained from lamentations. I arranged for the funerals then and there. I turned the Jizō hall into a cloister to be managed by the itinerant monk, and I had ten thousand monks participate in the memorial services. I gathered up my wife's bones and brought them here to Mount Kōya. I was twenty-seven then, and that was seven years ago."

When he finished there wasn't a single monk, including the head monk, who was not in need of wringing out his tear-drenched sleeves of black.

Next was a monk of very low origin, who had been sitting in the back. He had dark skin, one side of his head was bald and scarred, and the pus from an eye infection had run down his cheek. His yellowish brown under-robe was dirty, his black vestment was in tatters at the knees, his feet were chapped and cracked, and his shins were swollen from beriberi.

He came forward and spoke: "Revelatory tales are sacred.[29] We do not consider rank, high or low. Humble though I am, I too will tell my story."

The people in the room were rather dismayed. They averted their eyes, turned their heads, and chuckled. The monk seated himself respectfully in the lowest ranking seat and spoke:

"I am from Hata in Tosa.[30] On the twenty-eighth of the third month, when I was twenty, I got a scolding from my father, who was called the Dumb Monk: 'Gendayū, why don't you go collect firewood or dig up some potatoes or yams or arrowroot?' He made quite a fuss. 'If he feels that strongly about it . . . ,' I thought, and said I'd go. I stuck a

---

28. Here the narrative perspective becomes Toyora's again.

29. The text is very obscure here.

30. Hata was the southwest portion of Tosa and is now part of Kōchi Prefecture on Shikoku Island.

shovel into my belt, picked up an ax and a carrying stick, and headed for the mountain path. On the way I saw a young woman of seventeen or eighteen picking parsley near the marsh. Looking closely, I saw that it was Himekuma, with whom I had been in love for quite some time. She was the daughter of the monk Kaine no Muma.

"With my heart pounding, I approached her, longing to speak with her, but I hesitated. You could have compared me to Kashiwagi, whose heart followed the cat through a gap in the bamboo blind and then wondered if his love for the third princess was requited or not.[31] Or to Yūgiri, in whom Kumoinokari put her trust and who visited her secretly until he was found out by her father, Tō no Chūjō, and was forbidden to see her.[32] Surely he suffered a terrible longing for her. And there was Ariwara no Narihira, who fell in love with the shrine virgin even though he spent only a few hours with her. He climbed over the shrine fence to proclaim his love.[33]

"I tried to speak, but I was too embarrassed to utter a word. For a time I just stood there, shifting my weight from foot to foot. Then I remembered the saying: 'A man's heart and the pillars of the imperial palace are stout, but let me be stouter!' So I approached her and tugged on her sleeve. I spoke to her very gently: 'Excuse me, Miss Himekuma, will you marry me?' I asked.

"Himekuma shuddered. 'What would I want with a sunburned peasant like you?' She shook her sleeve to free herself from my grasp. Dispirited, I released her sleeve, and she left.

"Nevertheless, my heart overflowed with love. Though I tried to work, I couldn't keep my mind on it. Everything I did after that encounter by the sprouting bracken caused me sorrow.[34] Digging for arrowroot, I suddenly found myself full of resentment. When I dug for yams my bitter longing intensified. I made my way home in tears. I tried to eat but I could not swallow a thing, neither breakfast nor supper,

31. Kashiwagi fell in love with Genji's wife, the third princess, when a cat came running out of her room, pushing aside a bamboo blind so that she was revealed to his sight (see Seidensticker, *Genji*, 582–86).

32. This is described in *The Tale of Genji*, chapter 21, "The Maiden." Gendayū somewhat misrepresents the story. When Tō no Chūjō forbade Yūgiri to see Kumoinokari, the affection between the two youngsters had been rather innocent. The interference in fact romanticized and intensified the pair's feelings (ibid., 368–74).

33. The phrase *koe tatete* is a pivot word meaning both "to climb over" and "to raise one's voice" or "to speak up" and functions as a link between the narrator's hesitance to speak and this anecdote referring to episode 69 in *The Tales of Ise*. There, it is the virgin who visits the man in his quarters. They were only together between 11:00 P.M. and 2:00 A.M. See McCullough, *Ise*, 115–17.

34. This and the next few lines are presented in the poetic rhythm of alternating units of five and seven syllables.

neither rice cakes with horse chestnuts, nor millet gruel, nor deccan grass gruel, nor dumplings of millet.

"I realized that Shii no Shōshō must have lamented like this when, hopelessly in love with Ono no Komachi, he was forced to spend night after night sitting on the shaft bench of her carriage, waiting for her in vain.[35]

"I wanted to live no longer. Lying crumpled in a corner of the room dreaming of Lady Himekuma day and night, I was indeed in danger of dying.

"One day, my father, the monk, made a fuss, wanting to know why I hadn't cut the grass for Lord Chitō's horses. Ill though I was, I covered my chapped hands and feet and grudgingly got up. Picking up my sickle and some cord, I left for the fields. The grasses I cut were of many kinds. First I gathered longing-for-Himekuma grass, being-forgotten grass, more-tears grass, and mirror grass in which I saw the reflection of my beloved.[36]

"'Let me,' I thought, 'in my envy cut these grasses that are as deep as my vows of affection.' My love filled my breast to overflowing; not one mouthful could I eat. It was like cutting weeds in hell while being tormented by demons.

"I reaped the seaweed that rises and falls in the waves as I alternately hoped and despaired of seeing her. I wished that the mugwort from which Genji had brushed away the dew[37] might heal the unendurable love sickness that had settled in my chest.

35. There is some confusion here. The narrator has cited Shii no Shōshō's frustrating courtship of Ono no Komachi. She demanded that he come courting one hundred nights in a row before she would deign to welcome him in. Only his death on the one hundredth day prevented him from accomplishing this task. The story of Shii no Shōshō is found in *Sotoba Komachi* (see Keene, *Japanese Literature*, 270) and *Kayoi Komachi* (see Keene, *Twenty Plays*, 51–63). However, in the midst of this reference the narrator quotes a line that I have omitted. The line *kimi ga konu yo wa*, "nights when you don't come," suggests the reverse of the Komachi legend, that a woman waited in vain for her lover to come. This line might be a muddled reference to the anonymous *Kokinshū* poem 761: *Akatsuki no/ shigi no hanegaki/ momo hagaki/ kimi ga konu yo wa/ ware zo kazu kaku*, "On nights without you,/ I lie on this side and that,/ restless as the snipe/ beating and beating again/ his wings in the graying dawn" (McCullough, *Kokinwakashū*, 168). See also Rodd and Henkenius, *Kokinshū*, 268.

36. This list of grasses—with names that describe Gendayū's state of mind—and the three succeeding paragraphs are written in poetic cadence. I have omitted two indecipherable lines.

37. In *The Tale of Genji* it is Koremitsu, Genji's servant, who brushes the dew from the mugwort. The occasion is Genji's visit to the safflower lady. In the original context the tall, dew-laden weeds are suggestive of the lady's loneliness (see Seidensticker, *Genji*, 299).

"Lacking the leaves of a family crest, how could I have won Himekuma's affection? How could I have hoped to kiss her lips? Sinking beneath the weight of my boundless longing, I doubted that I would ever see her again.[38]

"I harvested all these various grasses for Lord Chitō. From where I was working in front of the barn I looked over at the main house, where they were holding a poetry meeting, composing in the poetic tradition of the Asukai and Mikohidari families.[39] Those serving as secretary and reader were holding brushes and narrow paper strips and a roll of linen paper. They were moaning as though they were in pain. The way Lord Chitō held his cheek with his left hand and cried out in a loud voice was exactly how my grandmother grimaced and groaned in pain when she had a toothache.

"I asked the Lord's retainers, 'What crime did our Lord commit in a previous life that he should suffer such punishment now?'

"'That is poetry,' they answered. 'The cuckoos that sing from the branches of trees, even water-dwelling frogs, all things express themselves so. It softens the hearts of fierce warriors. It moves invisible demons and gods to pity. It brings men and women together. For those who fall in love, it is with poetry that they compose letters to win another's heart,'[40] they explained.

"'I had thought that the only possible result of suddenly falling in love was to die young,' I said. 'Please teach me how to compose a poem.'

"'Explain how much your love affects you,' they told me.

"I went home, and when I had thought about it for three weeks, I composed the poem:

Loving Himekuma
Is like rubbing salt and soot over and over
Into the boils on my head.

"I said I wanted to have it written down and sent to Himekuma, but those who had told me about poetry asked, 'What kind of poetic spirit is this?'

---

38. What limited success these images had is lost in this paragraph, and I have thus omitted a final reference to grasses.

39. The Mikohidari family is that branch of the Fujiwara family that produced the great poets Shunzei (1114–1204) and his son Teika (1162–1241). Asukai Masatsune (1170–1221) was their student and one of the compilers, together with Teika, of the important imperial poetic anthology, the *Shinkokinshū* (1206).

40. This is a paraphrase of the *kana* preface of the *Kokinshū* (see Robert H. Brower and Earl Miner, *Japanese Court Poetry* [Stanford: Stanford University Press, 1961], 3).

"I explained, 'When you told me to describe how my love affects me, I thought, "There is nothing that affects me as piercingly as salt and soot on my head boils," so that is what I composed.'

"They burst out laughing so hard they had to hold onto their sides. So, in addition to the sorrow of love I had also humiliated myself. I shaved my boil-covered head and now it has been more than thirty years since I came to this mountain."

As he finished, loud guffaws broke out yet again.[41]

Next, everyone said it was the head monk's turn. "If that's the case . . .," he said, and he began to tell his story.

"When I was twenty-one I went to live in the capital to pursue a property dispute in Nanjō. Once, when I had been there for seven or eight years, I went to Kiyomizu Temple to pray. Then I went to the shrine of Tenjin on Fifth Avenue.[42] I prayed for the lawsuit to be settled to our advantage and for our land to be bequeathed to our descendants, and also for enlightenment. I vowed to make that sacred circuit one hundred times. With only two or three days left to go, at the foot of the bridge at the corner of Nishi no Tōin and Fifth Avenue, I came across a beautiful hair ribbon. I picked it up and looked at it. Words cannot describe its beauty. On a red background were gilded iris and cuckoo, over which was written, also in gold, 'The fence of the mountain rustic may fall to the ground. . . .' These were the first lines of the poem in *The Tale of Genji*, which ends, 'Rest gently, O dew, upon the wild carnation.'[43] In a corner was written, 'The willows of the timeless hall swayed gracefully in the wind.' This too was from *The Tale of Genji*, from the first chapter, which mentions Emperor Hsuan Tsung recalling the past.[44] Also, on the inside of the ribbon, in perfumed ink, was written 'The Maiden.'[45] I assumed that the owner must be about sixteen years old because all the references were to *The Tale of Genji* and the

41. For another view of the poetic skills of the lower classes, see *The Tosa Diary* (Earl Miner, *Japanese Poetic Diaries* [Berkeley: University of California Press, 1976], 59–91).

42. Kiyomizu Temple (founded in 798) is a very popular temple in the hills in eastern Kyoto. The shrine of Tenjin on Gojō enshrines Amaterasu and other heavenly deities of Shinto.

43. Recited by Murasaki's grandmother, this poem refers to her fears for the young girl should she herself die (see Seidensticker, *Genji*, 33).

44. This is not a direct quote from *The Tale of Genji*. The Chinese emperor Hsuan Tsung (685–762, r. 712–56) recalls that his beloved Yang Kuei-fei (719–56) was as graceful as the willows of the timeless hall (ibid., 12).

45. "The Maiden" is the title of chapter 21 of *The Tale of Genji* and refers to a Gosechi dancer who at one time caught Genji's eye (ibid., 377).

scent it gave off was incomparably fragrant. 'What young woman had lost such a ribbon?' I wondered, feeling curious about its owner.

"Just then I noticed a serving woman of about twenty-two or twenty-three who seemed to be searching for something in the road. I approached her and asked, 'What is it that you are looking for?'

"She said, 'You haven't, by any chance, found a hair ribbon, have you?'

"'I have the ribbon,' I replied. 'Tell me to whom it belongs and I will give it back.'

"The woman smiled: 'That is something to be kept secret. I cannot tell you her name. Just give me the ribbon.'

"'You are too reserved,' I insisted. 'On a pilgrimage one does not hide things. Come, tell me her name and I'll give you the ribbon.'

"The woman said, 'Perhaps there is no need for me to be so scrupulous. My mistress merely dashed off these phrases from *The Tale of Genji* in an idle moment. I might as well tell you about it. Why should I hide anything from you? She is Lady Koshōshō, who lives in the western wing of Lord Konoe's mansion. She recently lost her parents, so she has no one at all to rely upon. That is why she has been praying for support. For seven days she has gone first to Kiyomizu Temple and then to the shrine of Tenjin.' She spoke earnestly.

"Becoming more and more curious, I borrowed an ink stone at a nearby house and on some folded paper that I had with me I wrote out a poem:

> I would ask of the shrine maiden
> At my family shrine
> To what deity does this hair ribbon belong?[46]

I wrapped the ribbon in the paper and gave it to the serving woman. I watched as she went within the precincts of the shrine and handed it to a woman wearing a silk veil. The woman took it, glanced briefly at the poem, and immediately put it inside her sleeve.

"I called the serving woman back and cajoled her in various ways: 'If only she would deign to give me a reply! It would be a memento to treasure all my life. And you know, anyone who does not respond to a poem is reborn mute for seven lives.'

"The serving woman spoke with her mistress and returned: 'She told me to tell you this:

---

46. There is a pun in the poem: *kami* means both "deity" and "hair."

I saw the light
Shine through the sacred fence for the first time.
It is a manifestation of the deity.'

[Due to punning the poem simultaneously meant:]

Meeting you
For the first time,
My hair ribbon was returned to me.

"When the serving woman recited her mistress's poem, I became even more eager to meet the lady. From the shrine I went with the serving woman to learn the location of their lodgings. Subsequently I sought to make an ally of the serving woman by flattering her and giving her various presents. When it was clear that the lady not only had no parents, but no husband either, I asked, 'What should I do? I have written her any number of love letters. I have revealed the depth of my feelings, but she will not give me an answer any more substantial than the dew.'

"The serving woman explained that her mistress was still naive. 'She's reluctant even to mention this affair,' I was told.

" 'What am I to do?' I fretted.

"The serving woman explained that the lady's aunt on her mother's side was a nun living at Imakumano[47] and that I could ask her to intercede on my behalf. Being a woman of deep understanding, this nun became my intermediary, and the young lady and I secretly began to spend our nights together. After a short time my family's claim to our land was confirmed. I had intended to bring her home with me when I went, but just then there was an insurrection in Hōki Province and I had to rush away. At times our estate was surrounded by the rebels, and other times they blocked the roads. Before I knew it, two or three years had passed. When I was finally able to send someone to fetch her, no one knew where she had gone. Thinking she must have forsaken me for someone else, I felt deeply chagrined.

"Several years later I had occasion to make a pilgrimage to Kumano. I took a large retinue with me and arrived at the temple quarters of the Azechi Bishop[48] at the main shrine.

"I also paid a visit to the High Priest Takahara at the new shrine, and to a bishop at Nachi who lived near the hermitage of the retired emperor Kazan.

47. Imakumano in Kyoto is a branch shrine of the three Kumano shrines—Hongu, Shingu, and Nachi, all in Wakayama Prefecture.

48. Azechi is an honorary title, indicating high rank.

"This bishop extended an especially warm welcome to me, sending as many as fourteen youths to attend me. Although, needless to say, he was a recluse, he visited with me and arranged various entertainments on my behalf, including a delightful concert of flute and mandolin music. Among the youths was a lad of twelve or thirteen who seemed different from the others. There was a noble air about him and he looked pure of heart, like a peach blossom wet with spring rain or a budding willow bending in a breeze. He seemed a sensitive boy, and as I watched him my heart went out to him. 'How happy I would be if he were my child. How dear and what a source of delight he must be to his father and mother,' I thought, in an access of emotion.

"I asked about him: 'This boy, who are his parents? He has the air of someone from one of the most noble houses.[49] He does not look as though he is any ordinary boy.'

"The bishop smiled. 'This boy never knew his father. His mother was my niece. She loved that child more than anything in the world, but she always regretted having been forsaken by his father. Day and night she was lost in thoughts of him. Perhaps it was the result of being heartbroken, or perhaps it was her karmic fate, but she fell ill and died in the autumn of the boy's seventh year. Since he was an orphan, I had him brought here, and I am raising him in his mother's stead. He excels in his studies and he has a fine character, so I intend to have him succeed me. When your descendants make their pilgrimages to this mountain shrine, this youth will be the chief priest, so I hope your family will continue to come here for many generations.'

"Somehow, as I listened, I was deeply moved. 'Well then, what can you tell me about his mother's family?' I asked again.

"'My niece was called Koshōshō and lived in the west wing of Lord Konoe's residence,' the priest told me.

"How strange it was! I had been intimate with someone by that name. Yet, there are people in the world with the same name. Then again, she may have later become attached to another man and borne his child. I was doubtful but uneasy. I persuaded the boy to step forward. Calling him to my side, I asked him about his father.

"Tears welled up in his eyes, and he answered, 'I don't have either a father or a mother.'

"'They may be gone now, but at one time you had parents. Please tell me about them,' I said.

"'I didn't know my father. My mother was Koshōshō who lived on Lord Konoe's estate. My father abandoned her, and she spent the rest of

49. The text says specifically, "from one of the three aristocratic families [qualified to fill the post of great minister], or from one of the families qualified to become regent or chief advisor."

her life longing for him. She got sick, and when she realized she was dying, she called me to her side and said, "How wretched! Your father left me before you were born, and I don't know where he is. If the one and only person on whom you can depend dies, what will become of you? Why were you born into this human world only to face such sorrow? How you must resent your fate! Since I have little to live for, I don't regret losing my life, but to die before I can see you turn fifteen, that will be a hindrance to me on the road to the next world. If only I could see you at your father's side before I die, how relieved I would be! When you are lonely, take out these two mementos. If it is me you miss, look at this hair ribbon to console yourself. When you long for your father, comfort yourself by reading this letter. It is something he wrote," she explained. She took out a letter and a hair ribbon and gave them to me. "Life is transient and death is inexorable. You must not lament my death, but please do not fail to pray earnestly for my salvation," she said.

"'How I miss her! "Praise be to Amida Buddha." Those were her last words. She died at the age of twenty-five.' The boy gasped out the last of his story between sobs.

"Seeming to feel more trusting of me, he said, 'When I miss my father and mother I privately take out those mementos and comfort myself by looking at them. When I grieve for them, there is no one to take pity on me. I wonder why I feel close to you. From now on you must stay here whenever you come on a pilgrimage,' he insisted.

"As I listened I had realized he was my son. When I said I'd like to see the poem, he took it out of an amulet bag that he kept next to his skin. I saw that it was my handwriting and that the ribbon was unmistakably the hair ribbon that had belonged to the woman I had loved. I recalled her as vividly as if I had seen her only the moment before, and I was deeply moved.

"'I am not a stranger to all this. I am your father,' I said, identifying myself. For a while he was dumbfounded. Then he just sobbed. When I informed the bishop of these developments, he too wept. I told him that, having no other children, I wanted to take the boy home with me. His grief at the prospect of losing the boy was so great that I lingered there for four or five days. Finally, I left, taking my son with me. I bequeathed my whole estate to him and, taking leave of my family and kin, went to the capital. I unearthed the bones in Koshōshō's grave on Mount Funaoka and brought them to this holy mountain. That was thirty-one years ago."

When he pressed his black sleeve to his face and wept quietly, no one in the room tried to hold back their own tears.

The Three Monks

Part One

Mount Kōya is far from the imperial palace, distant from any village, a place where no human voices are to be heard. Its eight peaks[1] are rugged and towering. Its eight valleys are quiet and still. Here Kōbō Daishi entered his final, deep meditative state.[2] In this sacred place many await the coming of Maitreya, anticipating that dawn when he will enlighten all beings with his three sermons.[3] There are platforms for practicing *zazen* and halls for *nenbutsu* meditation. Living here and there on this mountain were three men who, each having his own reason for despising the world, had taken holy vows in mid-life. One day they met and started talking to each other.

"We all renounced the world late in life. Why have we done so? Let each of us tell the tale of his revelation. Since recounting these experiences is said to nullify past errors, there is no reason to be shy," came the proposal from one monk.

Among them was a monk of forty-two or forty-three who had grown thin and weak from his rigorous asceticism, but whose blackened teeth gave him an air of refinement. His clothes were torn here and there. He wore a slightly larger than usual stole.[4] He seemed lost in

---

1. Literally, the "eight-leaved peaks," an expression that refers to the idea that Kōya's eight peaks symbolize the eight petals of the lotus of the womb or matrix *mandala*, which form the backdrop for the depiction of the eight Buddhas and bodhisattvas who surround the central figure, Mahāvairocana.

2. Also, Kūkai (774–835), founder of the Shingon sect in Japan. See introduction p. 5.

3. Maitreya, the Buddha of the future, is to preach three sermons upon appearing in this world. All beings will thereby be saved.

4. A stole or *kara*, a square piece of cloth hung from both shoulders, is an abbreviated form of mantle (J *kesa*, Skt *kasāya*), a large rectangle of patched cloth originally used as a religious garment and later as a symbolic accessory. *Kesa* come in three sizes: widths of five, seven, or nine columns. The smallest was to be worn when performing manual tasks; the next was added for religious gatherings; and the largest was worn over the other two when fulfilling public duties. Ideally, a monk was expected to own only one of each, plus one begging bowl (see Mary Dusenbury, "*Kesa*: Robes of Japanese Buddhist Priests," Spencer Museum of Art, n.d.).

thought but he said, "Perhaps you will allow me to begin. Since it happened in the capital, you may have heard about it. It was while Ashikaga Takauji was shogun.[5] I was called Kasuya no Shirōzaemon and was an attendant to the shogun, having gone into his service at the age of thirteen. I accompanied him on pilgrimages to temples and shrines, and on moon- and blossom-viewing parties. I almost never left his side. Once when I was attending him while he called on Lord Nijō,[6] some colleagues of mine got together and two or three times sent messengers to urge my speedy return. I wanted to join my friends and hoped my lord would soon bring his visit to an end. I peeked into the room to see if that might be the case. It seemed as though they were drinking their second or third round of drinks. A young woman came in carrying on a tray a short-sleeved gown as a gift. She appeared to be in her late teens and wore a robe with a design of red blossoms and green leaves over scarlet trousers. Her hair was as long as she was tall, and it swayed gracefully as she walked. How can I explain how beautiful she was? People say that the Chinese women Yang Kuei-fei and Lady Li[7] and, in our country, Sotōri-hime, Ono no Komachi, the Somedono empress,[8] and other concubines were beautiful women, but they could not have been more beautiful than she. 'As long as I've been born human,' I thought, 'how I would like to talk with someone like her, and set my pillow next to hers! I wish at least that she would come out again and let me have another glimpse of her!' I fell immediately in love with her. My heart seemed to burn with longing. I tried to forget her but I could not. I was totally entranced by her.

"When the shogun went home, I also returned to my quarters. After that her image never left my mind. I couldn't eat, and when I stayed in bed for four or five days, neglecting my duties, the shogun sent word asking why I hadn't come. I reported that I was sick, and he immediately ordered that a doctor be sent to my quarters to see that I recovered. I got up and put on formal dress to receive him.[9]

5. Ashikaga Takauji (1305–58, shogun 1338–58) was founder of the Ashikaga shogunate, 1338–1573.

6. This is probably a reference to Nijō Yoshimoto (1320–88), a prominent statesman and poet of linked verse.

7. Yang Kuei-fei (719–56) was the concubine of the T'ang emperor Hsuan Tsung (685–762). Her beauty was said to be the indirect cause of the fall of the T'ang empire. Li Fujen was a concubine of the Han emperor Wu-di (157–87 B.C.).

8. Princess Sotōri was a consort of Emperor Ingyō (r. 412–53). Ono no Komachi (ca. 9th century) was an important poet and reknowned beauty. The Somedono empress was Fujiwara no Akirakeiko (829–900), empress to Emperor Montoku (827–58, r. 850–58).

9. He put on an *eboshi* (cap) and *hitatare* (jacket).

"The doctor felt my pulse for a while and then sat back to talk with me. 'How strange! You don't seem to be really ill,' he said. 'Are you holding a grudge against someone or are you concerned about a legal complaint of some kind?'

"I feigned nonchalance and answered, 'When I was a child I was sick like this; I recovered, but only after resting for fourteen or fifteen days. I think we should let it go for a while this time too. It's not a question of a grudge or anything like that.'

"What the doctor told my lord was, 'I don't think he has any disease. But perhaps he has something on his mind. There used to be a condition we called love.'

"'It could be love,' argued the shogun. 'It still occurs these days. Let someone ask him how he really feels.'

"Someone mentioned that Sasaki Saburōzaemon was a close friend of mine, and so the shogun sent for him.

"'Go to see Kasuya, take care of him, and ask him about his innermost feelings.'

"Following orders, Sasaki came to see me. First he reproached me saying, 'You and I are closer than any of the other retainers. We've been like brothers. Why didn't you tell me you were ill?' He complained at length.

"'I kept it to myself because I am not really very sick,' I replied. 'I haven't even told my aged mother, but I can see why you might be resentful. If it gets serious though, I will let you know immediately. But since you're just making a mountain out of a molehill, please go on home. It doesn't matter about me anyway, but if something should happen to our lord. . . .' I piled up excuses, but he insisted on staying and looking after me. For four or five days he never left my side. He asked about my deepest feelings, but I kept my thoughts to myself all that time. Finally, though, I realized I was being overly modest and I told him exactly what had happened.

"Sasaki listened, and then casually remarked, 'If it's just that you're in love, it's a simple matter.' He left my room, went straight to our lord's palace, and reported what he had found out.

"'This problem is easily resolved,' my lord declared. He graciously wrote a letter outlining the situation and had Sasaki take it to Lord Nijō. The answer, which my lord was so kind as to forward to my quarters, explained that the lady's name was Onoe, that it was inappropriate for her to leave the estate to visit someone of my modest rank, but that I could come to see her there. Never could I repay such generosity as my lord had shown me in this matter! Nevertheless, I was miserable. Even if I could meet Lady Onoe, it certainly would only be for one dreamlike night. I thought this was a good reason to renounce the world, but upon further reflection, I realized that people might snicker and say that though I had been in love with a lady in service at Lord Nijō's, and though the shogun himself had deigned to intercede on my behalf, I had been a coward and renounced the world without seeing her. I could never live down such humiliation. I decided I would spend the one night with her and not worry about how I might feel afterward.

"Though I had not intended to make any special preparations, I did look rather distinguished as I left with three young men as attendants. It was already quite late as my escort led the way to the Nijō estate. I was shown into a quaint room decorated with screens and Chinese paintings, where four or five splendidly dressed young women were waiting to welcome me. After everyone had been served two or three cups of saké we amused ourselves with tea aroma guessing games. Since I had only had one glimpse of her, I wasn't sure which of them was Lady Onoe. They were all so beautiful that I was confused. Then a woman came to my side and offered me her saké cup. Realizing that this was Lady Onoe, I accepted a drink from her.

"When the clamoring of roosters' cries announced the coming dawn and the tolling of temple bells urged my departure, we reluctantly disentangled our robes. Pledging her love far into the future, the lady left my side before daybreak. As she went out onto the veranda I glimpsed her beauty, her dark eyebrows and red lips, half hidden by her sleep-tousled hair. She was truly an enchanting sight.

"She composed this poem:

I am not accustomed to this
Dew on my sleeve:
Tears caused by a man I met unexpectedly.

"My answer was:

My longing fulfilled,
I will cherish the dew on my sleeve this morning
As a reminder of you.

"After that I continued to visit her at the palace, and she occasionally came to see me secretly in my quarters. Since the shogun knew that she was concerned about what people would think if word of our relationship got out, he granted her a modest estate in Ōmi.[10]

10. Specifically, it was an estate of 1,000 *koku*, 1,000 *kan*. These measurements refer respectively to the amount of rice produced on the fief and the cash value of the amount of rice owed in taxes. Ōmi, presently Shiga Prefecture, was quite near the capital. Perhaps they were to use this place for their trysts.

"Having put my faith in the god of Kitano, I had been in the habit of visiting his shrine on the twenty-fourth of every month.[11] Enamoured of this lady, however, I had been neglecting my prayers. On the evening of the twenty-fourth of the last month of the year, therefore, I went to the shrine to repent my previous negligence, and I intoned the Buddha's name deep into the night.

"I overheard someone say, 'Oh dear, how terrible! I wonder who she was.'

"It struck me as strange, so I questioned the man closely. A woman of seventeen or eighteen had been murdered nearby, and her clothes had been stolen. My fears aroused, I ran off without even picking up my things. It was none other than my beloved! I thought I must be dreaming. Not only had she been murdered and stripped, but even her hair had been cut off! I was completely at a loss for words. I was stunned. For what terrible sin was this retribution? I grieved to see her the victim of such a pitiful fate. I had been overjoyed to meet her. Now, conversely, it was cause for regret. Why had I fallen in love with this woman who had now preceded me in death? It was my fault that tender in years and highborn though she was, she had been slain by a sword wielded in malice. Try to imagine how I felt! I would have charged against any demon or hundreds of horsemen. I didn't care one whit for my own life. But I did not know who had done it. There was nothing I could do. Then and there, that very night, I cut off my topknot and became a monk. For twenty years now I have been praying for her soul on this mountain."

When he had finished, the black sleeves of the two monks who had listened to his tale were soaked with tears.

Next to speak was a monk of fifty or so. About six feet tall, he had a prominent Adam's apple, jaw, and cheekbones. His lips were thick, his eyes and nose quite large, and his complexion dark. A very gaunt man, he wore a tattered cotton robe, and he had shoved his mantle into the front of it.

Fingering a large rosary, he said, "Let me tell my story next."

"Fine, go right ahead," the others said.

"Strangely enough, I was the man who killed your lady."

Hearing this, Kasuya immediately stiffened and the color left his face. He looked as though he was about to kill the other man.

---

11. Kitano Tenjin in northwest Kyoto is the shrine where Sugawara Michizane (845–903) is worshiped. It was established in 942 to appease his vengeful spirit. The twenty-fifth is the anniversary of his death. While not an obvious place for *nenbutsu* practice, Buddhist influence there is attested by the fact that the shrine was under the supervision of Enryakuji from the middle of the Heian period.

The second monk spoke. "Please keep calm and let me tell you exactly what happened."

Kasuya settled down a bit and urged him to begin, "Hurry up then."

"You said you were from the capital," the rough-looking monk began, "so I expect you've heard of me. I am Aragorō of Third Avenue. I became a thief at the age of nine. I killed my first man at the age of thirteen, and I had murdered over 380 people when I killed your lady. I considered myself most talented at nighttime assaults and armed robbery. However, it may have been retribution for sins committed in a previous lifetime, but in any case, from the tenth month of that year, I had no luck. I even went up on the mountain roads, but I couldn't get my hands on anything of value. I had all kinds of good ideas, but something always suddenly went wrong. I did my utmost, but before long there was nothing to cook, and neither morning nor evening did any smoke rise from our hearth. Since my wife and children were miserable, I was depressed, and so sometime in the eleventh month I moved away from home. I spent my days wandering and my nights under the eaves of temple or shrine buildings. One day I went home to see how things were.

"My wife grabbed my sleeve and tearily berated me: 'Oh, I hate you! How can you be so cruel? I shouldn't be upset about your abandoning me: the bond between a husband and wife doesn't always last forever. In any case, if you don't care for me anymore, my telling you I love you won't bring you back. Why don't you hurry up and divorce me? As a single woman I wouldn't have any trouble making a living. But it'll soon be the New Year, and I have to do something for the children. You never had any land. You never practiced a trade or farmed. All you have ever done is taken other people's property, and now things are not going your way. You don't worry about what will happen to your children. You've even abandoned your home to sleep elsewhere. I suppose it's because of me that you find it so dreary at home, but how can you ignore the fact that your children are starving? These last two or three days we haven't had anything to eat. There has been no fire in our hearth. I can't bear to listen to the children crying for something to eat.' How she carried on!

"'It must be my karma from a former life catching up with me,' I said. 'I left because nothing I tried was working out, and it's precisely because I was worried about the kids that I've come back. I'll take care of things. Just wait. In a day or two everything will be fine.' What I was thinking was 'Surely tonight I'll have some luck.'

"I waited impatiently for dark. When temple bells tolled at twilight, I took my sword, 'Kuruma dachi,' hid in the shadow of an earthen wall and waited eagerly for someone to come along. As I gripped my weapon I thought, 'Let it be a swordsman like Fan K'uai or Chang Liang,[12] I'll still cut him down with one stroke.'

"The first to come were some young men lightly carrying an open litter and chatting among themselves. There was no use in attacking them. I let them pass. Then I noticed a fine fragrance in the air and thought happily, 'Aha! Here comes the right sort of person! My luck has changed!' The source of the fragrance and of the sound of a quiet tread was a woman whose beauty fairly illuminated the dark street. One of her serving women preceded her, while the other followed carrying an embroidered cloth bundle. They walked by, ignoring me. I let them pass and then chased after them. Frightened, the attendant in front screamed and fled. The other one dropped the bag and ran off calling for help. The lady, however, did not act the least bit upset. She did not even cry out. I approached her with my sword drawn and roughly stripped her of her outer clothes. 'I'll take your undergarments too,' I declared.

"'How can I give you my under-robe?' she said. 'I would be humiliated. Let me keep it.' She held out an amulet. 'Take this instead,' she said and tossed that to me.

"Heartless criminal that I was, I demanded her robe, 'That's not enough. Give me your under-robe!'

"'I'd rather die than take it off,' she answered. 'You'll have to kill me.'

"'There's nothing I'd rather do,' I replied as I stabbed her. Not wanting her robe to get stained with blood, I hurriedly wrenched it off her. Picking up the embroidered cloth bundle, I murmured to myself, 'How glad my wife and the children will be,' and ran home.

"When I knocked on the door, my wife asked skeptically, 'How can you be back so soon? You haven't accomplished anything, have you?'

"'Hurry up and open the door,' I insisted.

"When I tossed her the bundle she wondered how I'd gotten hold of anything of value so quickly. In her eagerness to see what it was, though, she didn't take the trouble to untie the cords on the bundle; she just cut them. As she began to examine the contents, I noticed that exquisite scent again. In the bag was a set of twelve robes. When my wife picked up a gown with a design of red blossoms and green leaves, and a pair of scarlet trousers, the fragrance filled the room. Such a perfume might have roused the suspicions of people passing along our

12. Fan K'uai (d. 189 B.C.) served Liu Pang, founder of the Early Han dynasty (206 B.C.–A.D. 23). Chang Liang (d. 187 B.C.) was a counselor to Liu Pang.

little street and startled our neighbors, but my wife was delighted. She happily tried on the under-robe. 'I've never had anything like this in my life! This would have belonged to a young lady. How old was she?'

"Thinking she had asked out of pity for the lady, I answered, 'It's hard to say because it was dark, but I'm sure she was still in her teens. She was probably eighteen or nineteen.'

"'I see,' she said, and then, without another word, she left the house.

"I wondered what she could be doing, but in a short time she came back. 'What an extravagant man you are,' she announced. 'If you're going to commit a crime you might as well get everything you can out of it. I went and cut off her hair just now. You don't often see hair as fine as this. I can make it into a wig. It's much better than the robes.'

"She rinsed the hair with hot water and then hung it over a pole to dry. She was so pleased that she danced her way around the house. 'What treasures I've got! Oh, I'm so glad!'

"As I watched her I thought, 'How despicable! How vile! Haven't we all been born human because we were touched by Buddhism in a previous existence?' I had received human form in this life, but not only hadn't I practiced Buddhism, not only wasn't I a virtuous man, I hadn't even shown the least bit of compassion. I was a terribly evil man, thinking day and night of nothing but killing and stealing. Since no one can escape retribution, I was bound to end up in hell. I had sustained my fragile life by committing evil deeds, as if I didn't know that life is no more durable than a dream. I was disgusted with myself. My wife was also inhuman. She was too horrible for words. I was repulsed by the thought that I was married to her, that I had been sleeping with her. Aware now how loathsome this woman's heart was, I regretted having killed the lady. I felt such pity for her then that I almost fainted. 'No, I can't go on like this,' I thought, and I decided to take her as my inspiration to faith. I would cut off my topknot, pray for her salvation, and seek enlightenment for myself.

"That very night I went to see Bishop Gen'e[13] at Kitakōji and First Avenue, and I became his disciple. He gave me the name Genchiku, and I came here." [Aragorō turned to the first monk:] "You must be outraged. Go ahead and kill me. Choose any means you like. Even if you cut me up into little pieces, I won't cry out. If you kill me, though, it will affect the lady's fate.[14] I'm not saying that because I don't want to

---

13. Bishop Gen'e (1269–1350) was a scholarly monk who served as imperial tutor to Emperor Godaigo (1318–39).

14. Perhaps because then she would no longer benefit from their prayers.

die. Just consider the Buddhist teachings. But now that I've told my tale, it's up to you."

He finished his story with sleeves soaked with tears.

"Even if some commonplace event had caused your religious awakening," Kasuya said, "we are both monks; how could I hate you? The fact that she was your inspiration endears you to me. She must have been a bodhisattva in human form. Manifesting herself as the Lady Onoe, she hoped to save two who were lost. When I think she herself was an expedient means employed by the Compassionate One, the past is ever more dear to me. Without her, how would you and I have come to take holy vows? How would we have learned to despise this world and to anticipate the incomparable bliss of paradise? This is the joy that arises from misery. I would be very glad if we could be companions from now on."

Tears had also dampened his black sleeves.

Finally, they asked the third monk to tell of his religious awakening. He too was well on in years. Over his tattered robe he wore a mantle of seven columns.[15] He had been quietly intoning a sutra. Ascetic practice had made him haggard and weathered his skin. Emaciated though he was, clearly he was of noble background. He gave the impression of having achieved enlightenment. Since he had dozed off, the other monks woke him and pressed him to begin his story.

"Having heard how the two of you came to your religious awakenings," he began, "I am moved beyond words. It must have been foreordained. My renunciation of the world, however, was nothing like yours. There is nothing to be gained in my telling you of it, but since you both told your stories, I must share mine, or you would think me unkind. It's a shame to take you away from your other efforts, but if you want to hear it . . .

"Mine was a branch of the Kusunoki family in Kawachi.[16] My father was Shinozaki no Kamonnosuke, and I was called Rokurōzaemon. Kusunoki no Masashige[17] regarded my father highly and always consulted him whether it was an important matter or not. He was widely known, within the clan and by the world at large, as Kusunoki's right hand man. My father committed ritual suicide during the battle in which Masashige was defeated. Masashige's heir, Masatsura,[18] treated

---

15. See note 4 above.

16. Kawachi is presently part of the Osaka metropolitan area.

17. Kusunoki Masashige (1294–1336), the staunchest supporter of Godaigo's southern court, was killed in battle by Ashikaga Takauji. See Ivan Morris, *The Nobility of Failure* (New York: Holt, Rinehart and Winston, 1975), 106–42.

18. Kusunoki Masatsura (1326–48) was Masashige's eldest son.

me kindly, and I did my utmost for him. I was wounded in the battle in
which he was killed, but the enemy failed to take my head. I was barely
still breathing when a monk I knew found me. He carried me to a safe
place and nursed me back to health. It is a wonder that I survived.
Kusunoki Masanori,[19] Masatsura's heir, was pleased to see me. He
trusted me just as his father, Masashige, had my father. But when I
heard second hand that he intended to surrender to Lord Ashikaga, I
was stunned. I went to see him: 'I can't believe it but I've heard that you
plan to surrender to Lord Ashikaga. It isn't true, is it?'

"'Since the emperor's behavior has been insufferable,'[20] he answered, 'that is just what I have decided.'

"'If you are angry with the emperor,' I told him, 'you should
renounce your responsibilities and abandon the world. That would be
the sincere way to register your complaint. To surrender to Ashikaga is
not to reproach the emperor but to rebel against him. People will say
that you betrayed the emperor because you didn't want to get caught on
the losing side, that you surrendered to Ashikaga for your own benefit.
You must never, never surrender. Why, when you had such an important decision to make, didn't you consult me, unworthy as I may be?'

" 'I didn't say anything because I was sure you would be against
it,' Masanori replied.

" 'If you thought I would be critical,' I argued, 'think about the
insulting things other people will say. Men of more than one generation
have died fighting for the Yoshino court, and their names will go down
in history. It is a shame to see such pathetic behavior in your generation. What quarrel could you have with the emperor? You hold your
land by the emperor's grace. In ancient times it was said, "Even if a lord
does not act as a lord should act, a retainer must act as a retainer
should."[21] Please, give up any idea of surrender.'

"After that Masanori went to the capital and met with the
shogun's deputy at Tōji. The emperor's cause was doomed. Even if I had
fought on alone, without the Kusunoki clan, there was little I could
have done. And I certainly wasn't about to surrender along with Masanori. I decided this was my opportunity to enter the way of Buddhism,
and thus I abandoned the world.

19. Kusunoki Masanori (dates unknown), Masashige's third son, went over to the northern court in 1369. He switched his allegiance back to the southern court in 1383.

20. Masanori tried to negotiate the peaceful unification of the northern and southern
   courts but apparently was frustrated in these efforts by the unreasonable demands
   of Emperor Chōkei (r. 1368–83). See H. Paul Varley, *Imperial Restoration in
   Medieval Japan* (New York: Columbia University Press, 1971), 120–21.

21. The Chinese source of this well-known expression is K'ung An-kuo's (156–74 B.C.)
   preface to the *Classic of Filial Piety* (*Kuwen hsiaoching*). See also Kitagawa and
   Tsuchida, *Heike*, 116 and McCullough, *Heike*, 77.

Part Two

"When I left Shinozaki in Kawachi, I left behind my three-year-old daughter, my baby boy, and my wife. I deeply regretted leaving my dear wife of many years, but, having decided that I must renounce the world completely, I immediately went out east.[22] I spent three years studying under the guidance of a priest in Matsushima[23] and then decided to head north[24] on an extended pilgrimage. I thought I would wander through the provinces and beg instruction from any wise monks I might meet. I could also take some comfort in visiting famous places and old ruins. In any event, since this unreliable world is not one in which we can hope to live forever, I was content to think I might die on the road.

"Eventually in my travels I turned westward and was surprised to find myself passing through Kawachi. I thought I'd see how things were in my hometown of Shinozaki. When I approached my former estate I saw that the wall around the perimeter had fallen into disrepair. The gate posts still stood, but there was no gate. The garden was overgrown with weeds. The main buildings had collapsed. There were only two or three rickety little huts left, nothing that would provide any protection from wind or rain. I couldn't bear to look. I passed by in tears. Nearby I saw an old man working in a paddy near the road. I was sure he would know about anything that had happened in the neighborhood. I approached him and asked, 'Hey, old man, what's the name of this place?'

"He came over, took off his straw hat and answered, 'This is Shinozaki.'

"I asked him to whom it belonged.

"'It's Lord Shinozaki's fief.'

"I wondered if he knew about my family. I sat down on the ridge between the paddies while the old man leaned on his hoe. He quietly told me the whole story, weeping as he spoke. 'Lord Kamonnosuke of Shinozaki was in every way a superior man, and so Lord Kusunoki relied heavily on his advice in making important decisions. Lord Kusunoki had greater respect for him than for anyone else in the clan. Shinozaki's son Rokurōzaemon abandoned the world in despair when Masanori surrendered to the Ashikaga forces. No one knows where he is now. I've heard he is up north, and I've also heard that he's dead, but there has never been any reliable news.'

22. This is to the Kantō, the region surrounding Tokyo.

23. Matsushima, in Miyagi Prefecture in the far northeast, is famous for its scenic beauty and was a popular site for religious practices from the late Heian period.

24. "North" renders *hokkoku*, which refers to the provinces facing the Japan Sea, including Wakasa, Echizen, Kaga, Noto, Etchū, Echigo, and Sado.

"As he wept, I suppressed my own tears and asked, 'Well, were you a relative or did you work on the fief?'

"He answered, 'I've been a farmer on this fief for many years. After Rokurōzaemon renounced the world, his family fell on hard times and all the servants left. Worthless nobody though I am, when I saw what a terrible state the lady and the children were in, I felt sorry for them. I put aside my own responsibilities and did what I could to serve them. In renouncing the world Rokurōzaemon abandoned a three-year-old daughter and an infant son. His wife somehow managed to make ends meet and take good care of them, but probably because she never got over the loss of her husband, last spring she fell ill. Recently she stopped eating, and soon after that she passed away. That was three days ago. I can't bear to see the children in their grief. It makes me feel as though I may faint. Her body was cremated near that pine tree you can see over there. The two children have been crying and visiting the site every day. I offered to go with them today too, but they said they didn't need me, so I'm hoeing this paddy as if it were an ordinary day. This isn't for my sake though. I'm thinking of the children's future. It's out of concern for them that I'm working this field. They call me "grandfather," and though I'm not their grandfather, I'm honored to have them rely on me. Since they're late in coming home today, I've been watching for them and can't keep my mind on this work.' He was weeping freely when he finished.

"It was overwhelming. This humble man had such compassion, while I had been heartless! I thought of telling the old man that I was Rokurōzaemon, but then I realized that to do so would be to nullify my years of religious practice. Instead, I said, 'You are indeed a rare person. Who else would have shown such kindness? But how sad for those children! Has there ever been a more pathetic situation? Trying to imagine their grief, I'm left speechless. I have not experienced anything as awful as they have, but I think I know how they must feel. There is nothing in the world as pitiful as a child being left an orphan.' I pressed my sleeve to my face and wept.

"The old man asked, 'So you too have faced such sorrow, have you?' and sobbed aloud.

"After a bit I said, 'Old man, you must never neglect those children. Though in another world, how thankful their parents must be! Your descendants will be rewarded for your kindness and will prosper. If you take good care of those children, the gods and Buddhas will watch over you. I must be going now, old man, since it's getting late.'

"When I stood up and started off he accompanied me. He came along for quite a while, talking earnestly the whole time. Everything he said brought more tears to his eyes. Finally, holding back my own tears, I said, 'Old man, really, this is far enough,' and he turned back.

"A little further along I saw what appeared to be the cremation site the old man had mentioned. 'I'd better not,' I thought, and went on. But then I reconsidered. When I had been inspired to faith and renounced my worldly ties, I had abandoned my wife, but now it was the third day after her death. To see her grave and pass it by would be impious. If I hadn't known, I wouldn't have had a choice, but as long as I was a monk, to go by without reciting a prayer[25] would be inexcusable. For one thing, her spirit would accrue some benefit, and for another, it would appease the resentment that she certainly had taken to her grave. Having decided to go back, I found two children crouched under the tree. Realizing that they were my children, I said, 'Do you mind if I ask why it is that you two are sitting here in such a place?'

"Without answering my question, they exclaimed, 'Oh, how glad we are to see you! This is the third day after our mother's death, and we're here to gather up her bones. How wonderful of you, a monk, to come along today of all days. Forgive us for asking, but, if you would recite a sutra, it would be of benefit to her in the next world.'

"As I listened to their insistent pleas, things momentarily went black before my eyes and I lost consciousness. I couldn't tell whether I was awake or dreaming. After a bit I pulled myself together and gazed at the children. The girl would be nine years old, her brother was six. They did not, after all, look as though they could have been the children of a worthless monk like me; they were an endearing pair. Every parent loves his children, how urgently I wanted to embrace them and tell them I was their father! But, I thought, if I were so weak-willed as that, the hardships I had endured for the past few years would be for nought, I would never be able to achieve Buddhahood. Can you imagine what a struggle it was to keep from telling them who I was?

"I don't know who had taught them, but with my daughter holding the interior box and my son the outer box,[26] they used a stalk of bamboo and a tree twig as a pair of chopsticks to pick up the bone fragments that remained after cremation. Now even more at a loss for words, I pressed my sleeve to my face and wept.

"'You are so young,' I said at last. 'Isn't there an adult to do this? Why are you collecting the bones yourselves?'

"'Our father renounced the world, and we haven't heard from him since then,' they explained. 'After he left there was only the old man who helped out but he didn't come with us today.' They spoke brusquely because they were choking on their tears.

---

25. "Prayer" renders *darani* (Skt *dhāraṇī*), which is a magical formula or prayer of mystical power, often recited in Sanskrit.

26. The girl is said to hold the "lid" (*futa*), but perhaps they are using a type of double box that has an inner compartment cradled within an exterior case.

"When they fell silent I tried to recite a prayer, but I could not utter a sound. Bitterly regretting having come back to my home, I reproached myself, 'No. This won't do.' I concentrated on reciting the prayer. Just as I was finishing, it suddenly began to rain. The drops that clung to the needles of the pine tree looked like tears.

"My daughter spoke: 'Our mother was from the capital, and she taught me about poetry. She told me that the most fearsome demon or cold-hearted person will soften when he hears poetry, and that the Buddhas also accept it as an offering.[27] She said it was deplorable for a woman not to study poetry. I've been copying out poems since I was seven years old. I've just thought of one.' Then she recited this verse:

Even the grasses and trees take pity on us!
Don't these raindrops
Show that they are weeping?

"My resolve instantly melted away. Had I been as fragile as the dew or frost I would have simply expired. No, I could not bear to keep it from them. I had to tell them 'I am your father, the monk Rokurō-zaemon.' But neither could I be so sentimental. 'Having long ago found the determination to renounce the world,' I thought, 'should I now once again take up the yoke of parenthood?' I accused myself of weakness for wanting to tell them. Finally, I merely remarked, 'That is an excellent poem. Surely the gods and Buddhas would be deeply moved. Even from their graves, your parents must be very pleased. Even I, insensitive, ignorant of compassion, and base as I am, cannot check the tears unleashed by your poem. Anyone with feelings could not fail to be moved by it. My passing by here just now and witnessing this pitiful scene must be the result of karma from a previous life. I find it hard to leave you, but please excuse me.'

"As I started off, my daughter spoke: 'Just as you say, taking shelter under the same tree, drinking from the same stream, everything depends on our karma from previous lives. Surely we shall meet again in some future lifetime. I'm truly sorry to see you go. And thank you so very much for saying a prayer for our mother.' She pressed her sleeve to her face and sobbed. Her brother didn't understand what was happening. He just held onto his sister anxiously and cried along with her.

"I thought I was going to faint. I had to avert my eyes. It was more painful than anything I could imagine, except perhaps stabbing myself in ritual suicide. They watched me as I left. Again and again I looked back at them. Having put their mother's bones in the inner box,

27. This is a paraphrase of the Japanese introduction to the *Kokinshū* (905), the first imperial anthology of poetry. See *Tales Told on Mount Kōya*, note 40.

they did not start back toward home. They headed off in another direction. I retraced my steps and asked, 'Why are you going that way? Where are you going?'

"'A venerable priest from the capital has come to preach at Hōninji,' they replied. 'Today is the fifth day of the one week he will be there. A great many people are going, and we want to hear him too. We were also thinking of having him consecrate our mother's bones. That's where we're going.'

"'How touching,' I said. 'That you children should think of such a thing must please your mother in the next world very much. How far is Hōninji from here?'

"'We don't know,' they answered. 'We thought we would just follow the other people going that way.'

"'Why don't you have someone go with you?' I asked. 'It is probably a strenuous trip. Surely the old man would take you tomorrow.'

"'We told him earlier that we wanted to go,' my daughter explained, 'but he scolded us saying we were too young. That's why we haven't gone before now.'

"'If that's the case, I'll accompany you,' I proposed. 'I will pay my respects to the priest, and I can benefit from listening to his sermons too.'

"We walked together, but I couldn't bring myself to chat with them. On the way my daughter remarked, 'If our father were still alive, he would be about your age. Oh, how wretched for us! I wonder what wickedness we are being punished for. To live apart from our father and to have lost our mother, how sad it is! If we had been older when our father left, we'd remember what he looked like and could console ourselves with our memories. What a heartless man!' She sobbed loudly. Then her brother said, 'Mother was always saying, morning and night, that father had become a Buddha. Please don't cry.' He sounded very grown up. It caused me such anguish that I couldn't see the road in front of me.

"Hōninji had been founded by Prince Shōtoku,[28] but during the strife of the Genkō and Kenmu periods (1331–36) its property had been confiscated and its buildings had fallen into disrepair. Thanks to the efforts of the Kusunoki clan, however, the lands had been repossessed and the buildings restored. I had heard that Priest Myōhō had been invited to come down from the capital to hold services, and I was glad for this opportunity to go and hear him myself. As we drew near the

28. Prince Shōtoku (574–622) was an important statesman and early advocate of Buddhism.

temple, the crowd grew dense. There were men and women, rich and poor, clergy and laity alike. There were uncountable thousands of palanquins of every sort, and men on horseback. People had come from miles around.[29] There was someone in every available space, under every tree and atop every blade of grass.

"It did not look likely that the children would be able to make their way into the main hall. I was wondering what they might do when they pleaded, 'Won't you let us through? We need to see the priest.' As they began to nudge people aside, it seemed the Buddhas and gods had taken pity on them because, one by one in turn, everyone stepped back to let them pass. When they came to the hall where the services were being conducted, the two children politely sat down just two or three rows from the priest. As I watched, again curious as to what they would do, my daughter set the inner box down before the priest and, kneeling there with her hands clasped, bowed three times.

"The priest gazed at her. 'Child, who are you?' he asked.

"'We are the children of Shinozaki Rokurōzaemon of the Kusunoki clan. When I was three my father had a disagreement with Kusunoki and renounced the world. We've never heard from him since. After that we lived in this sad world with our mother, but, to our sorrow, as all things change and pass away, we have now been parted from her. This is the third day since her death. There was no one else to gather up her bones, so my brother and I have done it. We put them in this box, but we didn't know what to do next so we've brought them with us to ask for your help. Our hope is that you will consecrate them and pray that she be reborn in paradise. Surely then she will attain salvation.'

"The priest was deeply moved. He did not say a word; he simply wept. All those who had come to hear his sermons were also moved to tears.

"Then my daughter took a scroll out of her sleeve-pocket and presented it to the priest. He picked it up and read it in a loud voice: 'No one knows how long they will live in this world,[30] but most children have their parents by their sides until they have grown up. It was my fate, however, to be separated from my father when I was three and now to have lost my mother. I am left with no one on whom to rely. In my anguish I have nowhere to turn. I am lost with no home to return to. My heart aches with longing. I cannot stop weeping these tears of sorrow long enough to dry my eyes. If there were another person like

29. Literally, "from three provinces," probably referring to Settsu, Kawachi, and Izumi. Most of this area is now part of the Osaka metropolitan area.

30. She refers to this world by the term *enbu* (also, *enbudai*, Skt *jambudvīpa*), which is a land said to be south of Mount Sumeru, the center of the Buddhist universe.

me, they might tell me of the bitter road they have traveled and console me. But I have not met such a person, even in my dreams, because I have been unable to sleep. The only thing that keeps me company is an ephemera so faint I can't be sure it's there. It has only been three days, but I feel as though it has been a thousand or ten thousand years. Nor is there any way I can escape a sorrowful future. Who knows how many autumns the dew will linger? Who would take pity on orphans like us? I pray only that we two be received in paradise on the same lotus leaf as our mother.' In quite proper fashion she had given the year and date at the end and then had added a poem[31]:

> Every time I look at this double box I am overcome with
>   tears.
> It is a reminder that
> I have lost both of my parents.[32]

"Before he had even quite finished reading, the priest pressed his sleeve to his face and wept. In the crowded hall there was not a single man or woman, high or low, clergy or laity, who was not wringing out their sleeves. In the audience was a man who cut off his topknot, offered it together with his sword to the priest, and became his disciple. There was also a woman who, under her wide-brimmed hat, cut her hair short and presented it to the priest as a sign of her religious awakening. Countless others also renounced the world.

"Just imagine the feelings that scene stirred within me! Much as I wanted to listen to the priest's sermon for a while, I realized I was in danger of being ensnared again by the bonds I had once severed. I shut my eyes. My mind was made up. Still, it seemed to me that to confront one thousand or ten thousand mounted warriors in battle singlehandedly, to face certain death, could have been no worse. It was far more difficult than leaving Shinozaki the first time.

"I traveled quite a long way before I stopped under a tree to rest and consider the situation. This was no way to gain enlightenment, I thought. Mount Kōya, where Kōbō Daishi rests, is a place made sacred by the presence of innumerable Buddhas. No other place is superior. I decided to build a hut near Kōbō Daishi's shrine and to devote myself to religious practice there. I made my way up this mountain in eager

---

31. There are in fact two poems in some versions. The second, nearly nonsense in English, translates, "Like the body of a case without its inner box, I am an orphaned child. Just as I have no way to tie up my hair, there is no way to describe my sorrow. What am I to do?" The poetry of it lies in a pun on the words "tie up" (iu) and "describe" (iu).

32. There is a pun on *futa oya*, which expresses both "two parents" and "double box."

anticipation. Since then I have thought of nothing else. I think neither of myself nor of others. Nor do I think of my old home. Every waking moment and even as I sleep, I spend all my days and months wholly absorbed in *nenbutsu* meditation. Today is the first time I have spoken with anyone. Last spring someone from Kawachi came here on a pilgrimage. I overheard him tell someone else that Kusunoki, having heard about my children's plight, had designated my son, who was then six years old, lord of Shinozaki. I also heard that my daughter had become a nun. It was quite a relief."

The two others said, "What remarkable religious devotion! How commendable!" Then they asked him what clerical name he used.

"Genbai."

It turned out that the monk Hankai went by the name Genshō, and that Aragorō was called Genchiku. The three monks simultaneously clapped their hands and spoke in unison: "How strange! The first character of our names is propitiously the same. The second characters of our three names form the auspicious word *shōchikubai*.[33] There must have been some bond between us in a former lifetime. Even if we all had studied under one teacher, such a coincidence is extremely unlikely. How rare and wonderful that our fates be so entwined! What a shame that we have lived here on Mount Kōya without having spoken to each other before this! From now on let us practice our faith together. Truly, the delusion and ignorance that fills the world stems from our deeds in past lives. To know this is good. Not to know this is to be an ordinary man. Status, pleasure, and knowledge, all are the result of actions taken in the past. Everyone thinks what he does is right and despises others, thinking that what they do is wrong. How pointless! Consider this well: the fact is that talent, knowledge, and wealth last only as long as you live. Realize that once the winds of transience blow, only a sincere religious commitment can lead to salvation.

"How would Hankai have come to a religious awakening without having met Lady Onoe? Each of us had a different experience, but we all were led unexpectedly to faith. We should not necessarily despise wickedness. Wickedness and goodness are the two sides of a single leaf. Nor should we despise love. It comes from vulnerability. If not for our vulnerability why would anyone turn to Buddhism? These facts of human life are the instrument by which we are taught to understand the true nature of things and by which we are inspired to enter into the way of Buddhism."

---

33. *Shōchikubai* means "pine, bamboo, and plum," a trio of auspicious symbols because all three are immune to the cold. Pine and bamboo are evergreen, and the plum blossoms in late winter.

The Seven Nuns

One day in the Jōwa period [1345–49], while drunk on the wine of darkness,[1] I watched blossoms swirling in confusion at the gust of an unseasonal wind in the vast sky of all existence,[2] and I decided to go with a friend to Zenkōji in Shinano Province. There, the innkeeper recounted the following tale.[3]

"Something very rare and wonderful happened here. I'd like to tell you about it. Some time ago there was a nun of unusually deep faith. For years she prayed regularly to the Buddha and chanted the *nenbutsu*. She felt all other people's sorrows as her own and was glad to see others happy. She made even her most casual comments in a gentle tone of voice.

"One day she realized that, though she had been so lucky as to be born into the human world, she had let yesterday pass and today would slip quickly by in idleness. When she quieted her heart and thought of the pain to come in the next life, she realized that above all other things we should lament our transmigrations in the cycle of life and death, that we should strive with all our might to break free of this cycle. 'I would like to sow the seed of my enlightenment,' she thought, 'but, I must have been stingy in some previous life. That is why I am a poor woman in this life. The best I can do is to find a place where firewood is available and heat water for baths for the rich and poor so they can wash

1. "The wine of darkness" is wine that, like darkness, clouds one's true mind.

2. The implicit meaning of this metaphorical comment is, "while still suffering from the illusion that reality is as I see it, I realized, thanks to the falling cherry blossoms, that the true nature of all things is emptiness." The phrase "vast sky" in the translation is an effort to render the double meaning of *sora*, "sky," also pronounced *kū*, "emptiness," or "void."

3. Because the text would be overburdened with quotation marks due to the triple level of narration, I have suppressed in the translation the quotation marks that would signal the pilgrim is quoting the innkeeper and those that would indicate the innkeeper is quoting each nun. Such marks are not part of the medieval Japanese orthographic apparatus in any case; quotations are made clear by grammatical devices. I occasionally use an identifying word or two to indicate the shift of the speaker.

away the grime of their worldly passions. This will be the seed of my enlightenment.'

"Looking for an appropriate place, she found that there was a plentiful supply of wood and water at Sekigawa[4] in the same province, and that it was located by a well-traveled road. She established a bathhouse and offered a bath service. Thus to all the tens of thousands of travelers, of high and low status, who made their way to Zenkōji from all over the country, she gave baths, scrubbing away the travelers' grime with her own two hands.

"Then one day another nun of about thirty came to the bathhouse after having made a pilgrimage to Zenkōji. She had a bath and stayed the night. Late that evening this nun said to the proprietress: 'The compassion you show in operating this bathhouse is a wonderful thing. When did you decide to do this? Ah, how I wish I could share the merit of working here! I would help bring water from the river and firewood from the mountainside. Every act would contribute to my future enlightenment.'

"'I am so glad [to hear you say that]!' replied the proprietress. 'What a good person you are to show such compassion!' Rejoicing, she added, 'Since you are already here, by all means, if you would like to, please stay on.'

"The second nun was overjoyed, and thereafter they heated the bathwater together. The nun who had come later was called Kon Amida Butsu, while the proprietress was called Ko Amida Butsu.[5] When one was hauling water, the other was gathering firewood. Though their work was hard and painful, their compassion was such that they did not mind it in the least.

"Now sometime after the twentieth of the ninth month, four or five travel-weary nuns came for baths and begged lodging for the night in the proprietress's quarters. It was autumn, when the evenings are long, and the dawn seemed slow in coming. The proprietress was concerned, fearing her guests might be in low spirits since they were lodged in a humble hut. As the hour grew late, the moon illuminated the gently sloping mountains and shone through the cracks in the walls. In that bleak setting, one of the nuns casually recited:

> Certainly this roof was not left unthatched
> For the sake of my moon-viewing.
> Tonight's lodging, a lonely hut.

4. The town of Sekigawa lies less than a day's journey, by foot, from Zenkōji.

5. Kon Amida Butsu means "the present-day Amida Buddha," and Ko Amida Butsu indicates "the old Amida Buddha." In the medieval period it was common for believers of the Jōdo schools, especially the Ji sect, to use "A," "Ami," or "Amida Butsu" as a suffix in religious names.

"In response to that murmured verse, another nun composed:

> We should look at the moon
> Through the cracks in the walls.
> Someday it will clear away the darkness in our hearts.

"From another nun came this poem:

> The light of the moon
> Filtering through the cracks,
> Do you think it will fail to illumine the darkness in our
> hearts?

"A nun of about sixty spoke up. 'Truly, however much we lament, what always remains is the darkness in our hearts. Though the moon

shines within, the fleeting clouds are dense, and we are lost in the long
night of the cycle of life and death. A sage once told me that an instant
of time is more precious than a thousand bars of gold. What is truly to
be held dear is each instant of time.[6]

Days and months do not pass pointlessly.
It is people who waste
Time in idleness.

"Overhearing all this, the proprietress knew these nuns to be
women of deep faith. She decided to approach them and ask about

6. Time is precious because it can be used to seek enlightenment.

cultivating enlightenment. She opened the sliding doors and said: 'I'm afraid you must be distressed to find yourselves in lodgings so bleak, but remember the lines of the poem: ". . . whether you live in a palace or a straw-thatched hut . . . You cannot live forever."[7] Think of it as a night's dream. Although many people come to take baths, since this place is little better than sleeping outdoors, I have never met travelers like you. Your concern with salvation suggests that you are women of refinement. To what sort of gentlemen were you married? What are your family backgrounds? How have you come to be nuns? Since this is such a sad and lonely time, perhaps you would share the stories of your revelations so we might console ourselves on this long, dark, autumn night.'

"'How kind of you!' the old nun replied. 'If we don't repent what hinders our enlightenment, the obstacles only increase. Let each of us tell of her revelation and eliminate those obstacles. Because we were born as women, because we are jealous and brandish banners of pride, disturbing the social order, we are very often despised. As it is the proprietress's express wish, we should, each with her own story, do as she requests.'

"So, in turn, the women told their tales of revelation. This record of their explanations as to how each had come to renounce the world, having once been a woman of considerable social standing, is called the Story of the Seven Nuns."

Shiragiku's Story
[The First Nun]

"Let a young person tell her tale," someone said.

"I'm ashamed to speak of my old self," a woman of about thirty said, "but if everyone will, I will too. I am the daughter of an imperial palace carpenter from Tōyama in Tamba Province. I was in the capital at the time of Lord Rokuhara's war,[8] and having managed to survive, I

7. Poem 1851 by Semimaru in the *Shinkokin waka shū* (1206), the eighth imperial poetic anthology (NKBT 28, 374): *Kono yo wa/ totemo kakutemo/ onaji koto/ miya mo waraya mo/ hateshinakereba.*

   In this world, whether you live in a palace or a straw-thatched hut,
   It's all the same.
   You cannot live forever.

8. The Lord of Rokuhara is a reference to Taira no Kiyomori. The Taira maintained a residence in the Rokuhara area of the capital, which was east of the Kamo River between Sixth and Seventh Avenues. The war referred to here is the Genpei war, between the Minamoto and Taira clans, the concluding battle of which occurred in 1185.

wandered from province to province, village to village, hamlet to hamlet, taking employment here and there. When there was no more work to be found and I was finally impoverished, I became a prostitute near Higashi no Tōin Avenue and called myself Shiragiku. At that time there was a famous poet called Akitada, head official of the Dazaifu,[9] a man of forty or so. I met him in the autumn of my nineteenth year. We developed deep feelings for each other and pledged to grow old together and share a grave.

"One day he left the capital to go back to his home province, but my fate was the sad and uncertain life of a prostitute. After that, the son of the deputy constable of Mino Province, Tokinokingo Toshiaki, took a liking to me and moved me from the capital to Mino. He was just over twenty and more gracious and kind than anyone in the whole world. Everyone was jealous that I had won the affections of such a man. However, before I'd had a chance to forget Akitada, the Dazaifu official, he came back to the capital and asked for me.

"'She was always talking about you,' people told him, 'but she was, after all, a woman who sold her love. She went off to Mino with another man.'

"He despaired of seeing me again in this life, but day and night he thought only of me. He had no friend whose conversation could distract him from his constant longing, so he cried his heart out alone. There was no chance for the dew on his sleeves, his profuse tears, to dry. In his melancholy he continually gazed toward Mino in the east, his feelings clearly apparent on his face. A young woman, Suke no Tsubone, who had been my attendant and who had remained in the capital, took a long, penetrating look at my lover of old, and feeling sorry for him, said: 'Can't you forget her? If you are suffering so much, send her a letter. It's a very simple thing to tell her how you feel.'

"'What useless advice!' he retorted. 'She is a prostitute. It was only a brief affair. How can you suggest such a thing?' His tears fell as though of their own accord, and covering his head with the sleeve of his robe, he lay down.

"'When Shiragiku left for Mino Province,' Suke no Tsubone replied, 'she called for me and said: "As a woman [my duty is to be faithful to one man], but I am only a prostitute; I can't love just one man. I have no choice but to start a new life with a new lover. I have to do this to keep a roof over my head." Shiragiku went on and on about

9. The head official at the Dazaifu, the imperial government headquarters in Kyushu, was responsible for defense against foreign invasions and for foreign trade matters. Posts such as this were often honorary and did not necessitate residence at the site.

it. Eventually she said: "If my lord comes back up to the capital, I will not have forgotten him. If he writes to me, still less will I be able to forget him." She repeated this over and over. Since she cared for you that much, stop agonizing and write to her.'

"'In that case . . .' he thought, and wrote to me. Suke no Tsubone, to stop her lord's fretting, told him what a happy occasion it would be to see me and talk with me again after all this time. She requested passage on a boat at Ōtsu Inlet, disembarked at Shina Inlet, and hurried down to Mino. In a short time she found someone to inform me of her arrival.

"'Why have you come?' I asked, crying for joy when I saw her.

"'The circumstances are these . . .' she explained, and handed me Akitada's letter.

"'This seems like a dream,' I said and read phrase piled on various phrase. At the end was the verse:

Though you have pledged your love
To a promising young blossom in Mino in the east,
Please don't forget this familiar old tree.

"His letter unleashed a flood of tears. I pulled the sleeve of my robe over my head and collapsed on the floor.

"Toshiaki stared at me. 'Who has written to you?' he asked. 'Has something happened to your parents? Why are you hiding something from me? If you don't tell me, it will cause an estrangement between us.'

"Although I tried to keep it from him, he insisted, and I had to tell him. I realized that my relationship with Akitada, fated from a previous life, had not yet run its course. My troubled feelings were as turbulent as the smoke that rises from Mount Asama, and I was sure that this was the end for me. With my cheeks turning red as autumn leaves, I replied, 'I am ashamed to tell you this, but I have received a letter from a man in the capital with whom I was once involved.' I took the letter out.

"'Let me see it,' Toshiaki said. Without a trace of anger he unfolded it, leaf after leaf, reading carefully. I didn't know what he was thinking, but after he pondered over it for a while, with tears rolling down his face, he spoke with an air of finality. 'Well, let our relationship end here. You are a prostitute. There's no reason for me to feel hurt.' Then he composed the poem:

Go and see
The blossoms in the capital before they are scattered.
Spring in the east does not matter.

"He ordered a carriage to take me directly to the capital. I felt like a fallen oak leaf at the mercy of the current in the river of love, but I had not thought, even in my dreams, that I would come to this. Since Toshiaki had loved me so well, I had put my trust in him and had thought that whatever happened, [I could count on him]. But he was strong-willed, so I decided to have no regrets this time. I was in no position not to go. Taking Suke no Tsubone with me, I left Mino Province. I wept as we departed, but as there was no reason to linger, we arrived at our lodgings in the capital in just five days.

"Well, Suke no Tsubone called on Akitada to announce my return, thinking that Akitada would be very pleased and would reward her. Contrary to her expectations, however, Akitada said: 'The color of the blossoms on this old tree have faded. I would be ashamed to have Shiragiku see me when I don't at all resemble my old self. Besides, how can I ignore the fact that the man in Mino parted from her while he still cared for her? That she should leave the Azuma blossom for the capital shows that our love is like two birds sharing a wing or the intertwined branches of two trees.[10] But, even so, how can I possibly see her?' His profound integrity and the reply he sent made me feel like a molting bird trying to fly.

"No matter what he said, we had been together for a long time, and he could not extinguish the embers of love burning in his breast. So the following year, distressed by the awkwardness of the situation but still yearning with desire, he fell ill with lovesickness and died.

"When I was told of his undying affection, [I pondered the situation]. He had applied the common expression 'think of other people's troubles as though they are your own' and had realized, 'though no chill wind of indifference stirs in my heart, just as I love her, the man in the east loves her too.'

"'Well, what will become of me?' I wondered. 'Shall I renounce this sad world? It is no good having my love facing two ways, like a two-sided cypress leaf.'[11] I decided to become a nun and pray for the salvation of the man who had died. That is how I came to be as I am now," she recounted, finishing her story.

"How gentle-hearted all three of you were!" the old nun commented. "The lord in the east, had he been like others, would have

---

10. These frequently used images are from Po Chu-i's well-known poem "Song of Everlasting Sorrow" about the love of Emperor Hsuan Tsung for Yang Kuei-fei. See n. 62 below.

11. Since both sides of a cypress leaf are identical, it serves as a metaphor for duplicity or divided loyalty.

been jealous and unsheathed a cruel sword. He must certainly have loved you deeply, because, on the contrary, his comment 'before the capital blossoms are scattered' reveals a compassion not to be found in this age. In choosing not to meet you, the man in the capital showed humility and integrity at the expense of his life. You don't find that among common men. If he had been an ordinary person who said empty things, you would already have given your heart to the blossoms of the young tree in the east, and forgetting the blossoms of the old tree, you would have thought that Akitada was saying pointless things, and you would not have felt so deeply about him. You might have, since you were a prostitute, no, anyone would have thought: 'I turned my back on my husband and, trusting in your letter, came up to the capital. What kind of love is this? If this is what you think of me, I should have stayed in the east. A woman's lot is burning resentment and endless regret.' But that never occurred to you. Since it is a rare thing even in a hundred generations, your wisdom in taking this as the seed of enlightenment and becoming a nun is a wonderful thing. From times long past until today, sorrow has been a source of religious inspiration and a seed that will blossom in future lifetimes. Surely the perfect enlightenment of the Three Bodies of the Buddha[12] can be attained."

The Wife from the Western Part of the Capital [The Second Nun]

Then a nun in her late thirties spoke: "I am from First Avenue in the capital. As people normally do, I got married and was intimate with my husband, but he regretted the fact that, despite the passing of years and months, we did not have a child. I, however, never felt that way. I was always thinking about the emptiness of this sad world and worrying about my fate in the world to come. On long, autumn nights when I lay awake until morning, a sense of the transience of things would come over me, and the fading cries of dying insects would arouse my sympathy. So when I made pilgrimages to worship the deities and Buddhas, I prayed only for the will to strive for enlightenment and for a life [as a nun] apart from this sad world.

12. The "Three Bodies of the Buddha" refer to the Buddha as absolute truth, the various bodhisattvas, and the historical Buddha.

"Nevertheless, I was married, and even though I did not especially want a child, in the natural course of events, I gave birth to a baby boy. He was an extraordinary child. He was not only very beautiful, but he was precocious and clever. He had a sweet voice and would hug his father and me and say things beyond his years. I was sure he would be a most wonderful person if he reached adulthood. Everyone who saw him said that a string of jewels could not outshine him. His father adored him beyond all limits. Because he loved his son so much, in the winter of the boy's fourth year,[13] he had decided to kill a crane with his own hand, to serve to his son.[14] At the time, our boy was at play on the other side of the carving board. The knife blade flew out of its handle and stuck in his breast, piercing him clean through. He screamed in fright, thinking his father had done it to chastise him. 'I won't ever again go near a bird,' he cried. 'I won't do anything bad; I won't be cross. I'll do just as you say, Father.' He pressed his hands together and began to sob.

"We ran to his side and did what we could to save his life. We sent for the most famous doctors in the capital, but his cries grew weaker and weaker until they sputtered like the thin flame of an oil lamp. Our prayers went unanswered. Finally, the next morning at dawn, he took our hands and passed away as though he had merely fallen asleep. My husband and I became hysterical. We screamed at the heavenly deities and wailed at the divinities of the earth. We felt no shame; we were quite crazed with grief.

"At length my husband regained control of himself, checked his tears, and observed consolingly: 'Everything is determined by our past actions.' He said nothing more and pretended to fall fast asleep. He waited until I was up and about, and then he stabbed himself with that same knife.

"'What are you doing?' I shouted, and grabbed his hand, but he had made up his mind to die. As it had done to our son, the blade pierced his heart and came out his back. Nothing could be done for him. As the day slowly passed, he told me what to do after his death. In the middle of the night three days later, he died.

13. Since a child was considered to be one year old at birth, and since age was counted from the New Year rather than from an individual's birthday, the boy would have been on the verge of turning five by Japanese count, and would have been between three and four by Western count.

14. Since the crane was a symbol of longevity, this was an extraordinarily unpropitious deed.

"In my terrible grief I thought of taking the knife to myself. I had almost decided to kill myself when someone came and scolded me: 'How foolish you are! Who will mourn the dead? If you are so determined, there's a better way to show your resolution, isn't there? There's a way to bring them salvation, you know. You may be thinking of sharing their pillows in death, but you must not!'

"'You're right! You're right! That's what the Buddhist law teaches. This is what is meant by "an inspiration to faith."' So, I used the knife to cut off my hair, which I threw away in the Kamo River. I went to a monk on Inokuma Street and took religious vows. Still, images of the two of them never left me. I couldn't sleep for picturing my husband and child in my mind's eye. Even though I had the appearance of a nun, I was concerned that my attachments to the world were profound, so I have undertaken many ascetic practices. Because I am a woman, I have memorized the Lotus Sutra,[15] and worship the Three Treasures."

Then an old nun commented, "Surely it was Kannon, appearing in some of his thirty-three manifestations.[16] He became your child, your husband, and the crane. He has promised to save all sentient beings. When we read the Lotus Sutra, we learn that he became the Lady Jōtoku and her two sons, Jōzō and Jōgen, in order to convert the king. By means of the eighteen magic feats that the brothers performed,[17] he saved their father, the king, and made him a great Buddha. If we read the sutra, we will understand. He became your husband, your child,

---

15. The Lotus Sutra is an important scripture for women because, although women were not considered able to attain Buddhahood, the Devadatta chapter tells how one woman, the Dragon King's daughter, attains Buddhahood. See Hurvitz, Lotus Blossom, 199–201.

16. Chapter 25, "The Gateway of the Bodhisattva Sound-Observer," of the Lotus Sutra describes the thirty-three manifestations to be used by Kannon in order to preach effectively to various people. Hurvitz, ibid., 314–15.

17. This reference is to the incident in chapter 27 of the Lotus Sutra, "The Former Affairs of the King Fine Adornment," in which Jōzō and Jōgen, the sons of the King Fine Adornment, ask their mother's permission to go and worship a certain Buddha. Their mother, Lady Jōtoku, advises them to ask their father's permission. In order to persuade their father, who was "attached to the dharma of the Brahmans," the two sons performed magical feats in mid-air: "walking, remaining still, sitting, lying down, emitting water from the upper part of their bodies, emitting fire from the lower part of their bodies . . . displaying a body large enough to fill empty space, then displaying a small one . . . vanishing in empty space and then suddenly appearing on the ground, sinking into the earth as if it were water, treading on the water as if it were earth." The Lotus Sutra lists sixteen such feats, but other scriptures list two additional feats (see Hurvitz, ibid., 325–27).

and the crane. It was all the bodhisattva's way of bringing you to salvation. We can trust in him. You are to be envied." Everyone rejoiced.

Hanakazura's Story
[The Third Nun]

Then a nun of about forty spoke.

"I am from the capital as well. My father was a palace guard stationed at the north gate, named Noriyuki; and although I'm embarrassed to talk about myself, I was called Hanakazura. I was introduced to, and subsequently married, a warrior named Okunoyama of Tōtōmi Province. After our marriage we were never separated by even a hair's breadth. We spent our days oblivious to the passing of time, concerned only with admiring the moon and spring blossoms. But my husband was a military man, and the day came when his lord was appointed governor of Kyushu and ordered to leave for his post immediately. Okunoyama was to accompany him. From the moment we got this news, we were deaf to what others said; we were blinded by our tears. But my husband had a lord, and I was a warrior's wife. It would have been shameful to have people talking [about our reluctance to do our duty]; though we lamented our fate, there was no alternative. Despite his tears, he would leave the capital.

"We had been saddened even when we parted briefly to dress in the mornings and evenings. How much more terrible would be this long trip to far-off Kyushu, not even knowing when he would return! Worse still, the life of a bowman facing battle is like that of a dewdrop. I could not hope for the wind to bring me letters from him. Worrying about him day and night, I would probably come down with lovesickness. If that was to be the case, I thought, I might as well take my chances with my husband. I longed to go with him. There were, nevertheless, other people's opinions to worry about, so instead I bemoaned the fact that I had to stay behind.

"Nor did my husband want to think of leaving. His love for me deepened,[18] but the dawn of his day of departure could not be held back. He set out amid tears and went as far as Yamazaki the first day. While he was still enroute, he surprised me by sending a messenger back to comfort me with word that when things quieted down in

18. There is allusive language here that does not make sense in this context and has not been translated. It seems meant merely to evoke the melancholy of autumn.

Kyushu he would send someone to fetch me. After that, however, I had no news from him. I wore myself out worrying about him; I spent all my time gazing toward Kyushu.

"In the autumn of the following year, Toyoda no Saburō, my husband's personal attendant of many years, came up to the capital. Nearly out of my mind with anxiety, I asked immediately how things were in the western provinces.

"'He was readily granted a fief in a place called Chikaku in Hizen Province, but he has not yet pacified the area,' Toyoda replied. 'Nevertheless, he longs only for you. He thinks of you day and night, so I have come to take you to him.' He handed me a letter.

"I was overjoyed and left immediately with Toyoda to guide me. Though I was not used to traveling, I was spurred on by the joy in my heart, for I was going to see my beloved husband. We found a fast boat and sped toward Kyushu. In about twenty days we arrived in Gifu in Chikuzen Province and immediately asked for news. The innkeeper replied: 'Whoever you may be, I'll tell you how the battle goes to take your mind off your travel-weariness. The governor was victorious in several recent clashes, scattering the enemy forces. He fortified Chikaku and went to Seburiyama. But the enemy regrouped, and things have been going badly at the fortifications in Chikaku these last four or five days. The general left Seburiyama yesterday with five thousand horsemen. Today or tomorrow they'll be trading arrows.'

"Oh, no! I thought, and my heart pounded with fear. I immediately dispatched Toyoda to tell my husband that I had come this far. Then three days later, in the late afternoon, Toyoda returned, his face pale. In a strange voice he said, 'Read this letter.' Then, choking on his tears, he spoke no more. At a loss for words, he fell to weeping.

"I was greatly alarmed and about to read the letter when I heard a commotion outside the gate. With a frightened cry I went outside and saw that a palanquin had been brought up. A feeling of premonition compelled me to run over to it, and I lifted the blinds to find my husband's lifeless body inside. Was this a dream or reality? When I had come so far, instead of the joy of seeing him again, what wretchedness to realize the futility of putting on travel robes and coming here! I embraced his corpse, alternately reproaching him and weeping. I knew no shame as I stubbornly clung to his body.

"'There's no good in carrying on like this,' said the innkeeper, taking hold of me and wrenching me away from the corpse.

"At this point Toyoda spoke through his tears: 'I arrived yesterday toward evening. Lord Okunoyama was very happy to get your letter. He said that he was going to the battlefield around dawn, but that he was overjoyed that you had come from the capital, and that he would

express himself in detail in this letter. But I wanted to find out how things were in the camp, so I stayed a while. I heard a great commotion among the ranks. Alarmed, I pricked up my ears. Officers were shouting that the enemy had attacked, that the troops should prepare for battle.

"'In today's clash, twenty thousand enemy approached in three groups. On our side were only five thousand men divided into three units. The battle began around eight in the morning, and they fought until about four this afternoon. Back and forth they surged, sons not knowing their fathers had been struck down, fathers not knowing their sons had been slain, until the wide plain of Chikaku was carpeted with dead men and horses. Up to this point Lord Okunoyama had clashed with the enemy many times, but he had not been badly wounded. He emerged from the ranks alone and charged into the thick of it. "That man is a great warrior," shouted the general. "He is not to be struck down!" Five hundred riders lined up and charged, smashing through the enemy ranks. As they retreated in two directions, our men regrouped to consider their strategy. Someone cried out: "I've lost sight of Lord Okunoyama, what has happened to him?" One of our warriors stepped forward and explained that Lord Okunoyama had been grappling with the younger Matsura brother, but that he had been separated from our lord in the fierce struggle and didn't know how Okunoyama had fared. Well, I thought, perhaps he is to meet his end. I must not fail to witness his last battle. I ran right out and quickly made my way to where the Matsura force was positioned. Then, as I had hoped, I caught sight of Lord Okunoyama's distinctive cape among the Matsura men.

"'I raised a great cry: "Ho there! Listen to me! I am Toyoda, from Lord Okunoyama's clan. I've come because I heard Lord Okunoyama was here."

"'"Well, whoever you are, Lord Okunoyama is here," someone shouted.

"'I realized that our lord was still alive, and that he must have said that he wanted to see me. How glad I was as I rushed to his side. But what use was my affection? He had been seriously wounded. I approached him where he lay and spoke to him, but he did not reply. He only looked at me, so I encouraged him: "Why are you so weak? This is Toyoda. Be strong. You must see your wife once more."

"'At this he took a breath with difficulty and struggled to say: "We never know how long we have to live, do we? With my life in such danger, I'm sorry that I sent you up to the capital. I can't bear causing my wife to suffer this way. Though I've been badly hurt, if I live two or three days, I'll only long to see her more. Yet I would be all the more ashamed to have her see me like this. Hurry and cut off my head."

"'"[Not] by someone else's hand," I thought, and with Lord Matsura's consent, I struck off our lord's head.' Toyoda stopped speaking, silenced by his tears.

"I looked at the letter. How pitiful! He had not known he was to vanish like white snow from a branch. 'I will definitely see you in four or five days,' he had written. His earnest words now were empty; this was the only letter he had left behind. I wept as I read it and I wept as I rolled it up. I could only protest: 'Isn't this just a dream?'

"I couldn't just stand there, weeping, indefinitely. He was cremated, and I cut off my long tresses. For these seventeen years I have been on a continuous pilgrimage throughout the provinces."

When she had finished her story, the old nun remarked: "Truly, as the Buddha said, a woman's terrible fate is to bear the burden of the Five Obstacles and Three Subjugations. Unable to view the moon of truth clearly, she is lost in the utter darkness of worldly desires, dwelling in the long night of endless rebirth, wandering round and round, like a wagon wheel, through the Twenty-five Worlds.[19] Though the Three Treasures—the teachings, the Buddha, and the clergy—suffuse the land, even when they are described with the use of illustrations, women make no effort to learn about them. Women have been doomed to choke and shrivel up in the flames of the Hell of Uninterrupted Suffering.[20] However, because the Buddha devises ways to save even women, he appeared as your husband. In that guise he has saved you. Those who have left their families to become monks and nuns are as numerous as rice, hemp, bamboo, and reeds, but one who earnestly pursues the faith is rare. Surely with this as the seed of enlightenment, your ancestors for seven generations will become Buddhas. Your relatives, from your great-grandparents down through to your great-grandchildren, will be reborn in paradise. There is no doubt of it."

Everyone rejoiced and wept for joy.

The Soldier's Wife
[The Fourth Nun]

Then a nun approaching fifty smiled and began, "I'm from Uji where I used to own some land. I don't have anything in particular to confess. I've never borne any grudges against the world, nor have I ever had a complaint against anyone. Unlike all the other stories, mine is not a tale of woe. It's just that I took a good look at the world. A blossom in full bloom is vulnerable to the breeze, and the light of the moon, which testifies to this throughout the land, is obscured by the clouds at dawn. Whatever imperial rank a person may have, however honored by the

---

19. The Twenty-five Worlds or the twenty-five forms of existence are the fourteen worlds in the desire realms (yokukai), in which beings are ruled by their desires for food, sex, and sleep; the seven realms of form (shikikai), where beings have transcended desire but retain physical form; and the four formless realms (mushikikai), where beings enjoy purely spiritual existence.

20. The worst of eight terrible hells. See nn. 21 and 37 below for a description of other hells.

world he may be, life is a moment's dream. Neither are the impoverished and ignorant long for this world. A child, newborn yesterday, becomes a corpse today. On the evening of a day of celebration, we
are confronted with lamentable events. What a terrible shame it is that
we don't recognize this truth, even though it is right before our eyes.

"We have only a fleeting self, which we should not even call our
own, but we hate people who say malicious things about us and smile
when people are compliant. In all the teachings it says there should be
no distinctions made between oneself and others, but though we hear
this teaching constantly, we fail to understand that both good and evil
are unchanging, and we are all caught in the cycle of rebirth. That is
why in our next lives we must face the judgment of the Ten Kings of
Hell and must dwell forever in the Hell of Scorching Heat, of Great
Scorching Heat, of Wailing, of Great Wailing, etc.[21] In our stupidity we
spin a silkworm's cocoon, and in the end it is no different from self-
immolation. How futile is human life!

"It is harder to be born human than for a one-eyed turtle to
encounter a hole in a floating log. Even when born as a man or woman,
it is highly unusual to be exposed to the Buddha's teachings. Even when
exposed to them, it is rare to have the opportunity to learn about the
schools of Mahāyāna Buddhism.

"After I realized that my body is like heavy dew in Adashi ceme-
tery, that it is as reliable as a letter arriving when there is no wind to
carry it, I decided to leave home to try to break free from this painful
cycle of life and death and to attain the sphere of the enlightened. I
decided to sever the conjugal bond of love and pray that I might gain
salvation in the next world together with my mother and father. I
believed the words of the text:

---

21. The dead confront each of the ten kings in turn until a judgment as to their fate is
    made. The first king is met after seven days, the next six at seven day intervals,
    the eighth after one hundred days, the ninth after one year, and the tenth after
    three years. The king most commonly named is Enma, the fifth King of Hell.
        The Hell of Scorching Heat is the sixth of eight. In this hell one is
    tortured by being put on hot iron, or in an iron cauldron. The seventh hell is the
    Hell of Great Scorching Heat. The Hell of Wailing is the fourth, where one is
    tortured with raging flames and boiling water and made to scream and wail. The
    fifth hell is the Hell of Great Wailing. The other hot hells not mentioned in the
    text are the first hell, where one suffers and is revived by a cold wind in order to
    suffer over and over; the second hell, in which one is bound with hot iron chains
    and cut to pieces; the third hell, in which one is crushed by falling iron mountains
    and where birds with flaming iron beaks peck out one's intestines; and the eighth
    and last hot hell, where one dies and is continuously reborn to suffer endlessly.
    There are also eight cold hells. See n. 37 below.

While still caught in transmigration through the Three
    Worlds,
I cannot sever the bonds of attachment.
Abandoning affection, I enter the realm of causelessness
    [enlightenment].
That is the true expression of affection.[22]

"I asked my husband to let me go, but he would not. In my bitter disappointment I devised a scheme for making myself distasteful to him in every possible way. So, doing just as I pleased, I did not comb my hair or wash my face or blacken my teeth[23] or cut my finger- and toenails. I made myself repugnant to look at, one-eyebrowed and coarse.

"When I went to pray to the gods and the Buddhas, I asked only to be allowed to renounce the world. At that time, I saw in the mountains to the east and west of the capital, and in the city itself, miserable beggars who were clinging to life, worthless as it is, by soliciting passersby. Their voices as they cried out to me seemed like claps of thunder. Some were crippled or blind. There were also lepers and other beggars holding straw hats to their chests. I asked a religious leader what past deeds they were being punished for.

"He explained that if you read the Sutra of Cause and Effect,[24] all causes and effects are quite clearly explained. A starving, destitute beggar is someone who, thinking of his possessions as something enduring, was stingy in his former life. Such is the recompense for those who ignored the Buddhist teachings. The blind and the dumb are those who hoodwinked and lied to others in their previous lives. Anyone who is deaf is someone who shunned sermons and sutra expositions and concerned himself only with affairs of this world, who took every minute and hour to indulge in moon- and flower-vewing and who was happy only at those times. Such people will not be released from the cycle of rebirth even after tens of thousands of aeons. The sacred teaching says:

---

22. This is a scriptural verse recited when one takes the tonsure (see *Hōon jurin*, *T* 53:448, no. 2122). This verse is also cited in *The Tale of the Heike* 10.10 (see also Kitagawa and Tsuchida, *Heike*, 618 and McCullough, *Heike*, 345–46).

23. It is not known when the practice of blackening one's teeth originated. Through most of the medieval period, both men and women of the upper classes did so. In the Edo period the custom died out among men. The practice ended among women during the Meiji period (*Nihon rekishi daijiten* 3:83).

24. *Ingakyō* (properly, *Kako genzai ingakyō*), the *Sutra of Past and Present Cause and Effect* (*T* no. 189), tells of Śākyamuni's life and the principles of karmic retribution.

If you want to know past causes,
Look at the present effects.
If you want to know future effects,
Look at present causes.

It is as obvious as the lines in the palm of your hand.

"I reflected deeply on these truths, and I thought constantly that I must somehow make my husband understand and let me go, but he would not. Once I thought that if he would not give me permission, I would cut off my hair, leave it by my pillow, and just run away to some temple. Then I grew concerned that his resentment would present an obstacle to my religious efforts. He was too stubborn! In my frustration I went first to Kitano Shrine to pray that I might enter the path to salvation and that my husband might quickly be made a believer.

"On my way home an old skull lying in the grass by the roadside caught my eye. There was no reason to find this sight shocking, but the eyeless skull with some of its teeth missing and its sex indistinguishable reminded me of the verse:

Skin-deep is the difference
Between men and women.
As skeletons we are all the same.

"Well, someday, sometime, I too will be nothing but forgotten bones, I thought. Though the sun may set behind the ridge of the eastern mountains and heaven fall to earth, how can I avoid becoming an old skeleton?[25] I put the skull in my sleeve-pocket, went home, and that night set it by my husband's pillow as he slept. After a while, when he awoke and was speaking to me of love, I took his hand and placed it on the skull.

"'What's this?' he screamed, shuddering.

"'You shouldn't be so surprised,' I said. I took his hand again and had him feel my face at length. 'What's the difference? This skull is only as different from my face as a frame with or without silk stretched over it. You must not have any feeling for me! However much a husband and wife care for each other, it's not a bond that lasts long. Though it should endure for two lifetimes, our fates are controlled by past causes. When we are reborn we remember nothing of previous existences, so how can our paths in the next life be the same? How can we be born on the same

25. See pp. 10–12 for a discussion of this concept.

lotus? It is true that we must inevitably suffer the pain of separation from our loved ones[26]; it is a fact that we cannot avoid parting from whomever we may meet. You too must seek enlightenment.[27]

"'Kūkai said that the four hundred and four ailments[28] are caused by deeds done long ago, and that we are born into the cycle of life and death through women. If you don't take this opportunity to break out of the round of rebirth, when will you be able to free yourself? If you won't, then find some other woman and love her as your wife instead of me. If you will aid me in my quest for enlightenment, I will shave my head and abandon this world. I will become an itinerant nun, calm my mind, and make pilgrimages to various temples and sacred mountains. Since I am set on seeking enlightenment, I won't think anything of it [if you take another wife].' I held his hand and pleaded earnestly the whole night through. I did not try to control my sobbing, and with tears streaming, I argued insistently.

"Then he responded: 'I am neither stone nor wood. Do you think I have not noticed your behavior these past few years? However much you are motivated to seek enlightenment, you are a woman, and something will dim your fervor before long. Now let me tell you a story. Recently there was a happy couple in the capital, like you and me, who were leading a good life. The husband, however, for some reason lamented the emptiness of this world day and night and thought only of matters pertaining to his next life. He often asked his wife for permission to leave, and finally he cut off his hair. Because he was so intent on his enlightenment, he ate none of the five grains.[29] "The five grains," he reasoned, "are cultivated by the plow and hoe, which kill insects and worms. That is how they are grown. Therefore, to eat them is to participate in killing living things. Moreover, if you mix salt and plum vinegar to flavor your food, you obstruct the pursuit of enlightenment.[30]

---

26. This is one of eight kinds of suffering or sorrows: birth, growing old, disease, death, parting from a loved one, meeting with someone hateful, unattained aims, and all the ills of the five *skandhas* (physical sense organs plus four types of mental processes).

27. A phrase, *shokushointonyokuiho*, attributed to Myōchi Daishi has been omitted since Myōchi Daishi is unknown and the statement attributed to him is indecipherable.

28. There were thought to be 101 ailments caused by each of the four elements, earth, water, fire, and wind: 202 fevers caused by earth and fire and 202 chills caused by water and wind.

29. The five grains are wheat, rice, beans, and two kinds of millet.

30. Salt and vinegar were basic flavorings. The logic of this sentence is that an interest in food, as an attachment to worldly things, obstructs enlightenment.

""'Kūkai pointed out that human toil is required to produced even one bowl of rice or one cup of oil. Thus, rather than eating the five grains when it necessitates pain and death, rather than living wastefully, I will eat only what I can glean from the forest." People thought it extraordinary that he lived on only the fruit of trees and grasses for month after month. Later he was called "the Reverend Forest-gleaner" and "Forest-gleaner Amida Buddha." So, you see, everyone knew about him. But then, somehow, he lost his will. He began to relax his adherence to his forest-gleaning regimen, perhaps because he had grown old.

"'About this time news of his strict asceticism reached his former wife, and she judged him to be a Buddha in this decadent age. She took every opportunity to visit him. Concerned for his welfare, she saw him more and more frequently. Sometimes they spoke of the past and wept. Because of their deep affection for each other, they were unable to remain free of their old attachment. Finally, people began to say their behavior was disgraceful. Since they had reunited as husband and wife, people ridiculed them and made them the subject of gossip throughout the capital. The popular saying, "He's just a former Forest-gleaning Buddha,"[31] dates from this affair.

"'Moreover, when you look at the state of the world, you see that there are many people who have been inspired to seek enlightenment, who at the beginning follow a forest-gleaning regimen and wear robes woven of grass. They own nothing but their three robes and one begging bowl, and are considered bodhisattvas incarnated as saints. Later, however, they throw off their clerical mantles and robes, learn the lyrics of popular songs, gather young boys around them, bury the sutras and sacred commentaries in dust, and enjoy themselves at drinking parties. Many revert completely to lay life, become the butt of people's jokes, and are called "monks who regretted it."

"'It's not that I can't bear to part with you. It's just that, as a woman, you hear the teachings from someone once and immediately undertake to follow them, but it is not faith that comes from wisdom. For your sake, I cannot agree to dissolving our marriage and sending you back to your parents. There is a text that says that faith is like a great boulder: it is difficult to set upright, but it is very easy to abandon. Rather than going ahead with this ridiculous plan and becoming a laughingstock, if you remain a lay person and if your convictions are

---

31. The phrase "former Forest-gleaning Buddha" (*tada moto no mokuami*) came to mean "one who had achieved more glory than his social position led him to expect but who blundered and lost the status he had gained."

strong enough, then try to uphold the five layman's prohibitions,[32] don't neglect to make pilgrimages to temples and pagodas, and remain as my wife. If you pray for salvation in the next world, you will immediately find peace of mind in this one, and you will be reborn to a good station in the next. Isn't that as good as leaving home? Give it up! Besides, as the *The Net of Brahma Sutra*[33] says, the bodhisattvas's vows are to benefit laymen. How could the scriptural lessons we have been studying all our lives be only for those who take the tonsure? You must change your mind.'

"Then I said: 'As a woman I hesitate to continue to object, and I am deeply grateful for the story of the Forest-gleaning Amida, the laughingstock, that you have told me out of your compassion borne of our years together. Yet, even if I wavered in my commitment to seek enlightenment, how could my belief in the net of the Buddha's teachings be fruitless? I have heard of a commentary that says the merit of having taken the tonsure for twenty-four hours will keep you from falling into hell for two hundred thousand aeons.[34] Can my desire for enlightenment be futile? I may revert to my previous lay state,[35] but since I have made up my mind, please give me your permission. Though I may not see it through to the end, I certainly have that intention. And, if you are concerned [about my safety because] I am young [and attractive], there is something I have kept from you, but would like to tell you now. Look at this.' From the bag in which I kept my amulet, I carefully drew out a dagger with a blade as sharp as ice.

"'I have this knife so that if, after I become a nun, some rascal makes sport of me, I can pay him back with this through the heart. Since I am firmly resolved, please, I beg you, let me do as I wish.' I was insistent, and he said nothing for a time, while he pondered my words.

"'Your argument rings quite true, quite true. Though I have a man's body, I have less than your woman's heart. Truly, though we are like the fragile banana tree leaf, easily frayed in the wind, and like froth on the water, we think things will always be the same; yet how long will we be together?' He wept as he recited:

---

32. These are prohibitions against killing, stealing, lewdness, lying, and drinking.

33. *Bonmōkyō* (T no. 1484) gives the Mahāyāna disciplinary code, including ten major and forty-eight minor rules.

34. Aeon renders kalpa, a virtually limitless unit of time. Defined poetically, it is more time than it would take for a gigantic mountain to be worn away by a heavenly being brushing it with a soft cloth once a year.

35. Here the text reads *moto no mama no tsugihashi naritomo*, "revert to my previous state as the bridge in Mama." *Mama no tsugihashi* is a *utamakura* or pillow phrase, used here to no apparent advantage.

He who is not stout-hearted
Will have difficulty
Breaking free from the cycle of life and death.

"He cut off his hair and placed it at my knees. He did not bother about his property, but left the house at dawn just as he was. I don't know where he finally went. He may even be in the capital.

"Delighted to be able to do as I wished after he left, I shaved my head and set out on a pilgrimage through the provinces."

"Yours was certainly a true renunciation," a nun of some years remarked. "Since everyone experiences sorrow, no one can avoid it. There are many who leave their families and renounce the world, but you had no particular woes. There was no one against whom you had a grudge or complaint, and not only did you free yourself of your marital relationship, an especially deep bond, but when your husband wouldn't consent, you plotted various things, and accomplished your own and your husband's religious awakening as well. How wonderful in a world such as this! The Godai'in[36] shows that there is no real Buddha of the future and ultimately no historical Buddha. Everyone should free himself as you did."

With that, all present exclaimed: "How rare and wonderful!" They joined their hands in prayer and rejoiced.

Lord Kikui's Wife
[The Fifth Nun]

Then the elderly nun told her story. "Since all of my companions have told their tales, if I don't tell mine, I would seem to have encouraged you insincerely. Please forgive my lack of modesty in talking about myself, but I have a strange and wonderful tale to tell.

"I was born in Awa Province. When I reached a marriageable age, I wed a man called Kikui no Ukon. When he went off to the capital on business, I waited impatiently for him. I asked, 'Is the capital this way?' and day and night I did nothing but gaze in that direction. I would call together my attendants and chat through the night, speaking of nothing but him. I was still obsessed with thoughts of him and burning with love when my husband came home three years later. I was so happy that, ignoring people's stares, I ran out of the front gate crying: 'You've been so long in coming home.'

"'So I have,' he replied, not looking particularly happy to be back.

"'That's an unexpected attitude,' I thought, and for two or three months I wondered what might have happened in the capital to upset him. Then I heard a rumor on the wind: 'Lord Kikui has brought a beautiful woman back with him. She's young and has the elegant and aristocratic diction of someone from the capital, a woman with the grace of a willow in a spring breeze. He has established her in a house that he found for her.'

"Now I understood. Judging from the expression on his face when I ran out to meet him at the gate, this rumor was quite true. Well, if there was another woman, I would have to do something about it.

---

36. The *Godai'in* is one of thirteen sections of the womb or matrix *mandala*.

Being from the distant capital, she wouldn't have any friends here, while I had many relatives. Since others would certainly take my side in this matter, I decided to teach this woman a lesson. I would make an example of this degenerate, husband-stealing female and wrest her away from my husband. But then, on second thought, I reasoned 'No, my husband is not an irresponsible man, [he isn't likely to abandon me].' Besides, I was approaching thirty, and I couldn't look forward to very many more years. And it certainly wasn't unusual for a man to be fickle. As long as he didn't shun me, I'd let things be. And so I slept alone on a pillow dampened by my tears, and the bells at dawn echoed my desolation.

"I had spent several months being patient and understanding, when one day my husband said listlessly: 'I can't hide this from you indefinitely. I brought a wonderful woman home with me from the capital. I can't send her all the way back now. There's no point in your getting angry. I don't intend to replace you. You mustn't hold this against me.'

"What he said seemed reasonable. 'It's a very common thing,' I replied graciously. 'Why should I be upset? It's not a question of this one woman from the capital, there certainly have been plenty of other cases of this kind of thing. That's how men are.'

"'I'm so glad [to hear you say that],' he replied happily. 'You are indeed a well-bred woman.'

"Some months went by, but things were not as my husband had said. The number of days he spent with his mistress increased, and I was brushed aside. No matter what I said, he was cold toward me. At first I worried about what people might think and about my future. 'Well,' I thought, 'even if that's how it is, as long as he will provide for me . . .' But I felt he was very cruel, and although I did not show it outwardly, inside I resented him terribly. Night after night, day upon day, I brooded about the two of them, and then I developed a strange condition on my back. I had it examined and learned it was something like scales. I was horrified. Another day, looking at myself in a mirror, I noticed that my hair was tangled and my eyes gleamed brightly. My mouth had broadened and two horn-like lumps had risen on my forehead. Until then I had thought that this kind of thing only happened in old tales to other people, but now I was in more and more pain. I began to feel as though my body were on fire. Everyone who noticed these changes in me were frightened, and after a while all my attendants left me. Well, the world would soon know, I thought, sighing deeply. I spent months just gazing off into space.

"There was, however, one attendant who had served me for years and who still kept me company at times. One day when an ascetic came begging, this attendant said to him: 'This woman's jealousy is causing

physical changes in her. Won't you instruct her in the sacred teachings and save her?'

"'Of course,' he replied.

"Then my attendant said to me: 'This ascetic is a rare and wonderful man, let him guide you to faith.'

"I was furious. 'I'll do no such thing! I'm not going to listen to a word about Buddhas or Buddhist doctrine. All I want is to turn this place into a swamp and cover it with black clouds. I'll spout flames like those of the Red Lotus and Deep Red Lotus hells[37] and drive that hateful

37. These are the seventh and eighth cold hells, in which it is so cold that one's skin and
    flesh crack and look like red lotus flowers. The first six cold hells are: one, where
    the cold causes skin to blister; two, where the cold causes blisters to burst; three,
    where the cold is such that frozen lips can only utter the sound "asetta"; four,

woman away from my husband. If I could just swallow her up in a gulp, I'd be satisfied. After that my husband and I will live together in the Three Evil Realms[38] and wreak havoc for the rest of eternity. I want only to become a great villain.' I gave a great angry shout that shook the mountains and valleys and made the earth tremble. My attendant was frightened out of her wits. Then I remarked, 'If he is an ascetic who has been wandering throughout the provinces, he must know everything. I'll see him.'

"'What can I do for you?' the ascetic inquired.

"'I'm ashamed,' I answered, 'to have you see me looking like this and embarrassed to ask you about this, but a hateful woman has been making me miserable. There must be a way to kill her. Teach me.'

"'That's easy,' the ascetic replied.

"I was delighted and explained, 'I have hated that woman for years. I can't begin to tell you what my days and nights have been like. I haven't even been able to sleep. I have harbored a fire in my breast; three times a night and three times a day, I feel as though flames are shooting out from my body. Look at this. When I put water in this tub and hold it in my arms, it comes to a boil, and I suffer all the more. If I could kill that woman, my suffering would come to an end, so [please tell me how to do it].'

"'It's very simple,' said the ascetic. 'To kill someone you must take a certain attitude. If you do as I teach you, it may at most take fourteen or fifteen days, but surely not so long as sixteen or seventeen.'[39]

"'Whatever it is, I'll do as you say,' I agreed.

"'Think of nothing,' the ascetic told me. 'Let no thoughts arise. Forget good and bad. Don't think about the person you care for, and don't think about the one you hate. Abandon all thoughts. Let your mind be as empty as if your head had been cut off. If you do this, your original, fundamental self will emerge. This is said to be the way most favored by the Buddhas to do away with hated people. If you still have an occasional thought that suddenly occurs to you, don't abandon it, but think hard where it came from, and what kind of thought it is. Think well, think and think.[40] Devote your mind to the question of the

---

where "kakukakuba" is the only sound utterable in this even colder hell; five, where "kokuba" is the only sound that can be made; and six, where skin is frozen blue.

38. The Three Evil Transmigrations are realms into which one is reborn as a result of negative karma: the realm of hells, of hungry ghosts, and of beasts.

39. The text reads "it won't take six or seven days." I assume the meaning to be sixteen or seventeen days, considering the context.

40. "Think well, think and think" renders *minen, yokunen, nenneni*, which seems somewhat garbled. The translation does not account for *i*.

four origins of all things.[41] You will see there will be no source for your evil thoughts. There will be the ultimate reality of the *Lotus Sutra*, the single truth behind all things. At that time all those you hate will be slain at once,' he explained.

"I put my faith in his words and quieted my mind. I made myself oblivious to the passing of time, and when, whether walking, standing, sitting, or lying down, I had an evil or wrong thought, I meditated, practiced religious rites, or confined myself to a quiet place. I sought in various ways to accomplish what I had been taught. But none of this had any effect at all.

"After fourteen or fifteen days, the ascetic summoned me. 'What has become of the woman you hate?' he inquired.

"'I am not aware of her at all,' I replied.

"'Then what is most noble in your true self has appeared. When you conquer the thoughts that arise, love and hate are destroyed like snowflakes falling into a fire, and evil and goodness are indistinguishable. There is no you and there is no other. The other is you and you are the other. This is the true way to do away with those you hate. This is vanquishing the source and annihilating life and death.'

"No sooner had he finished speaking than I clapped my hands and said that truly, truly, the awful woman was gone, that my dear husband was gone. I heaved a great sigh of relief. My chest felt unbound. I awoke from my dream. The traces of snake scales were gone. Physically I was back to normal. I suddenly understood. I realized that past, present, and future are like an illusion, and immediately I became the ascetic's disciple."

When she had finished, the proprietress responded: "Leaving aside what you did, how wonderful the ascetic's teaching! He did not reprove you for your malice, but guided you to enlightenment. Surely such is the true Mahāyāna doctrine. Tendai commentaries explain that good and evil are the same, that wickedness and virtue are one,[42] and we recite verses from scripture on escaping the cycle of rebirth. However, with words alone, lacking the sutras, such activity is no more than the buzzing of insects, they say.

> I have abandoned this sad world,
> Which should be shunned.
> Now I search for the true way.

---

41. Living things are categorized into four groups according to how they are born: creatures born from a womb, from eggs, from moisture, i.e., insects, and by self-transformation, i.e., heavenly beings, the inhabitants of hell, etc.

42. The translation omits *henshakaichū*, which is not decipherable.

The true way is everything the historical Buddha did. Enlightenment is not in the Buddha, nor in humankind. It is not in the past, nor is it in the present. It is where time and space are transcended. The Buddha explained this place as the Pure Land of a bodhisattva of universal compassion. The many Buddhas of the past, present, and future, the Buddhas of the Ten Directions,[43] the various [sacred] ornaments and utensils, Śākyamuni's eighty thousand teachings,[44] and the twelve categories of the Mahāyāna canon,[45] all reveal the absolute truth of the one reality, the wonderful law.

"You were ridiculed as an abandoned woman, looked down upon and despised, but your heart, especially, has been ennobled by the clear and bright light of the moon that penetrates to every corner. How marvelous! How wonderful! It is said that sharing the shade of a single tree and sipping from the same stream is due to karma from another life. I am grateful for the religious inspiration that I have gained from meeting you. I have provided lodging for countless travelers whose understanding of Buddhism was questionable. I have never met anyone who has achieved enlightenment as profoundly as you have." The proprietress rejoiced greatly.

The Lord Miike Affair
[The Sixth Nun]

"Well, proprietress, why did you renounce the world?"

"I was an attendant to the wife of Lord Miike of Chikugo in Tsukushi,"[46] she answered. "After Lord Miike went to the capital to press a lawsuit, his lady, never receiving any letters from him, was always distracted. She hardly ever spoke, and there were always tears in her eyes. Downcast and sorrowful, she made a pathetic figure. One day,

---

43. The Ten Directions are east, west, south, north, southeast, southwest, northwest, northeast, nadir, and zenith.

44. "Śākyamuni's eighty thousand teachings" is an abbreviation for "the eighty-four thousand teachings," which means all of the Buddha's teachings.

45. All the scriptures are categorized into twelve types based on form or content. The twelve are: the Buddha's sermons; metrical pieces; poems; solicited addresses; narratives; stories of former lives of the Buddha; miracles; parables, metaphors, illustrations; discussions by question and answer; impromptu or unsolicited addresses; expanded sutras; and prophecies.

46. Chikugo is located in the southern part of modern Fukuoka Prefecture. Tsukushi refers to Kyushu.

not being able to bear the sight of her like that, I remarked: 'It's strange that we have not had any word from our lord. However much I'm concerned about what will become of you, I am distraught with worry about your son's future. I have been thinking it over. What do you think of taking the boy and going to the capital to look for our lord?'

"'I am so glad to hear your suggestion,' the lady replied. 'I have been thinking of doing just that for a long time, but days and months have gone by and I have done nothing because I am a helpless woman, and because I haven't been able to tell how you felt. But you have been very sensitive. Let's go.'

"With the twelve-year-old Fujiwaka at the head of our small party,[47]

> We set off for an unfamiliar place, with only our determina-
> tion as a guide.
> When we arrived at Anrakuji[48] in the latter part of the
> second lunar month,
> As we longed for our lord in the capital, we remembered
> the history of the deity and prayed to him for
> protection.
> At Hakozaki,[49] which we had heard of but never seen, the
> wind blew fiercely through the pines.
> We passed through the Moji checkpoint,[50] where times past
> are recorded.
> At Itsukushima,[51] where days pile up, we put our trust in
> the deity's pledge.
> We crossed the steep slopes of Au Mountain,[52] hoping to
> meet our lord,

47. What follows is *michiyuki bun*, poetic prose of alternating five- and seven-syllable lines that evokes the emotional and physical hardships of travel while it describes places along the route. It is characterized by the use of place-names, associative words, pivot words, pillow words, and allusions to classical poetry.

48. There is a temple called Anrakuji in Usa, Ōita Prefecture, but this is in eastern Kyushu, and not on their route. There is no indication that they made a detour to pray there. This reference may be to an Anrakuji that is no longer in existence or reflect the author's ignorance of the geography of Kyushu.

49. Hakozaki is in modern eastern Fukuoka Prefecture.

50. Moji checkpoint is at the northern tip of Kyushu, where one crosses to Shimonoseki on Honshu. The pillow phrase, *sono mukashi o mo shirushi oku*, "where times past are recorded," comes from the meaning of the word *moji*, "written words." The place-name *moji* is now written with characters meaning "gatekeeper."

51. Itsukushima refers to Itsukushima Jinja, the tutelary shrine of the Taira clan, located on Miyajima, in Hiroshima Bay. The pillow phrase, *hi kazu wa tsumoru*, "where days pile up," comes from the meaning of *itsu*, "when," or "what time?"

52. No specific Au Mountain between Hiroshima and Onomichi can be located in available reference works, but it is similar to a common name for mountains, written *ao* "green," which suggests *au*, "to meet."

And quickly climbed Ura Mountain in Onomichi.[53]
After some days, we arrived in Suma and Akashi.[54]
There we remembered that Genji had spoken of 'the waves
    close by.'[55]
Seeing the birds at Ikutagawa,[56] we felt sure we would find
    our lord, and passed on happily.
We soon arrived in the capital,

took lodgings in the Fifth Avenue and Muromachi area, and asked the innkeeper if he knew where Lord Miike might be.

"'Yes, indeed I do. Lord Miike won his suit and was granted rights to land in Sumiyoshi, in Echigo. He has gone there.'

"What a disappointment to hear that! We had counted on finding him 'in the capital,' but now it was some strange place called Echigo. How could we get there in this state of exhaustion? I felt like a molting bird struggling to fly. Then I composed myself and said to my lady, 'If we turn back now, we will never find him. Since it's probably no further than we have come so far, however long the way, and since we have already staked our lives on finding him, if you will take the Koshi highway to Echigo, I will go with you.'

"'If only you will come with me,' she answered, 'for my lord's sake, I would be happy to go even to Soto no Hama in Tsugaru[57] or Chishima in Ezo.'[58]

"Thus we decided to leave the capital for Echigo.

Departing the capital, we put Arachi Mountain,[59] the very
    name of which is frightening, behind us.

53. Onomichi is a city on the Inland Sea in the eastern part of modern Hiroshima.

54. Suma and Akashi are cities on the Inland Sea in Hyōgo Prefecture, made famous as the two sites of Genji's exile in *The Tale of Genji*.

55. "The waves close by" is a phrase from *The Tale of Genji*, chapter 12, "Suma." The larger context is: "When Genji raised his head from his pillow to listen to the storm raging around him, he felt as though the waves were close by" (*Nihon koten zensho* 2:148; Seidensticker, *Genji*, 235–36).

56. Ikutagawa is a river in modern Kobe city. There is a legend incorporated in *Yamato monogatari*, a poem tale from about 951, which tells of a woman wooed by two suitors. As a trial to win her hand, they were asked to shoot at waterfowl. When both men succeeded and the woman was unable to choose between them, she drowned herself in Ikutagawa, and the two men followed her example (*NKBT* 9:311–16). The presence of live birds at Ikutagawa, strangely enough, here is taken as a propitious sign.

57. Tsugaru Peninsula is at the northern tip of the main island of Japan.

58. Ezo is modern Hokkaido.

59. Arachi Mountain, in Tsuruga City in Fukui Prefecture, was the site of an important checkpoint on the main road to the north. Arachi may be written with the characters meaning "rugged land." Another passage of *michiyuki bun* begins here.

By day we were beckoned by the mountain winds,
Which seemed to murmur doubts of our return, feeling as
   though our lives were falling blossoms of melting snow;
Our nights were spent in mountain fields.
Brushing aside grasses as we went, we arrived in Shino-
   hara[60] and Port Ataka.

A boat was setting sail just then, so we requested passage and were taken to Kashiwazaki, a famous place in Echigo. When we asked there about our lord, we were told, 'Lord Miike is living in the Third Ward,' so we took lodgings in that area and sent a detailed letter, which we entrusted to our innkeeper. However, Lord Miike was at that time in Sumiyoshi, not at his Third Ward quarters. In charge of the house was a disreputable woman who came out to receive the innkeeper. When he told her the details of his errand, she realized that our appearance made her position precarious.

"'The letter is undoubtedly from Lord Miike's wife,' the woman guessed apprehensively. 'This is terrible! I am sure to be dismissed immediately. The lord is always saying that he longs day and night for his wife and child in Tsukushi. What will become of me?'

"'I've got it!' she thought. 'The best scheme is to use money. I've heard it said that the best way to breach a fortress or conquer a country is with riches.' Taking care to avoid attracting notice, she showed the messenger into the house, gave him various presents, plied him with food and drink, and entreated him to help her. 'I'm relying on you,' she cajoled him. 'You can do your utmost for someone from a distant province, but there is no profit in it. If I were the lord, I'd see to it that not only you, but your whole clan, were well taken care of. Find some way to get rid of those travelers.'

"'I will certainly see that your wishes are fulfilled,' the man replied. He returned to the inn and said that when he had given the letter to Lord Miike, the lord had read it carefully and exclaimed: 'This is very suspicious! Who has come and said such a thing? She is a fake. I have no wife in the west, and since I do not, I have no child either. I don't know these people. Anyone who makes up lies like these must not be given lodging in my fief even for one night. Anyone who puts them up will have his whole clan punished.'

"'I should have known better than to run an errand for you!' the innkeeper complained. 'What a mistake to let liars like you stay here

---

60. Shinohara, in Kaga City in southern Ishikawa Prefecture, means a "field where the
   bamboo grass is lush and deep," in which case it could be waist or shoulder high.

even this long! Hurry up and get out of here! Oh, what frightful people! Hurry up! Go on!'

"He chased us out, brandishing a stick. The baseness of the creature! Dazzled by presents and food and drink, he threw us out of the inn without a moment's notice.

"There was nothing we could do. Weeping as we went, we left the Third Ward area. With no destination to set our sights on, with nowhere to point to and say 'That's the place we'll go,' with nowhere to stay, fearful for our lives, we came, weeping, to a hall dedicated to the worship of Zaō.[61] We spent the night praying there, asking what was to become of us, but the deity gave us no sign. Then toward dawn, the mistress said: 'Although, as men do, my lord has come to hate me, Fujiwaka is truly his child. If somehow we can present his son to him, will he be able to abandon the boy? I have come this far and suffered sorrow and shame for the sake of my child's future. I hesitate to ask you, but take this letter, and bring the boy to see his father. Explain the situation, leave Fujiwaka with him, and hurry back here. Since we can't go home now, we should treat this experience as the seed of enlightenment, become nuns, and wander the provinces.'

"'Yes, yes, just as you say,' I agreed. I accepted the letter, excused myself, and hurried toward the Third Ward with Fujiwaka, leaving my mistress behind at the Hall of Zaō by herself.

"However, around noon that day, two or three mountain ascetics overtook us. They were speaking sadly among themselves. Listening intently, I heard one of them say: 'Yes, but she was a beautiful woman. People will be talking about her for a long time to come. Even though she was dead, she looked like a bodhisattva. Yang Kuei-fei and Princess Sotōri[62] must have resembled her. What long and beautiful hair she had. She couldn't have been an ordinary person. I've never seen anyone like her even in the capital. How sad! I wonder what sorrow made her do it.'

"My heart pounded with fear and I approached them with a sense of foreboding. 'What were you speaking of just now?' I asked.

---

61. Zaō is a deity of fierce demeanor who conquers evil spirits. Worship of Zaō was initiated at Mount Kinpu in Nara Prefecture, by En no Gyōja (b. 634), who is considered the founder of Shugendō, a popular sect that combines esoteric Buddhism with mountain worship and stresses ascetic practices to cultivate miraculous powers.

62. Yang Kuei-fei (719–56) was the consort of Emperor Hsuan Tsung (685–762, r. 712–56). Her beauty and talent led the emperor to neglect his imperial responsibilities and thereby caused the fall of the T'ang dynasty. The legendary Sotōri-hime, whose radiance shone through her garments, was the supposed consort of Emperor Ingyō (r. 412–53).

"'It's this,' they explained. 'A beautiful woman has drowned her-self at the river crossing. A crowd has gathered and people are weeping by the roadside. We were moved too, and though we hadn't known her, we intoned a verse of scripture before we passed by.'

"'There's no doubt about it,' I thought, and hurried back toward the Hall of Zaō. But I was both exhausted from traveling and stricken with sorrow; although I put one foot in front of the other, I trod the same ground. I did not have the heart to go forward. I hoped it was a dream. 'If only I would wake up,' I wished. I returned with wavering steps, asking everyone I met along the way, but they all said the same thing. They told me they had seen her when they had passed. So we hurried back and came running up to where a crowd had gathered.

"Her long hair, weltering in the current, was twined round her body. The cord of her skirt had been fastened tightly. She had put stones in the sleeve-pockets of her layered silk robes so that she would be sure to sink. Her ebony rosary was wrapped around her hand. Rocked by the waves that brushed the shore, she seemed to be sleeping.

"Fujiwaka held her face in his hands and moaned tearfully: 'What do you want me to do now? If you were just going to abandon me, why did you bring me here? I understand that you were overwhelmed with bitterness and resolved to die because of father's cruel heartlessness, but I am embittered that you have deceived and abandoned me.' He wept with sorrow, and I, in an access of grief, decided to follow her example, but Fujiwaka suddenly embraced me. 'I have had a terrible shock. I have lost both of my parents. If you leave me, what will become of me?' Clutching my hand, he collapsed on the ground. With him clinging to the skirt of my robe, my resolve weakened; I was near fainting when, strangely, four or five large boats on a leisurely excursion came down the river in a line, making quite a magnificent sight.

"The boats, which seemed to be those of a warrior, headed toward an island in the middle of the river. Those aboard were entertaining themselves with singing and drinking when they noticed the crowd gathered round the corpse. 'What's that?' asked the lord, and someone who knew said: 'A traveler threw herself into the river,' and explained what had happened. 'Well,' said the lord, 'that's strange. Who was she?' He had his boat brought nearer, and taking a long look, said: 'How sad! I wonder who she was? I have a child about that age back home, so although I don't know him, I feel sorry for him.' The lord ordered his boat brought to the river bank and asked: 'Where are you from?'

"Fujiwaka covered his mother's body with his sleeve. 'I'm from the western provinces,' he replied.

"The lord asked: 'How did this happen?'

"'Let me tell you. I came with my mother through the provinces looking for my father, but since he had forgotten us, in her bitterness, she . . .' Weeping, he clutched at his mother's corpse.

"His suspicions aroused, the lord jumped out of his boat and pulled the boy's sleeve away from my mistress's face. It was clearly his wife. 'Oh, no! How could it have come to this? It isn't true, is it? Isn't this a dream? Heedless of people's stares and what they might think, the lord embraced the corpse and wept. Taken aback, everyone seated in the boats became very somber, wondering what relationship there could have been between them.

"'Why should I hide anything now?' said the lord after a time. 'Everyone, look. This is my son. And this woman was, in Tsukushi . . .' His voice broke. He pressed his sleeve to his face, collapsed on the ground, and wept, pathetically. There was no one, neither friend nor stranger, who did not need to wring out his own sleeves.

"'This journey, the whole trip, from the day we left Tsukushi, has been hard to bear,' I said. 'Even a man would have found it so. My mistress traveled with Fujiwaka the long distance to the capital, where she heard that you had gone to Echigo Province. She wandered wearily along the Koshi highway, which she had never seen before, yet in her joy at the prospect of seeing you she forgot the gloom and pain. But coming all this way was fruitless. You had heartlessly forgotten her. On top of that was the awful matter of the night's lodgings. Hardly able to stand up, by your order she was refused quarters and cast out. Deeply resenting you, she stayed alone at the Hall of Zaō, having sent Fujiwaka and me on a useless mission. Then she did this.' I berated him at length, clutching his sleeve. Raining tears, I cast the blame on him.

"When I had said all there was to say, he reproached himself: 'If that is what truly happened, it is no wonder that she was bitter. I was planning on going to Tsukushi to see Fujiwaka soon. How could I have forgotten my own son?'

"'Well then, my lord's heart was not false. Here is a letter she wrote this morning,' I said, taking it out of my sleeve and giving it to him. He opened the missive and found that it reiterated what I had told him.

"'Forgive me [for writing to you]. I realize that your gate is not open to me, that your feelings for me are faint as the wan morning moon. I am in an abyss of misery because you have abandoned me.[63] I never thought I might end up like this, but I don't matter. I will vanish like the white snow on the road we traveled to Echigo. But Fujiwaka is your son. If you deny that, my life has been wasted. If he loses both parents, on whom can he depend?[64] I have resolved to die, but my concern for him will hinder my progress toward Buddhahood in my next life.[65] With bitter thoughts I wait for morning to break and for dusk to

---

63. There is substantial word play here. The sentence contains three associated words, *wasurei*, "a well of forgetfulness," a metaphor for a place of abandonment; *asamashi*, "wretched," which suggests *asai*, "shallowness of water or feeling"; and *fuchi*, "deep pool" or "abyss," connnoting pain and difficulty.

64. A string of associated words joins the previous two sentences: *ikite kai naki namidagawa, namida no tsuyu no tama kushige futa oya tomo ni nakariseba*. *Naki* of *kai naki*, "futile" or "wasted," puns with *naki*, "to cry," and evokes *namidagawa*, "a river of tears." *Namida*, "tears," is repeated and evokes *tsuyu*, "dewdrops," which evokes *tama*, "jewel," of *tama kushige*, "comb box," which is a pillow word for *futa*, "lid," of *futa oya*, "two parents."

65. There is more word play here. *Kiru*, "to cut," of *omoikiru*, "to resolve," evokes *kuretake*, a kind of "Chinese bamboo," which is a pillow word for *yomiji*, "the next life."

fall. I am prostrate; my sleeves are drifting in a bed awash with dew. This sorrow must be retribution for transgressions in a former life. But even if you hate me, won't you take a little pity on me? Pray for my soul.'

"On that sad note, the letter ended. What a pathetic message! She obviously had wept as she wrote, for the letter was stained with tears. The handwriting was stiff and cramped; it had been written with a trembling hand. What emotions must have been raging within her! When I imagined her final moments, I wanted to follow her in death, but I resolved to pray for her soul. First we took her body by boat to the Hall of Zaō, weeping as we went, and soon we had reduced it to smoke.

"The lord reprimanded the innkeeper's clan, more than twenty people, and told his son: 'Fujiwaka, take revenge for your mother. Vent your wrath.'

"Fujiwaka was delighted. 'As a lesson to future generations,' he said calmly to his father, 'this man and his clan cannot be punished enough, but even if we take his life, it won't bring back mother. For her soul's benefit, let us spare him. Moreover, though my stepmother was cruel, it was said in ancient times that to revere your stepmother is to be filial toward your father, so we must not bear a grudge against her.'

"His father wept at this sentiment. 'If your mother could hear your words of wisdom,' he said, 'she would not argue with you. The sandalwood tree is fragrant from the time it first sprouts; you are indeed a worthy heir for the Miike clan.'

"The lord relinquished his position as head of the clan to Fujiwaka, made a wooden grave tablet for his wife's spirit, and mournfully recited this poem:

I never thought
I would see those who came to Echigo
In this state.

"In the garden he cut off his hair and left, never to be seen again. With that turn of events, I became a nun and went to Zenkōji to pray for my lady's salvation. For twenty years I practiced difficult and painful austerities, and then I established this bathhouse to accumulate merit on her behalf."

When she had finished, the old nun said: "You have achieved enlightenment in this life. I rejoice that we took lodgings here and have heard your rare and wonderful story." All five nuns rejoiced together at their good fortune [in having been able to hear the proprietress's inspirational story].

The Story of the Retired Emperor Kazan's Daughter [The Seventh Nun]

Kon Amida Butsu, who had fallen asleep behind a partition while listening to everyone's revelations, stretched and scratched herself, making a rustling sound. The travelers heard the noise she made and wondered if there wasn't some rascal about. "Our guests have shared their precious revelations, long, intimate stories, and thirty-one-syllable poems," the proprietress said. "They have stayed awake all this long autumn night with only tears to counter their sleepiness, but you haven't listened. You are despicable.[66] And how strange that you found it possible to sleep! You have no more sensitivity than a tree or a stone. You are a wretch, someone whom these nuns should avoid. You can't go on sleeping. As it says in the *Sutra of Grouped Records*,[67] even if a person is not originally evil, if he associates with evil people, he will surely become so. We revere these words of truth. Get out of here immediately!"

At that point Kon Amida Butsu recited as she lay there:

A quiet, prone figure is a pleasant sight,
Why should anyone listen to
People talking in their sleep?

"Proprietress, what a senseless thing you've said. You asked me to leave these temporary quarters. Even if you begged me to stay, how could I possibly do that? Do you still fail to comprehend the dwelling of unchanging eternal abiding?[68] You quote the *Sutra of Grouped Records* saying, 'Don't associate with evil people,' but which of us do you suppose is the evil person? Certainly you have heard over and over again that good and evil are not two different things, that wickedness and righteousness are indistinguishable. Perhaps you are getting senile as you grow old. Besides, isn't the *Sutra of Grouped Records* only one of the four Hīnayāna sutras?[69] The Buddha called them 'merely Hīnayāna,' saying they might be employed once, but that using them again was like referring to last year's calendar."

She had spoken over her shoulder as she headed for the door, but the other nuns said, "We didn't expect someone like you to be able to quote scripture and to compose thirty-one-syllable poems. We are perplexed. Yet to call our revelations 'talking in our sleep' is vulgar and rude."

---

66. This display of ill temper is out of character for the two bathhouse nuns, but such discontinuity is not unusual in medieval short stories.

67. On the *Sutra of Grouped Records* (Zōichiagongyō) (T no. 125) see n. 69 below.

68. This is a metaphor for the concept that existence is eternal, without change.

69. The four Hīnayāna sutras are the *Sutras of the Tradition* (Āgama) and refer to early Buddhist teachings that include: (1) Jōagongyō (T no. 1), *Sutra of Long Records*; (2) Chūagongyō (T no. 26), *Sutra of Middle Length Sayings*; (3) Zōagongyō (T no. 99), *Sutra of Miscellaneous Records*; and (4) Zōichiagongyō (T no. 125), *Sutra of Grouped Records*. See Earl Miner, Odagiri Hiroko, and Robert E. Morrell, *The Princeton Companion to Classical Japanese Literature* (Princeton: Princeton University Press, 1985), 379–80. Hīnayāna ("small vehicle") is a pejorative term for such early Buddhist teachings as these and is used only by adherents of the later Mahāyāna tradition.

The proprietress reproached her too: "How can you call it 'talking in our sleep?'"

Kon Amida Butsu laughed loudly. "Look! All of your tales were 'talking in your sleep' though you stayed up the whole night telling them. Outwardly you are nuns, but in your hearts you are still lay women. Do you think tonight's teary encounter is proper behavior for someone who has renounced the world? Because it is taught that if we don't realize our transgressions, our karmic burden will be heavy, you have each told a tale. But why haven't you told of true revelations?"

At this another nun retorted: "Are there two or three kinds of revelations, those of lies and those of truth?" The young nun laughed merrily.

"As far as all of you are concerned, there aren't two or three kinds of revelations," Kon Amida Butsu replied. "But that is not how it is for a Buddha. A Buddha distinguishes between different kinds of revelations. That is to say, they can be divided into two main groups. One is the Revelation Regarding Phenomena and the other is the Revelation Regarding Ultimate Reality.[70] All of your revelations tonight were shallow revelations, like the kind of frivolous talk that lay people exchange over tea. The Revelation Regarding Phenomena is explained in the *Sutra of Meditation on the Bodhisattva Universal Vow*, which says: 'If you would "repent," seat yourself properly and contemplate true reality. Transgressions are nullified through wisdom, just as frost and dew vanish in the sunlight.'[71] Thus it is the revelation of transience by which means all our transgressions that are rooted in the six causes of illusion—seeing, hearing, smelling, tasting, touching, and thinking—are cancelled out, just as frost or dew is burned off by the morning sun. Let me put it this way: If you examine the source of all transgressions, the frost and dew of worldly passions cannot survive in the light of the realization of the ultimate truth of the emptiness of all existence."

At this another nun said: "This is no ordinary person. She is not at all what she appeared to be. Let us ask her about all the things we don't understand." Addressing Kon Amida Butsu, they inquired, "Revelation is the repentance of trangressions, but you mentioned the Revelation Regarding Phenomena and the Revelation Regarding Ultimate Reality. What is the reason for distinguishing between these two?"

"How could I, ignorant as I am," she replied, "know something that you, wise as you are, don't know? Nevertheless, whenever I meet

---

70. For a discussion of the subject of *ji no sange* and *ri no sange* see pp. 24–25.

71. The *Sutra of Meditation on the Bodhisattva Universal Vow* is *Fugenkangyō* (T no. 277, *Kanfugenbosatsugyōhōkyō*), the third sutra of the threefold *Lotus Sutra*.

wise monks from the Tendai, Shingon, Zen, and Ritsu schools, I question them, and they have said that the two kinds of revelations are particularly hard to comprehend. Recently I questioned a monk who said that distinguishing between phenomena and ultimate reality is very difficult. He picked up a piece of crystal to make a comparison. The relationship between phenomena and ultimate reality is like a crystal that possesses the property of fire. An ignorant person certainly wouldn't realize it, but when you focus the rays of the sun through a crystal and light a fire on a signal flare, you know without a doubt that the jewel has the property of fire. Phenomena and ultimate reality are similar. The fact that the crystal possesses the property of fire is a fundamental principle that never changes; a burning signal fire is a phenomenon that is ever changing. Moreover, though the signal flare catches fire, the property of fire in the jewel has no form, no appearance. It cannot be ascertained by the eye nor held in the hand.

"The whole universe, however, is the manifestation of ultimate reality. [Ultimate reality] is uncontainable. It is neither wide nor narrow. Only the fire that burns on the signal flare has form and appearance, a time when it goes out and a time when it is burning. Form and appearance depend on distinct causes that occur in time. Unfortunately, people are mindful only of the phenomenal aspect of the burning fire, which has a distinct cause, and do not try to understand the wonderful realm of unchanging eternal existence. These things cannot be understood easily. We must devote ourselves completely to the Buddha's way and study day and night. A revelation based on an understanding of both phenomena and ultimate reality would be rare and wonderful indeed.

"It says in the Vimalakīrti Sutra[72] that if you would cleanse the outside, first cleanse the inside. If the inside is clean, then the outside will be clean. Also, it says in the precepts that a hundred joys arise from a religious awakening. Speaking as you all did, out of love and sorrow, with tears flowing freely, isn't that 'talking in your sleep,' as I said? Besides, your storytelling began with the poem:

> Certainly the roof hasn't been left unthatched
> For the sake of my moon viewing.
> Tonight's lodging, a lonely hut.

---

72. The Vimalakīrti Sutra is Jōmyōkyō (T no. 475), an alternate title for Yuimakitsukyō, an early influential Mahāyāna sutra featuring Vimalakīrti, a wise and virtuous layman.

"I sense the idea of a permanent dwelling in the mind of a woman who would recite lines like 'tonight, one night's lodging.' Where in this world is a permanent dwelling? To speak of permanence is a mistake. The Three Realms are composed of the Six Heavens of the world of sensuous desires, the Eighteen Heavens of the world of form, and the Four Empty Regions of the world of formlessness.[73] At the summit of these three realms is the heaven of neither thinking nor nonthinking.[74] Life in this heaven is very long; it is eighty thousand aeons long. When after eighty thousand aeons your karma is exhausted, there is what is called 'falling into the Three Paths.' After a long, long time you will fall into one of the Three [Evil] Paths.[75] *The Ten Stages of the Development of the Mind*[76] explains this. Furthermore, in this world, one lifetime is sixty years. If you count how many months there are in those sixty years it comes to only 720, and if you count the number of days there are, you'll find there are over 26,000 days.[77] That is the life span of a healthy person. It goes without saying that the old will not necessarily die before the young. To speak on any particular night of 'one night's lodging' is ridiculous. As I said, all of your tales were 'talking in your sleep.' Let me conclude by reciting:

Everyone's temporary lodgings are ramshackle.
The moonlight that comes filtering in
Is the proprietor.

"Put aside the kind of faith in scripture that the proprietress shows. The Three Virtues[78] are all found in the wonderful truth of

---

73. See n. 19. Although there are variant enumerations of these realms, this accounting does not match the standard ones.

74. *Hisōhihisōten* is the fourth of the heavens in the realm of formlessness, in which one has almost attained *musō*, the "absence of thinking."

75. The Three Paths are the evil worlds of hell, hungry demons, and beasts.

76. This Shingon text, *Jūjūshin ron*, was written by Kūkai around 830. It describes the ten stages of understanding represented by Confucianism, Taoism, and various schools of Buddhism. See Hakeda, *Kūkai, Major Works*, 163–224 for a translation of "The Precious Key to the Secret Treasury," Kūkai's own condensed version of this text.

77. Whether by lunar or solar calendar, the number of days in sixty years does not approach 26,000. At 365.25 days per year, there are 20,115 days in sixty years. There would have to be 36.1 days in a month for her calculations to be correct.

78. The Three Virtues are *hōshin*, the embodiment of truth; *hannya*, wisdom, or knowing all things in their reality; and *gedatsu*, deliverance, freedom from all bonds.

ultimate reality. Nothing exists outside of our minds. What is there to be given up? What is there to be held dear? What is there to be mourned? Nothing, for worldly desires imply enlightenment."[79]

In response, the proprietress observed: " 'Worldly desires imply enlightenment' is, as you say, a point of doctrine common to all the sects. We all follow that principle. Let me explain how. Like me, these women have all had sad, tragic experiences. We have had enough of love and sorrow. Learning first hand about evil conduct and worldly desire in this sad world, we then turned away from worldly desire and toward enlightenment. Doesn't that truly reflect 'worldly desires imply enlightenment'? Take down your banner of pride."

"That is a very unique interpretation of 'worldly desires imply enlightenment,'" Kon Amida Butsu replied. "That is not my understanding of the phrase. The nature of worldly desires and of enlightenment cannot be grasped directly. The statement refers to the wonderful truth of absolute reality. Let me give an example. Hard ice, though solid, is commonly understood to be water insofar as that was its previous state. To draw the analogy, consider carefully the meaning of the word 'imply' in 'worldly desires imply enlightenment.' As you all see it, one turns away from worldly desire, and then one turns toward enlightenment. Think of the example I gave. Ice forms in cold weather but melts with the warmth of spring and becomes water. In that case, the word 'imply' is not appropriate.

"The anecdote of Bodhidharma's[80] three enlightened disciples illuminates the meaning of this concept. The nun Tsung-chih said to Bodhidharma: 'Extinguishing worldly desire, we become enlightened.'

"'You have gained my skin,' said the master.

"'Being lost in illusion,' Tao-yu said, 'is the equivalent of worldly desire; to perceive the truth is to be enlightened.'

"'You have won my flesh,' said the master.

"The third disciple, Hui-k'o said, 'Ultimately, as there is no worldly desire, there is only enlightenment.'

---

79. "Worldly desires imply enlightenment" (*bonnō soku bodai*) is a Tendai phrase and the highest expression of Mahāyāna thought. *Bonnō* is pain, affliction, distress, and whatever causes these; *bodai* is perfect wisdom, enlightenment. *Soku*, "to be inseparable," in Tendai thought means (1) the union or unity of two things, (2) the inseparability of front and back, and (3) the inseparability of substance and quality, e.g., water and wave.

80. Bodhidharma was the twenty-eighth Indian and first Chinese patriarch, said to have arrived in China in 520 and to have established the Ch'an (Zen) sect there.

"'You have gained my marrow,' commented the master.[81]

"Thus, the degrees of enlightenment attained by the three are called skin, flesh, and marrow. The extent of your understanding is that of the skin, which the nun Tsung-chih gained. You have not even won the flesh. How could it be said that you have gained the marrow?

"The founders of different sects distinguish between the doctrine that good and evil are different but united and the doctrine that good and evil are the same but assume different forms. Moreover, the fact that we are born with the propensity for both good and evil reveals the meaning of 'worldly desires imply enlightenment,' but since you can't understand when I speak in terms unfamiliar to you, I will say it simply:

> Colors to our eyes, sounds in our ears;
> The wind rustles through the withered
> Grasses of Naniwa Bay.[82]

> The innocence of one who calls out
> 'Moon, oh, moon, blossoms, oh, blossoms';
> That is the way of ways.[83]

---

81. The *Ching-te ch'uan-teng lu,* volume 3, gives a somewhat different version. As translated in *A History of Zen Buddhism,* by Heinrich Dumoulin, p. 73:

> Nine years had passed and he [Bodhidharma] now wished to return westward to India. He called his disciples and said: "The time has now come. Why does not each of you say what you have attained?"
> The disciple Tao-fu replied: "As I see it (the truth) neither adheres to words or letters nor is it separate from them. Yet it functions as the Way."
> The Master said: "You have attained my skin."
> Then a nun, Tsung-chih, spoke: "As I understand it, (the truth) is like the auspicious glimpse of the Buddha Land of Akshobya; it is seen once, but not a second time."
> The Master replied: "You have attained my flesh."
> Tao-yu said: "The four great elements are originally empty; the five *skandhas* have no existence. According to my belief, there is no *dharma* to be grasped."
> To him the Master replied: "You have attained my bones."
> Finally there was Hui-k'o. He bowed respectfully and stood silent.
> The Master said: "You have attained my marrow."

82. The point of this poem is that one knows the wind is blowing by the sight of the grasses swaying and the sound of their rustling, metaphors for worldly desires, which reveal the wind, a metaphor for enlightenment. This poem reflects the concept of "worldly desires imply enlightenment" held by the proprietress, that one comes to enlightenment having renounced worldly desires.

83. This poem reflects Kon Amida Butsu's concept of "worldly desires imply enlightenment," that the way to attain enlightenment is to take things just as they are.

"To recite the *nenbutsu* in this frame of mind, I calm my mind; I neither think about the Buddha, nor fear any hells. Not allowing myself to become distracted, I recite the six characters of the *nenbutsu*. What can be found outside my own mind? In any case, I never concern myself with academic knowledge. Under the moon of ultimate truth and equality, I take the universe as my dwelling: I dance my way along. When I see the moon, I sing of the moon; when I see blossoms, I sing of blossoms. I chip away at the steel of my mind and tear apart the sheer silk of my flesh.[84] Passing through distant checkpoints, I travel on and on. I don't put up at night within castle precincts; I think of Vairocana as the proprietor of my lodgings, and I have peace of mind. Rather than spending my time with small-minded people and staying in cramped houses, I just take an old straw hat and begging bag, and go."

She added:

A cloud drifts on when the wind blows,
And lingers when there is no breeze.
It is the wanderer who has peace of mind.

"Please excuse me, everyone," she said, intending to leave the brushwood hut, but the nuns reached out [to hold her back].

"What is your name? Who are you?" they asked. They caught her sleeve, asking all sorts of questions to make her stay.

"I have no name and no self. A self is an illusion," she replied, and she left after all, without more ado. Since Kon Amida Butsu had so amazed them, the nuns subsequently asked about her.

"She is the daughter of the retired emperor Kazan [968–1008, r. 984–86]," their informant said respectfully. "Since she was so beautiful, it was decided early that she should serve the emperor at court, and so she was called the imperial princess.

"In the spring of her sixteenth year, when the emperor came from the Omuro Palace to view the retired emperor's garden in bloom, a well-known youth called Lord Hanawaka was in the retinue. The boy was so lovely that the party goers forgot to notice the blossoming trees when the drinking had begun. The blossoms were just past their prime and ready to fall, so when a strong evening breeze arose, it seemed just as though snow were drifting down from the trees to the front of the garden. In the course of the entertainment the wine cup came to the retired emperor Kazan. 'Come now, Hanawaka, offer His Majesty a cup of wine,' directed the reigning emperor.

---

84. She needs to overcome mental illusions that are strong as steel and to become oblivious to desires of her weak and fragile body.

"Since Hanawaka was a good dancer,[85] he opened his fan a bit and danced while he recited a line from a song: 'The blossoms lay scattered in confusion after a swirling wind.'[86] Hanawaka himself might have been taken for a blossom. A heavenly being would surely look just as he looked then. At that moment, when a breeze opened a crack in the blinds, Hanawaka and the princess exchanged a fleeting glance. From that instant on, although they had no hope of meeting again, like fireflies in summer, their hearts glowed with love for each other.

"The princess could not forget the sight of Hanawaka dancing; she thought of him constantly. Hanawaka also lost himself in yearning for her and had a relative deliver a letter. When the princess read it she found only the poem:

> I am afraid I shall die of
> This forbidden love.
> If only I could tell the world.[87]

"'Who is this from?' she asked.

"'It's from the youth who danced here once,' came the reply. 'Ever since he caught a glimpse of you, he has been distraught. He has fallen in love with you. For you to help him would be an act of compassion worthy of a bodhisattva. Send him an answer.'

"'Since I too am a confused tangle of emotions on his account, I want to follow my heart, but a relationship is unthinkable,' the princess decided. 'He must forget me before people find out. What would happen if the world knew?' She never sent a reply.

"However, the feelings one locks in one's heart ultimately always break out, and soon they were exchanging letters and meeting secretly. They were cautious, but since he came to her often, like the fisherman who cast his nets in Akogi Inlet in Ise Bay,[88] word leaked out. 'She is supposed to become an empress,' said the miserable rumor-mongers, 'but if word of this scandal gets to the emperor, where will she end up? She's too much in love to heed anyone's warnings. What she's doing is like picking up a boulder and jumping into an abyss.'

---

85. Apparently it was the custom to perform a song or dance in such a situation.

86. *Wakan rōei shū*, poem 129. The text gives only the first half of the verse. It concludes: "The nightingale sings dejectedly when rain falls" (NKBT 73:79).

87. The translation omits the pillow phrase *tama sudare*, "a bejeweled blind," which alludes both to the blind that opened briefly by accident and the blind that properly separates them so that they cannot meet.

88. Akogi Inlet was the exclusive fishing ground for offerings to be made at Ise Shrine. According to legend, an old man poached too frequently and was caught.

"There was nowhere she could go without becoming the subject of gossip. The capital is a vast city, but rumors flew thick and fast. She was forced to flee with her wet-nurse and Hanawaka, just the three of them, on foot. She and Hanawaka exchanged vows to stand by each other even if they found themselves in a tiger-infested moor, on the Island of Demons, or in Koryō.[89] Thus they made their way as far as Naniwa Bay. The wet-nurse had a relative in Shikoku, and they had decided to seek refuge there.

"Now the mistress of their inn, having taken a long look at the princess, said to her husband: 'She is incredibly beautiful and probably still in her teens. She couldn't be anyone ordinary. I'm a woman too, but I was so taken with her, so entranced, that I dropped what I was holding in my hand. For a sight you'll never forget as long as you live, go steal a glimpse of her.'

"Indeed he would, he thought, and looked through a crack in the door. She was even more lovely than his wife had told him. She was so radiantly beautiful that all else was obliterated. He felt like a cloud floating in the sky, gazing at the moon as it drifted along nearby. He watched her, spellbound. He became distraught. 'I can't live on after she leaves. I will win her love,' he resolved, looking around. 'There's only one young man accompanying her: it'll be no trouble to take her.'

"Later that night he called the wet-nurse aside and gave her an ultimatum: 'Hand over the young lady. Even if I can't have her in this lifetime, I'll die and sink to the bottom of hell before I give up trying. If you don't cooperate, you'll all be dead by morning.'

"The wet-nurse was terrified, but she calmed herself and tried to reason with him: 'I realize you've given me an ultimatum but please reconsider: she is from the capital and on her way to Shikoku. Her single companion is a youth with whom she has exchanged vows of love. They have sworn to grow old and be buried together. Please, you absolutely must forget her.'

"There was, however, no way to sway the man from his desire. He was determined, no matter what, to drown the youth and kidnap the princess. He readied a small boat, and while the couple, exhausted from their journey, were fast asleep, he drew the youth aside. 'This way, this way,' the innkeeper said, leading the youth out through the gate. The youth's mind was blurred with sleep, and he stumbled along, unaware that he was about to be murdered. He assumed the boat bound for Shikoku was casting off. But no, only he was brought on board.

---

89. The Island of Demons, or Kikai, is one of the northern Ryukyu Islands, south of Kyushu. Koryō was an early state in southern Korea that existed from 918 to 1392.

"When the innkeeper grabbed him round the waist to push him into the sea, the youth cried out over and over in great distress, 'What are you doing? Princess, don't you love me anymore? Why aren't you coming?'

"'There's nothing you can say to save yourself,' grumbled the innkeeper. 'Hurry up. Over you go!' He grabbed the youth by his sash and threw him into the sea.

"Murderer though the innkeeper was, tears blurred his vision as he returned to the inn. He found the two women confused and in a panic. He tried to embrace the princess on the spot, not knowing that she had hidden the flute and sword that had been under the youth's

pillow. He didn't expect her to offer any resistance in the darkness. She was his, he was sure. But the princess, recognizing the wicked inn-keeper, stabbed him once in the chest. Though she had not struck a hard blow, the sword was a fine sharp one, and the man seemed on the verge of breathing his last.

"Despite the pain, however, he clutched the weapon, clinging to life. 'Would you kill me to avenge your poor husband?' he gasped. 'Oh, of course you hate me. But I don't mind losing my life for your sake. Pray for my soul. Flee from here before anyone finds out about this. A kind nun lives on the far side of the mountain west of here. If you can get there, you will be all right.' Even as his voice weakened and his life ebbed away, he wept and worried about her fate. Early in the morning, he died.

"Thus, this terrible affair led to the deaths of two men. Although the princess had been designated to become one of the emperor's wives, she had committed a common crime. It must have been the doing of the guardian deity of the palace; it was miraculous that both men should have been killed.

"Now the princess went to the nun of whom she had been told, cut off her hair, and changed her flowerlike appearance to that of a nun. In linen robes, carrying a mendicant's bag, her makeup gone, her natural complexion revealed, she wandered through the provinces as a tattered beggar.

"For the sake of the spirits of those who had died on her account, she visited learned monks in various temples and listened to sermons. Then she left the capital and eventually found herself in Kaga Province. After some years during which she lived among other religious itiner-ants and social outcasts, she decided to go to Zenkōji. There was a subtemple to one side, the abbot of which was greatly revered as some-one who had attained enlightenment. She felt this was the kind of place she had been looking for and stayed in the area for two years. Sometimes she secluded herself in mountain valleys, sometimes she begged with other mendicants. She did not neglect the practices of either the completely enlightened cleric or the partially enlightened one.[90] It was said by many that she had grasped the meaning of 'the absolute in everything.' One day, borrowing a brush from a temple servant, she wrote:

90. The fully enlightened cleric is one who has transcended the concerns of lay life and therefore mingles freely in towns among people (NKD 12:512). The partially enlightened cleric has not yet freed himself from worldly concerns and therefore secludes himself in the mountains (NKD 10:460).

An arrow shot from a spindletree bow,
Aimed at no target,
Will ultimately hit its mark.

"When he saw this poem, the abbot thought she was an extraordinary person and wrote:

Since that's the case,
There's nothing to do but set off like
An arrow shot from a spindletree bow.

"Deeply grateful for his words, the princess left to wander the provinces with the wind as her only guide. Meanwhile, she spent a few years at this bathhouse. When she was hungry, she ate, and if she grew tired, she slept."

Oh, how true these words; all the scriptures are for the purpose of revealing a single truth. We must seek to become enlightened. The Buddhas and bodhisattvas, in their compassion, strive to bring us to this most precious goal by one means or another. People who take even the sound of the wind blowing as a prowler's footstep[91] are confronted with sorrow so that faith may be stirred up in their hearts. How wonderful it is! Even if we do not understand these teachings, we should immediately renounce our selves and take up an ascetic life. We should be concerned only with sowing the seeds of virtue that will bear the fruit of enlightenment in our future lives. Unfortunately, though provinces and towns everywhere overflow with people who know such sorrow, few learn from their experiences and abandon this sad world. Among those whose suffering leads them to take religious vows, there are many whose resolve soon weakens. However, while the wise princess has grown old and is nearing her end, her faith has remained strong and firm. What a truly rare and wonderful thing!

I have stained my writing brush with these many words hoping to inspire piety in my worthy readers. If anyone who might learn from this tale has the opportunity to read it, I shall certainly accrue religious merit for having spread the faith.

---

91. This metaphor suggests someone who worries about material things.

Analyses

The Tale of Genmu

The opening lines of *The Tale of Genmu* summarize the basic message of religious awakening tales: that all things are transient. Readers are informed of a second principle in the next few lines: that attachments to worldly pleasures, such as the beauties of nature, cause "perpetual rebirth," that is, they obstruct enlightenment. In addition to introducing the theme of the tale, these prefatory remarks function as the narrator's self-introduction. They are a statement of his faith and world view and advise the reader of the nature of the story to follow. "If even the lay person should shun these ties [attachments to worldly pleasures]," the narrator says, "how much more so the Buddha's disciple." The disciple he has in mind is obviously the protagonist of his tale, Genmu. The reader naturally assumes that the story of Genmu will be an illustration of the principles the narrator has presented.

These are the meanings implied in the words of the preface, but the opening lines further serve to establish the narrator's relationship with his narratee. In pronouncing religious truths and chiding his audience for failing to heed them, he is adopting the stance of a religious teacher. The narrator's attitude presumes a conventional narratee who grants the narrator the considerable authority he asserts and relinquishes the potential for his own interpretive freedom.

Having established authoritative status, the narrator can afford to efface himself in the telling of his tale. Only in the conclusion does he again directly address his audience, to evaluate his own story by rejoicing that Genmu and others were able to achieve salvation. His stance vis-à-vis his tale is to claim that it reveals religious truths. It is an example of "foolish talk and dazzling rhetoric," he asserts, "an expedient means useful in teaching the unenlightened." He warns his audience not to fail to seek salvation and promises that they will achieve it. These few intrusive remarks at the opening and closing of the story constitute explicit directions to the narratee on how to interpret the story of Genmu. He shows that he expects his audience to cooperate and accept the tale as he has presented it, as a religious lesson. Insofar as readers tend to identify themselves with the narratee and the author with the narrator, readers are likely to comply, to think of the author as

143

a proselytizer and to limit their interpretations to the obvious, didactic level.

In the case of *The Tale of Genmu* the narrator leaves much of his didactic work to Genmu himself. The story is told wholly through Genmu's perspective. We learn only what this character thinks, says, witnesses, or hears. Like the narrator, however, Genmu is a figure who commands respect. He is introduced as a scholar who has studied difficult doctrinal treatises. In pondering the same truths expressed by the narrator, he quotes several of the most venerated of Japan's Buddhist theologians: Genshin, author of the influential *Teachings Essential for Rebirth*, Saichō, founder of the Tendai sect, and Kūkai, founder of the Shingon sect. Genmu himself interprets his experience of loving and losing Hanamatsu as a lesson on transience and an answer to his prayer for religious awakening.

Secondary characters echo Genmu's interpretation of the world and share his response to it. Hanamatsu's colleagues, Sotsu and Jijū, are inspired to religious awakening by the youth's death, and the old abbot is keenly aware of the religious significance of Hanamatsu's untimely demise. The ranks of the faithful are further swelled by the young Ono's religious awakening, although he is inspired less by having lost a loved one than because he identifies with his victim, a peer. Thus the tale presents as exemplars five characters who experience religious awakenings and includes interpretive commentary by both narrator and characters.

These are the most common and obvious didactic means at a storyteller's disposal, but in *The Tale of Genmu* imagery is also employed to didactic ends. The practice is found even in the title. Genmu is the name of the protagonist, but its constituent parts suggest another meaning. *Gen* means "illusion," and *mu* is "dream." The title therefore could be rendered as *A Tale of Illusion and Dream*, referring not only to Genmu's encounter with Hanamatsu's spirit, but also to the protagonist's initial unenlightened state.

Genmu himself comments on the traditional significance of clouds and flowers. He muses that "in the morning glory that wilts as the sun rises and in the clouds of dawn that gather to veil the night moon" is evidence of the essentially transient nature of all life. But a deeper religious meaning for these two basic images has been established in the narrator's preface: clouds that "obscure the thirty-two natural features of the full moon" are a metaphor for ignorance and illusion, and the scattered "blossoms of the Ten Shining Virtues" refer to obstacles to enlightenment. Thus these images allude both to transience and to Genmu's ignorant attachment to transient things. When they are used in the scenes in which Genmu meets and falls in love with Hanamatsu, they suggest the potentially religious meaning of that love.

After Genmu prayed to be inspired to faith at the main hall, "clouds gathered in the sky." This alerts the reader to the fact that Genmu is going to experience a worldly passion that initially will interfere with his religious goal but that is actually the means by which he will achieve it. Genmu catches sight of the lovely youth whose hair has the luster of dew-touched cherry blossoms and composes poetry comparing the snow on the trees to spring blossoms. The youth's very name, as we later learn, incorporates *hana*, "blossom." By associating Hanamatsu with the blossoms of spring, the narrator foreshadows his death.

The suggestive use of imagery intensifies with Genmu's trip to Shimotsuke to visit Hanamatsu. The sight of cherry trees in full bloom increases Genmu's longing and compels his decision to undertake the long journey to the east. Having arrived at the hall on Mount Nikkō, where he has been told to pass the night, Genmu finds that "the light of a misty moon on this cloudy spring night shone in, mingling with the radiance emanating from Amida's brow." From this description we can assume that although Genmu is still deluded, his religious awakening is imminent. The next paragraph juxtaposes images of scattering blossoms and moonlight: as the beauty of the cherry blossoms makes him "long all the more for his beloved," his sleeves, wet with tears, glisten in the moonlight. We may understand this symbolic language to mean that the light of religious truth will free Genmu from the pain that his love is causing him. Thus, having established the metaphorical meaning of cherry blossoms, clouds, and moonlight, the author uses these images to describe the secular settings in which Genmu falls and is lost in love, but simultaneously also to point out the higher, religious meaning and outcome of that love.

Even if *The Tale of Genmu* treated only Genmu's experiences of falling in love and awakening to religious truth, it would leave its readers satisfied with respect to their literary and religious needs. It would then fit squarely in the tradition of religious awakening stories. *The Tale of Genmu* continues, however, to describe Genmu's encounter with the young man who killed Hanamatsu, a meeting that in form foreshadows the *zange monogatari* genre. The symmetry of the two men's experiences—one is the murderer, the other the victim's lover—is both an effective literary device and part of the religious lesson. According to the secular code of warrior ethics Ono was right to kill Hanamatsu, but by Buddhist law it was wrong. And yet it effected Ono's and others' religious awakenings and therefore was a benefit. Genmu broke Buddhist precepts in loving Hanamatsu, but that love taught him religious truth. Thus, both Genmu and Ono exemplify the idea that right and wrong are relative, that the only absolutes are the transient nature of this world and the need to seek salvation from the pain and sorrow caused by our ignorance of that reality.

Also effective is the relative credibility of *The Tale of Genmu*. The religious awakenings are quite convincingly motivated. Meeting (or dreaming of meeting) the ghost of one's beloved is certainly the kind of traumatic experience that might inspire a radical response such as Genmu's, especially insofar as he was predisposed to it. The young Ono also received a terrible shock. His father's body not yet cold, he finds himself grinning in justifiable pride for having apprehended and slain his father's killer. That pride is suddenly turned to pain, however, when he learns the following morning that his victim was a boy only a year or two younger than himself. (We may note here the similarity to Kumagai no Naozane's experience of slaying a boy who reminded him of his son and thereby being inspired to renounce the world.[1]) Grieving now both for his father and Hanamatsu, it is credible that Ono should resolve to become a monk and devote his life to praying for their and his own salvation.

Less immediately credible is Genmu's reaction when he meets Ono, the young man who killed Hanamatsu: he weeps, tells of his love for Hanamatsu, and then becomes Ono's closest friend. Genmu's equable reaction cannot be explained by the fact that Ono was justified in killing Hanamatsu. A picture of Genmu considering the extenuating circumstances, that Hanamatsu had taken a calculated risk in avenging his father and that the young Ono had only exacted common justice in slaying his father's killer, is not emotionally honest. Genmu's magnanimous response to Ono is indeed implausible and can only be understood as an illustration of the miraculous power of Buddhism to transform hatred into love through forgiveness. It is similar to the situation presented in the *The Three Monks*. In that tale the monk Kasuya is initially outraged when he meets his wife's brutal murderer. However, upon listening to the villain's account of the murder and learning that his wife's death inspired the murderer's religious awakening, Kasuya forgives the murderous thief. This example is even more astonishing than that of Genmu and Ono: Kasuya's wife was cruelly murdered and humiliated in death. There were no extenuating circumstances in this case. Nevertheless, Kasuya declares that he feels affection for this fellow monk. Thus, both tales present the harsh lesson that all is transient, but also offer the consoling hope that through Buddhism you may heal your emotional wounds and come to love your enemy.

1. Kitagawa, *Heike*, 561–63 and McCullough, *Heike*, 315–17.

One curious note in *The Tale of Genmu* is that the text advocates the severing of all worldly ties, characterizing romantic love as that which obstructs enlightenment, but condones the bond formed between Genmu and Ono in the forty years they spend together on Mount Kōya. Their attachment to each other, reflected in their prayer to be reborn on the same lotus leaf in the Western Paradise, seems contradictory to their goal of enlightenment. Genmu appears merely to have exchanged his passion for Hanamatsu for a religiously acceptable form of love, clerical collegiality with Ono. Genmu's homoeroticism has been thinly sublimated. Perhaps this paradox may be understood as a concession to those who find the demands of the religious life too harsh. The concept of the Western Paradise itself is admittedly a fictional device intended to entice people to faith. The important thing is to take up religious practices, for whatever reason. In the process of performing rituals such as the *nenbutsu* and services for the salvation of the deceased, one gradually comes to understand the meaning of Buddhist teachings. Genmu and Ono may properly be understood to have taken only the very first step on the long path to enlightenment.

Modern readers might prefer to interpret the tale more freely. On a yet broader level of meaning, love causes Genmu great turmoil until he abandons lay life to find peace and companionship in the clerical community. Thus the tale exemplifies the proposition that romantic love is a negative, destructive force that is transformed by religious faith into the constructive power of compassion, a proposition relevant in many cultures in any age. A cynical reading, furthermore, might emphasize the bond between Genmu and Ono and conclude that homoeroticism has been condoned.

Tales Told on Mount Kōya

The opening remarks of the primary narrator of *Tales Told on Mount Kōya* are a description of the setting: the sacred precincts of Mount Kōya, which is the site of Kongōbuji Temple, headquarters of the Shingon sect, and the resting place of Kōbō Daishi. The narrator's stance is revealed in this expression of reverence for that holy place and respect for the men who practice their faith there. His comments on the natural environment refer metaphorically to his hopes for the readers' attainment of enlightenment.

The primary narrator soon relinquishes center stage to the monks of Mount Kōya, specifically, to the ascetic who is head of Kayadō. It is this ascetic who proposes the sharing of revelatory tales. His highly authoritative status is immediately established: having renounced great wealth and prestige to become a monk and head of a large cloister, he is a venerable and credible speaker. His contact with his audience, the monks at Kayadō, is that of a caring and sympathetic leader and teacher. In remonstrating with them for proposing to spend an evening in composing poetry, he is as gentle as he can be. In asserting that revelatory tales nullify wrongdoing and aid in the quest for enlightenment, his stance is that of an advocate.

The first tale refers self-consciously to the act of reading inspirational stories. It presents a model for the reader: if the character Shun Amidabu was moved to renounce the world by an old story, so then may readers of *Tales Told on Mount Kōya* be likewise moved. After these obvious cues are given in the first pages of the *Tales*, interpretation by narrators and characters is reduced to a minimum. The narratees' approval of the tales they are told is reflected in an occasional and terse remark that they were moved to tears. The didactic intent of the author is firmly and explicitly established, but after that the reader is left to read independently, unaided by narratorial comment.

The strength of *Tales Told on Mount Kōya* lies in part in the variety of its six component stories. They range widely even in length: two tales are only one or two pages long, two are about four pages, and two are seven or eight pages in length. These are arranged in a pattern that provides both balance and variation: short, medium, short, long, medium, long.

There does not appear to be any meaningful structure with regard to content in the order of the six tales, such as can be found in *The Seven Nuns*, but both variety and continuity have been provided. The first four stories deal alternately with witnessing evil and with emotional loss. The first story describes a son who is repelled by his father's cruelty to others while the third tale tells of a man who is repulsed by his wife's extreme callousness plus the horror of his own deed. The second story relates the battlefield death of a teacher and ally. As an account of the murder of a faithful second wife by a vindictive first wife, the fourth tale is a combination of the themes of evil and loss. If unrequited love and humiliation can be seen as losses, the fifth tale repeats a major theme, but it is anomalous insofar as it is the only story with a comical element. The sixth and last tale treats a favorite Japanese theme, the separation and reunion of parent and child, specifically a father and son. It is a fitting subject for the concluding story since it echoes the very first tale in presenting a father and son pair. This time however the speaker is the father, not the son. Another reversal is that it ends the whole sequence on an uplifting, positive note—a loving reunion of admirable characters leads to religious awakening—in contrast to the negative experience and critical attitude that triggers the religious awakening in the first account. Stories four and six are comparable insofar as both include a discovery that a woman falsely accused of infidelity had in fact been faithful.

The best of *Tales Told on Mount Kōya* is certainly the fourth story, which tells of the murder of Toyora's second wife. The final tale is as long, but it lacks drama and suspense. The murder story, though, incorporates a clever scheme to frame the second wife as an adulteress, a chilling appearance by the ghost of the murdered woman, a brave bystander who risks his life for compassion and justice, and the pathos of the revelation that the victim was not only innocent of adultery but also was pregnant with her husband's son. This story of Toyora's is also interesting as a rare example of a man admitting to having committed evil deeds himself. To get revenge against the monk whom he presumed had seduced his wife, Toyora murdered any monk who wandered within his reach, thus committing the most heinous of all crimes according to Buddhist law.

Toyora's tale is, moreover, told with careful attention to vivid detail and provides realistic motivations for all its characters. The only flaw is that the narrative voice strays so far from the original point of view as to create the incongruity of a narrator quoting himself extensively from the perspective of a character.

The third story also merits particular comment, and comparison with its possible prototype, which is found in *Shasekishū* (Sand and Pebbles, 1279–83). In *Sand and Pebbles* the thief's tale[1] is more briefly told than in *Tales Told on Mount Kōya*, and it is paired with an account by the husband of the thief's victim (as in *The Three Monks*, which will be analyzed later).

In *Sand and Pebbles* the thief has no children and only turns to crime out of love for his wife—she suggests that he steal to provide for her, advice that he resists until she threatens to leave him. That he is then repulsed by her callousness and leaves her is poetic justice, a much more interesting development than the situation in the *Tales* version, where the wife encourages Kō Amidabu to become a thief for their children's sake. However, in the version in the revelatory tale, the wife's inhumanity is depicted in far more detail and is much more vivid and shocking. In *Sand and Pebbles* the wife is merely said to have smiled at her husband's news of the murder, while the wife in *Tales Told on Mount Kōya* is shown to possess macabre knowledge: she is truly grotesque

---

1. Robert E. Morrell, trans., *Sand and Pebbles*, (*Shasekishū*): *The Tales of Mujū Ichien, A Voice for Pluralism in Kamakura Buddhism* (Albany: State University of New York Press, 1985), 249–50.

> 10A:7 Religious Awakening from an Evil Influence
> In the capital lived a couple who passed their lives in poverty.
> "I can't stand this miserable existence," the wife told her husband. "People will do anything to improve their condition in life. You can support me by becoming a robber or a highwayman!"
> "Lots of people are poor. How could I possibly do what you ask?" But his wife cried and whined bitterly.
> "If that's the way you feel, then give me a divorce. I'll find a real man to live with."
> And so, because of his deep affection for his wife, the man set out in the direction of Uchino, looking for an opportunity. Around sunset a woman with a young girl attendant passed him. There was no one in sight, so the man killed them both, stripped them of their clothes, and returned home.
> "Here it is! I got what you asked for." The man handed the blood-stained garments to his wife, telling her what he had done. He expected her to say something about its being a wretched business even though she had urged him to do it. Instead her face wrinkled with smiles, giving an appearance of utter delight.
> The man was repelled, and the love and affection which he had felt for her vanished. He immediately left the house, cut off his locks, and became a monk. Then he went up to Mount Kōya, where he earnestly prepared for the next life. Profoundly aware of his sin of senseless murder, he prayed for his victims' happiness in the next world.

> The anecdote goes on to tell how this monk met the monk who had been the victim's husband. That monk declares: "The woman was my beloved wife. After that day of bereavement I abandoned the world . . ."

when she cheerfully disengages the severed hand from the stolen gown. While it is credible that the man in *Sand and Pebbles* repents of his violent crime, it is harder to forgive that character in *Tales Told on Mount Kōya*. He did not resist his wife's wicked suggestion. And despicable though the wife may be, this reader is not inclined to forget that it was the husband who cruelly severed the young woman's hand in the first place. Even if his motivation—to provide for his children—should absolve him from guilt for the theft, surely he used excessive force in slicing off the young woman's hand to get that one robe, especially when he already had several other gowns in his grasp. These complaints are, of course, the result of a modern perspective; the issue for the medieval author was not justice or situational ethics, but the outcome of this deed—religious awakening, in light of which all else becomes irrelevant.

The fifth story, of unrequited love and humiliation as a poet, was perhaps intended merely to provide a change of pace, some mild comic relief, but its effect is to undermine the serious didactic thrust of the whole. Despite the earnestness with which this monk tells his tale, even the audience of venerable monks chortle rather than weep. There is, moreover, an illogical ironic distance between the story and the discourse of this tale. While the object of this narrator's description is himself as an ignorant peasant, he alludes in poetic cadence to the classics of aristocratic literature, *The Tale of Genji* and *The Tales of Ise*, and indulges in extensive and sophisticated punning. It is unlikely that this man, who had not the slightest poetic sensibility when he became a monk, has received an education in classical Japanese literature since arriving on Mount Kōya. It is preposterous that this lovelorn but base peasant uses the elegant discourse of the classics to tell his story. This device might have been effective had the narrator been someone refined, someone appropriately familiar with that discourse. A sympathetic account by such a narrator would have lent dignity to the poor peasant's sad experience. Perhaps the author was blinded to the unfortunate effects of this particular combination of narrator and discourse by the weight of convention—classical allusions were a rigid requirement when recounting a love affair. As written, however, the disparity between this peasant narrator's status and his aristocratic discourse is implausible and contributes not to the sense of pathos that has characterized the tales up to this point, but an element of comedy, which conflicts with the other tales and undermines their impact.

Overall, *Tales Told on Mount Kōya* shows mixed results as a didactic text. It begins strongly, but part way through the author seems to have lost interest in proselytizing. The fifth, comic story undermines the seriousness of the other tales, and the lack of any concluding interpretive commentary by the primary or secondary narrators is a lost opportunity to drive home the point made by the revelatory accounts. With the exception of the fourth tale, the individual stories are of minor interest. While a crisscrossing of certain themes gives the varied whole some coherence, there is no sense of any underlying organizational principle. *Tales Told on Mount Kōya* serves, however, a very useful function by providing the contrast that makes more obvious the strengths of the other revelatory tales.

The Three Monks

The Three Monks has the least obtrusive narrator of all the revelatory tales. Opening commentary sets the scene as the sacred precincts of Mount Kōya, just as in *Tales Told on Mount Kōya*, though more briefly. While the narrator identifies the monks only by physical description, this conveys their class backgrounds and the intense rigor with which they have pursued religious practices over the years. After each description of religious awakening, the narrator notes that the men were moved to tears. Thus, the narrator very efficiently endows his characters with religious authority and their stories with credibility.

Commentary by the characters within the tale is also relatively sparse. Their stance toward their individual tales is enunciated in the call to revelation: "Since recounting these experiences is said to nullify past errors . . ." The only significantly interpretive passage in the story is the conclusion in which the three men deliver *in unison* a short sermon on the nature of this world and the value of religious practice. They expound general lessons drawn from the tales just told and exhort the reader to faith and practice. They are ostensibly speaking to each other, but the tone and content of the passage is that of an author addressing his readers.

Another manifestation of didactic intent is the effect on Kasuya of Aragorō's tale. When Kasuya first learns that Aragorō is the man who murdered his wife, Kasuya is ready to kill him. After hearing Aragorō's story, however, he declares himself a friend of his former enemy and finds joy for the present in the misery of the past. Just as in the first account in *Tales Told on Mount Kōya*, here too the point is that if Kasuya can be redeemed by a story, so also can the reader.

The content of *The Three Monks*, surprisingly, does not directly serve the didactic purpose, at least not in the way that it does in other revelatory tales. The first example of religious awakening, Kasuya's story, is the unexpected, brutal murder of his wife. Other tales do not delve deeply into a character's emotional reaction to dreadful news, but merely recount that the character responded by renouncing the world. The reader in those cases assumes that the renunciation was the result of having recognized the truth of the Buddhist teachings on transience and suffering. In *The Three Monks*, however, Kasuya relates that he first felt angry with his wife, that he next blamed himself, and that finally he turned his rage against the unknown murderer. He was angry but powerless. It appears to have been frustration, not pain or sorrow, that motivated Kasuya to take religious vows. There being no evidence of any appreciation of religious doctrine, this seems an unproductive approach if the author's intent is really to proselytize.

Unlike the monk in *Tales Told on Mount Kōya* who only stole once when he was in dire need, Aragorō is a hardened criminal, an unlikely role model. He tells us that his wife's utter lack of pity led him to reflect upon Buddhist teachings. Perhaps Aragorō could not see his own cruelty until it was reflected in his wife. It is only in passing that he mentions the traditional message of revelatory tales, the transience of the things of this world and personal suffering. Instead he worries about the principle of retribution—he realizes that he has doomed himself to hell with his many crimes. His final remarks focus not on himself but on his wife and his victim. As he concludes his story, it seems that, vile as he himself is, it is indeed his *wife's* cruelty that was the major reason he regretted killing Lady Onoe. He remembers that it was at his wife's urging that he went out with murder on his mind that night. Had he perhaps exercised some discrimination in choosing his victims prior to that? He seems most offended at the fact that a beautiful, aristocratic, young lady was murdered on behalf of the wife he now sees as a vile and loathesome creature. If we weigh the last sentences of this passage most heavily, his story is seen as a case of witnessing evil rather than one of repenting evil. Even more so than in the version in *Tales Told on Mount Kōya*, it is hard, at least for this reader, to forgive Aragorō. A rather greater sense of personal remorse on his part would be appreciated.

It seems unlikely that readers would take Aragorō's account as personally relevant. It is conceivably inspirational, however, insofar as this religious awakening account is amazing rather than credible. Like Kasuya's miraculous spirit of collegiality with Aragorō, it reflects not mundane reality but the supernatural possibilities of the sacred. The tale is not a rational argument based on Buddhist truths. Instead it appeals on the level of faith.

Shinozaki's religious awakening is a simple case of professional disappointment. His implication that it was a long-standing intention, conveyed by his reference to taking an "opportunity to enter the way of Buddhism," is not borne out by his story. Shinozaki renounces the world because his lord ignores his advice. Could he have felt this as an emotional loss? He may have lost the respect and trust of his lord, but he does not say that this is the cause for his despair. Since he himself had counseled his lord to renounce the world as a political statement aimed at the emperor, we must interpret his renunciation similarly. It is a means of preserving his honor and self-respect. His integrity and pride as a samurai do not allow him to follow his lord in surrender. To renounce the world is, for Shinozaki, to resign in protest.

Shinozaki does not truly renounce lay life until six years later when he meets his children and leaves them again without revealing his identity. This part of his account forms the second half of the text of *The Three Monks*. Most scholars refer to this second half of *The Three Monks* as *gojitsudan*, "a tale of what happened afterward," almost as if it were a postscript. The understanding has been that while part one describes the pre-renunciation experience, part two describes post-renunciation experience.[1] Shinozaki's reunion with his children, however, is *not* typical of a monk's religious life. Most of the monks in revelatory tales go directly to Mount Kōya. Shinozaki's encounter with his children occurs because he has not yet broken with his past, he is still curious about his old home. Confronting his children provides Shinozaki the opportunity to undergo the religious awakening he had failed to experience when he first became a monk.

Seeing his children causes Shinozaki excruciating emotional pain. It is, however, pain of his own choosing. In fact, the two children constitute a possible *gain*, not a loss. In meeting his children he is given the chance to reestablish his parental bond in their time of greatest need, three days after their mother's death. Love and joy, the *positive* aspects of emotional attachments, are available to Shinozaki if he declares his identity. It is his decision whether to accept or reject that happiness. Unlike other characters in revelatory tales who react in the aftermath of some tragedy, Shinozaki faces a choice. It is not that the changeable ways of the world have taken his loved ones from him, but that he must decide whether or not to sacrifice his relationship with his children.

Shinozaki's account of this reunion is extremely redundant. His renunciation of the world is retold no less than five times—three of them by his daughter, who of course focuses on the disastrous effect it has had on her life. Four times he describes his urge to reveal his identity to his children and the agony of deciding to keep it concealed. In other revelatory tales redundancy is used to enhance the message that renunciation is a wise choice, one that brings relief from suffering. In this account redundancy is used to show the awesome difficulty of sacrificing familial ties. It also shows the sorrow and suffering it causes those left behind. This is not a simplistic sermon aimed at quickly

1. Nishizawa Masaji, "Chūsei shōsetsu kō ichi—*Sannin hōshi*," *Bunkyō ronsō* 10.1 (December 1974):26.

inspiring religious commitment, but a cold, hard, honest picture of the terrible demands of a religious life. It should discourage anyone whose interest in Buddhism is superficial. It constitutes fair warning to the serious seeker of religious truth that renunciation of the world is an enormously difficult struggle. Such an account is unique among revelatory tales and seems rather at odds with both the first two tales and with the monks' interpretive commentary that unreservedly urges religious commitment. The lessons the monks draw in their conclusion include transience, the principle of karmic cause and effect, and the meaninglessness of secular value judgments of goodness and wickedness in view of religious ends. These lessons are based on the two stories told by Kasuya and Aragorō. The monks essentially overlook any implications that might be found in the story of Shinozaki's encounter with his children. The didactic thrust of The Three Monks is divided, then, making it a more interesting, if less immediately persuasive, text.

While the first two stories are intimately interwoven, content analysis does not reveal anything that unites all three of the tales. That broad coherence was at least attempted, however, can be seen in the several superficial links revolving primarily around the characters' names. The monks' secular names incorporate the numbers four, five, and six: Kasuya Shirōzaemon (four), Aragorō (five), and Shinozaki Rokurōzaemon (six). The primary link, that the second character of each monk's clerical name forms part of the word shōchikubai (pine, bamboo, and plum), is made explicitly in the tale. Each character is also subtly associated with one of these plants. Kasuya prays regularly at the shrine of Kitano Tenjin, which is famous for its plum trees, the second element in Shinozaki's name. Aragorō is described as bony, which evokes the knobby joints of the bamboo plant, the second character in his own clerical name. Shinozaki mentions having studied at Matsushima (Pine Island) and finds his children mourning their mother under a pine tree, which is the second element in Kasuya's clerical name.[2] Rather than a direct one to one relationship between associations and names, the associations of pine and plum with the first and third monks is reversed in their clerical names. Another symmetrical feature is the political alliances of the characters.[3] In secular life the first and third monks were on opposite sides of the imperial schism; Kasuya served Ashikaga Takauji, the military mainstay of the northern court, while Shinozaki fought with the Kusunoki clan for the southern court. While

2. Sekine Kenji, "Sannin hōshi shiron," Ryūkyū daigaku hōgakubu kiyō (Kokubungaku ronshū) 26 (January 1982):67.

3. Nishizawa, "Chūsei shōsetsu kō ichi," 24.

these patterns seem to be mechanical devices without profound significance, they do constitute evidence that the author was quite concerned with the question of unity.

Continuity, limited though it may be, is achieved by means of the consistent concern with family relationships shown in all three tales. The most obvious binding tension in the tale is the fact that Kasuya and Aragorō form an antagonistic pair because Kasuya is an indirect victim of the crime perpetrated by Aragorō. At the same time, they are united by the fact that Aragorō comes to mourn the death of Kasuya's wife, Lady Onoe. However, they form a pair of opposites in one other way: Kasuya renounced the world because he lost the wife he loved, while Aragorō was motivated, at least in part, by hatred of his wife. Shinozaki, on the other hand, is nearly oblivious to his wife. He chooses to stop and pray for her salvation not out of affection but to provide her with religious benefit and to placate her angry spirit. It is his children whom he loves and pities. Indeed, he found it easier to risk his life for his lord in battle than to abandon his children. His act was a measure of the value of religious practice. It is not just a haven in times of distress, not merely a way to escape pain and suffering, but worth more than the joys of the secular world, worth making what was for Shinozaki the ultimate sacrifice.

The limited and superficial unity in the The Three Monks parallels its lack of a single, focused doctrinal message. Instead it issues a call to faith. This is the function of the miraculous prospect of a hardhearted murderer experiencing a religious awakening and of the victim's husband embracing the murderer as a colleague. This is also the function of the example of a religious awakening that is not caused by, but rather is the cause of, much suffering. This is daunting testimony that a religious life demands, and deserves, profound sacrifice. As a didactic text the impact of The Three Monks is equivocal. The conclusion presents a rational argument for religious practice, but the stories strain credulity, eschew logic, and instead appeal to a reader's faith. Thus, The Three Monks represents a new dimension of the revelatory tale genre.

The Seven Nuns

The Seven Nuns is the most overtly didactic of the four tales translated here. It has two judgmental narrators, nine characters who renounce the world, frequent and extensive evaluative commentary by characters, and it contains passages that amount to two lengthy sermons.

The first narrator is someone on pilgrimage to Zenkōji. His brief self-introduction is laden with religious metaphors: ". . . drunk on the wine of darkness, I watched blossoms swirling in confusion at the gust of an unseasonal wind in the vast sky of all existence." These familiar metaphors indicate that the pilgrim is on a quest for enlightenment: aware of being lost in illusion, and that all things are transient, he seeks to deepen his understanding of the principle of emptiness. Thus he undertakes a pilgrimage to Zenkōji. These remarks also serve to forewarn the reader that the tale to follow treats these issues.

To encourage the reader to believe these accounts, the pilgrim cites his source: "The innkeeper recounted the following tale." The innkeeper's introduction is minimal: "Something rare and wonderful happened here. I'd like to tell you about it. Some time ago . . ." For an innkeeper, telling stories is one aspect of the hospitality he offers his guests, but with one short phrase he has also indicated his positive evaluation of the tale he will tell. His status, moreover, is that of a local authority.

First the innkeeper explains how two nuns came to operate a bathhouse near Zenkōji in order to accumulate religious merit, and how one nun, seeking religious instruction, begged five visiting nuns for the stories of their religious awakenings, their revelatory tales. Thus, the stance of the narrators on each of the multiple levels is didactic: the telling and retelling of the seven accounts to follow are seen to be motivated by religious faith.

The structure of *The Seven Nuns* is subtle. The unifying principle is the fact that the tales comprise a list of concrete examples of four of the eight kinds of suffering[1]: parting from a loved one ("Shiragiku's

---

1. These are the latter four kinds of sufferings. The first four of the full eight are life, old age, illness, and death.

Story," "The Wife from the Western Part of the Capital," "Hanakazura's Story"), meeting with a hated one ("Lord Kikui's Wife"), unattained aims ("The Lord Miike Affair"), and intense suffering ("The Story of the Retired Emperor Kazan's Daughter"). Otherwise, however, the seven tales are unrelated; indeed, they present a wide range of variety. For example, although there are four instances of love triangles, each case differs from the others.

The text is also divided in half by two sermons, one presented by the fourth or middle nun and her husband, and one by the seventh and last nun. This division reflects a categorization of the events that triggered the nuns' religious awakenings and serves the didactic purpose of the text.

The first three revelatory experiences are the result of circumstances that are not malevolent. The behavior of the characters whose actions cause these three women to take the tonsure is blameless. On the contrary, it is more or less admirable.

The first tale is one of unusual irony. Shiragiku's lovers sympathize and defer to each other, leaving her without a patron. Toshiaki is touched by his elder rival's depth of feeling and sends Shiragiku back to him. Partly out of consideration for Toshiaki, who has been so noble as to relinquish Shiragiku, Akitada refuses to see her again. Shiragiku is left to renounce this world in which the two men's respect for each other outweighs any practical regard for her welfare. Her victimization is a kind of unintended by-product of the admirable behavior of her two lovers.

In the second story, "The Wife from the Western Part of the Capital," preparations for a celebration end in the accidental death of the child. It is wholly understandable that the man who caused the fatal accident is driven to commit suicide. Although the reader may judge as terribly unwise the decision to slaughter a crane, a propitious creature, for a celebratory meal, there is no hint in the text that the wife found fault with her husband for this. Her role in these events was merely that of an innocent bystander.

In "Hanakazura's Story" we meet Lord Okunoyama and his wife, who are a devoted couple. The husband is only doing his soldierly duty when he departs for the front in Kyushu. His death is untimely, but heroic; he dies in battle having been praised as a great warrior by his lord. Hanakazura had been well aware of the danger: "the life of a bowman facing battle is like that of a dewdrop." She too could only lament her husband's fate. There was no one to blame.

The fourth storyteller provides a respite from tragedy and is the transition between the two halves of the text. This nun never suffered any particular loss; her awareness of transience is grounded in scripture, not experience. She describes the debate with her husband, in the course of which she quotes scripture and saints and recites poetry. Her neglect of personal hygiene as a act of passive resistance and her handling of the discarded skull are startling, but these are acts she chooses. She is the instigator, not the victim.

The second half of *The Seven Nuns* is quite different. The tragic events depicted in the last three tales are all caused by contemptible behavior, particularly lust. Men prove fickle, and a rival is duplicitous.

Lord Kikui's wife, whose story is the fifth revelation, is happily in love when her husband takes a mistress. Her first impulse is to persecute her rival, but she soon decides to acquiesce. She reasons that her basic needs are still being met, that she is getting old, and that men are inevitably fickle. Her husband, however, is too flagrantly faithless, and jealousy gets the better of her. Lord Kikui's wife begins to show eerie signs of metamorphosis. Without the intervention of the itinerant monk who teaches her to meditate, she would have turned into a dragon. Tragedy is averted only because she saves herself from falling prey to the jealousy caused by her husband's infidelity.

The sixth tale is that of the bathhouse proprietress, who tells the story of Lord Miike's family. Having gone to the capital on business, Lord Miike fails to return. His crime is neglect, though he admits only to procrastination. The tragedy is caused by his mistress, who is threatened by the surprising appearance of Lord Miike's wife and son. She bribes a man to deliver a false message from Lord Miike denying the existence of both wife and child. When Lord Miike discovers that his wife has drowned herself in despair, he is moved to renounce the world, an act that serves to redeem him. All the blame, therefore, falls on the mistress and her accomplice, the innkeeper. The storyteller suffers because she sympathizes with Lady Miike, her employer.

The story of the seventh nun's religious awakening is preceded by her sermon on the true meaning of renunciation of worldly ties, the second such didactic presentation. Her revelatory experience is then recounted by an unidentified character, but it is the most dramatic of all. The daughter of a retired emperor, she ran away with an aristocratic youth. An innkeeper murdered the youth in order to make the princess his own. She stabbed the innkeeper to death to save herself from being raped by him. The innkeeper's lust led him to murder the youth, and it forced the princess to kill him in self-defense.

Clearly, *The Seven Nuns* distinguishes two possibilities: the three stories of the first half depict unfortunate circumstances causing grievous results, and the three stories of the second half present the tragic consequences of condemnable behavior. (The fourth story is transitional and therefore not counted here.) The emphasis, however, is on the lamentable results, not the deplorable causes. Lord Kikui's wife, for example, offers to tolerate her husband's infidelity: "there certainly have been plenty of other cases of this kind of thing. That's how men are." By ideal standards, Lord Kikui is guilty, but insofar as his wife is a practical realist, he is forgiven. In the sixth tale the mistress who pushed Lord Miike's wife to suicide and the man who colluded with her are forgiven by the saintlike son. He argues that forgiveness will benefit his mother's soul and that filial piety requires that he revere his stepmother, cruel though she was. The lustful innkeeper is depicted as the victim of the princess's beauty. Because his wife found the princess "entrancing," she encouraged him to take a look at her. Following that advice, he becomes "spellbound." It is implied that he was helpless to act other than as he did.

The behavior that seems shameful is, in fact, all motivated by love. Lord Kikui, Lord Miike, and the innkeeper love unwisely. Similarly, the women who became nuns can be said to be guilty of loving too much. By simultaneously making and de-emphasizing the distinction between fault and no-fault tragedy, The Seven Nuns highlights its religious lesson that worldly attachments, especially love, inevitably cause sorrow.

There is, however, another message in the seventh nun's story. Her sermon on the two kinds of revelations and the meaning of "worldly desires imply enlightenment" conveys a significantly different lesson than that presented in the revelation accounts. While the other nuns talk about emotional pain and suffering and renouncing bonds of affection, Kon Amida Butsu exemplifies one who has severed her attachments and found peace of mind in an itinerant life, drifting like a cloud. Her carefree attitude is interpreted as rudeness, but it is actually a reflection of the depth of her enlightenment. Her exposition, which represents a deeper level of religious understanding than that revealed by the first six nuns, is probably the primary message of the tale, but it is a lesson presented only once.

Several devices underline the moral of the seventh nun's story. The note of discord with which her participation begins is a dramatic change in the previously saccharine tenor of the discussion. She is not modest, mournful, or pious like the other nuns, but self-confident, cheerful, and insouciant. Her name signifies her religious authority: Kon Amida Butsu means "the present Amida Buddha," suggesting that she is a living Buddha or a manifestation of Amida Buddha. Kon Amida Butsu's refusal to participate in the sharing of self-revelatory stories sets her apart from the other nuns, highlighting her role in The Seven Nuns as a whole. She is also endowed with authority by virtue of her quotations from esoteric scripture, both Hīnayāna texts and Mahāyāna sutras, by virtue of her superior social status (she was an imperial princess), and because her religious awakening was the result of events far more dramatic than the others' experiences. She is the only one to have caused a scandal in having eloped, which in her case is no less than an offense against the emperor. While the other women lost their loved ones to war, suicide, or another woman, the seventh nun's lover was murdered. She alone suffered the violent assault of attempted rape. Only the seventh nun took the life of another. We can detect a logic here which predicts that the worse one's trials are, the more profound one's enlightenment will be. Clearly the concept "worldly desires imply enlightenment" is a more difficult lesson than that all things are transient and therefore life is full of suffering. It is a lesson entrusted to the character who is by far the most impressive of the seven. Endowed with this considerable authority, the seventh nun becomes a persuasive proselytizer.

As a whole, then, *The Seven Nuns* appears to have been carefully designed to fulfill a specifically didactic purpose. Individually, too, the seven stories are vignettes of surprising variety and considerable interest.

"Shiragiku" is ironic. We might expect men involved with a prostitute to be rather callous, but Shiragiku's problem is caused by profound sincerity. The second story is the simple account of a rather horrible accident. This nun is a practical and straightforward woman who tells her tale concisely. There is romantic flavor in the third tale of a rare, happy couple. The passionate Hanakazura tells her story melodramatically. The middle story provides a change of pace: "Unlike all the other stories, mine is not a tale of woe. It's just that I took a good look at the world." The soldier's wife shows equanimity and formidible tenacity. Her superior resolve is attested by her husband: "Though I have a man's body, I have less than your woman's heart." The story presents a battle of wills rather than a conventional, action-oriented plot. Fictional debates have often been used as the setting for doctrinal expositions, but this is a particularly engaging one. Starting off with the disadvantage of her inferior status as a woman and a wife, this woman has the greater will to win.

One delightful aspect of the fifth story, "Lord Kikui's Wife," is the irony in the presentation of the idea that the heroine is metamorphosing into a dragon: "Until then I had thought that this kind of thing happened to other people, in old tales . . ." Inasmuch as this, too, is a tale, the reader may interpret her condition as a psychosomatic disorder, symptomatic of the intensity of her jealousy, rather than as a supernatural phenomenon. There is also irony in the wandering ascetic's instructions on how to eliminate undesirables. He pretends to teach Lord Kikui's wife how to kill her rival, but he actually teaches her how to meditate, how to conquer her emotions, a fact of which she is naively unaware until the goal has been accomplished. Contemplation proves to be medication that cures both the symptom and the disease.

The sixth tale is distinguished by a long passage of *michiyuki bun*, or poetic travel itinerary. The quest to find Lord Miike takes his wife, her son, and her attendant all the way from Kyushu to the capital and then to Echigo, on the Japan Sea coast, a prodigious journey. The names of many of the places through which they pass are given in the poetic cadence of alternating phrases of seven and five syllables and with elaborate word play involving puns, allusions, and associations.

The seventh story is the coup de grace. Following the difficult lecture on the nature of abiding qualities versus transient phenomena, the weary reader is indulged with a rather spicy drama including both murder and attempted rape.

The Seven Nuns is profoundly didactic, but thanks to the discrete organization and the manipulation of the status and stance of the several narrators, there is interest in the achievement of that didactic effect. Because *The Seven Nuns* does not allow much latitude for the modern preference for novel interpretations, contemporary readers may be inclined to read this text as an historical artifact. It may well be, however, that the seven memorable stories and their well-wrought lessons prove timeless.

Bibliography

Andrews, Allan A. *The Teachings Essential for Rebirth: A Study of Genshin's Ōjōyōshū*. Tokyo: Sophia University, 1973.

Araki, James T. "*Otogi-zōshi and Nara-ehon*: A Field of Study in Flux." *Monumenta Nipponica* 36.1 (Spring 1981):1–20.

Arikawa Mikao. "Zangemono no keisei ni kansuru ichi kōsatsu." *Gunma daigaku kiyo: jinbun kagaku hen* 4 (1954):1–20.

Barnhart, C. L., ed. *American College Dictionary*. New York: Random House, 1969.

Brazell, Karen, trans. *The Confessions of Lady Nijō*. Garden City, New York: Anchor Press/Doubleday, 1973.

Brower, Robert H., and Earl Miner. *Japanese Court Poetry*. Stanford: Stanford University Press, 1961.

Childs, Margaret H. "*Chigo monogatari*: Love Stories or Buddhist Sermons?" *Monumenta Nipponica* 35.2 (Summer 1980):127–51.

———. "Religious Awakening Stories in Late Medieval Japan: The Dynamics of Didacticism." Ph.D. dissertation, University of Pennsylvania, 1983.

———. "*Kyōgen-kigo*: Love Stories as Buddhist Sermons." *Japanese Journal of Religious Studies* 12.1 (March 1985):91–104.

———. "The Influence of the Buddhist Practice of *Sange* on Literary Form: Revelatory Tales." *Japanese Journal of Religious Studies* 14.1 (March 1987):53–66.

———. "Didacticism in Medieval Short Stories: *Hatsuse monogatari* and *Akimichi*." *Monumenta Nipponica* 42.3 (Autumn 1987): 253–88.

deBary, Wm. Theodore. *The Buddhist Tradition in India, China and Japan*. New York: Random House, 1969.

de Visser, M. W. *Ancient Buddhism in Japan*. 2 vols. Leiden: E. J. Brill, 1935.

Dumoulin, Heinrich. *A History of Zen Buddhism*. Translated from German by Paul Peachey. New York: Random House, 1963.

———. "The Consciousness of Guilt and the Practice of Confession in Japanese Buddhism." In *Studies in Mysticism and Religion*, 117–29. Jerusalem: Magnes Press, Hebrew University, 1967.

Dusenbury, Mary. "*Kesa*: Robes of Japanese Priests." Lawrence, Kansas: Spencer Museum of Art, n.d.

Foard, James H. "In Search of a Lost Reformation: A Reconsideration of Kamakura Buddhism." *Japanese Journal of Religious Studies* 7.4 (December 1980):261–91.

Fowler, Alastair. *Kinds of Literature: An Introduction to the Theory of Genres and Modes.* Cambridge: Harvard University Press, 1982.

Fujii Ryū, ed. *Mikan otogi zōshishū to kenkyū.* 3 vols. *Mikan kokubun shiryō.* Toyohashi: Mikan Kokubun Shiryō Kankōkai, 1956.

Fujimoto Kōsaburō, ed. *Nihon shaji taikan.* 2 vols. Tokyo: Meicho Kankōkai, 1970.

Fujimura Saku, ed. *Nihon bungaku daijiten.* 8 vols. Tokyo: Shinchōsha, 1950.

Genshin. *Ōjōyōshū: Nihon jōdokyō no yoake.* 2 vols. Translated into modern Japanese by Ishida Mizumaro. Tokyo: Heibonsha, 1976.

Goodwin, Janet R. "Alms for Kasagi Temple." *Journal of Asian Studies* 46.4 (November 1987):827–41.

——. "Building Bridges and Saving Souls: The Fruits of Evangelism in Medieval Japan." *Monumenta Nipponica* 44.2 (Summer 1989):137–49.

Gorai Shigeru. *Kōya hijiri.* Tokyo: Kadokawa Shoten, 1975.

Hakeda, Yoshito S. *Kūkai, Major Works: Translated with an Account of His Life and a Study of His Thought.* New York: Columbia University Press, 1972.

Hall, John Whitney. "Terms and Concepts in Japanese Medieval History: An Inquiry into the Problems of Translations." *Journal of Japanese Studies* 9.1 (1983):1–32.

Hanawa Hokinoichi, comp. *Genmu monogatari.* In *Zoku gunsho ruijū* 18, 395–411. Tokyo: Zoku Gunsho Ruijū Kanseikai, 1958.

Hastings, James, ed. *Encyclopaedia of Religion and Ethics.* 12 vols. New York: Charles Scribner's Sons, 1951.

Hatano Takekuni. "Kōya hijiri to zange bungaku." *Mikkyō bunka* (January 1947):44–55.

Hayashi Masahiko. *Nihon no etoki.* Tokyo: Miyai Shoten, 1982.

Hayashi Masahiko, and Tokuda Kazuo, eds., *Etoki daihonshū.* Tokyo: Miyai Shoten, 1983.

Hori Ichirō. "On the Concept of *Hijiri* (Holy-man)." Parts 1, 2. *Numen* 5.2 (April 1958):128–60; 5.3 (September 1958):199–232.

——. *Folk Religion in Japan.* Chicago: University of Chicago Press, 1968.

Hurvitz, Leon, trans. *Scripture of the Lotus Blossom of the Fine Dharma.* New York: Columbia University Press, 1976.

Ichiko Teiji, ed. *Komachi no sōshi.* In *NKBT* 38 (*Otogi zōshi*), 86–101. Tokyo: Iwanami Shoten, 1965.

——, ed. *Sannin hōshi*. In *NKBT* 38 (*Otogi zōshi*), 434–59. Tokyo: Iwanami Shoten, 1965.

——. *Chūsei shōsetsu no kenkyū*. Tokyo: Tokyo Daigaku Shuppankai, 1978.

——. *Chūsei shōsetsu to sono shūhen*. Tokyo: Tokyo Daigaku Shuppankai, 1981.

Ihara Saikaku. *Five Women Who Loved Love*. Wm. Theodore de Bary, trans. Rutland, Vermont: Charles E. Tuttle, 1971.

——. *The Life of an Amorous Woman and Other Writings*. Ivan Morris, ed. and trans. Norfolk, Connecticut: New Directions Books, 1963.

Kageyama Haruki. *Hieizan to Kōyasan*. Tokyo: Kyōikusha, 1980.

Kamo no Chōmei. *Hōjōki: Hosshin shū. Shinchō Nihon koten shūsei*. Miki Sumito, ed. Tokyo: Shinchōsha, 1979.

Karaki Junzō. *Mujō*. Tokyo: Chikuma Shobō, 1965.

Katō Bunnō, Yoshiro Tamura, and Kōjirō Miyasaka, trans. *The Three-fold Lotus Sutra: Innumerable Meanings, The Lotus Flower of the Wonderful Law, and Meditation on the Bodhisattva Universal Vow*. New York: Weatherhill/Kosei, 1975.

Kavanagh, Frederick. "Twenty Representative Muromachi Period Prose Narratives: An Analytic Study." Ph.D. dissertation, University of Hawaii, 1985.

Keene, Donald, ed. *Anthology of Japanese Literature*. Rutland, Vermont: Charles E. Tuttle Company, 1963.

——, ed. *Twenty Plays of the Nō Theatre*. New York: Columbia University Press, 1970.

——, trans. *Essays in Idleness: The Tsurezuregusa of Kenkō*, by Yoshida Kenkō. New York: Columbia University Press, 1967.

Kelsey, Michael William. "Didactics in Art: The Literary Structure of *Konjaku Monogatari-shū*." Ph.D. dissertation, Indiana University, 1976.

Kinsei Bungaku Shoshi Kenkyū, ed. *Kinsei bungaku shiryō ruijū, Kanazō-shi hen* 10, 3–221. Tokyo: Benseisha, 1973.

Kishi Tokuzō. "Shichinin bikuni oboegaki—sono 'katari' to 'etoki' ni tsuite." *Kokugo kokubun* 28.4 (April 1959):42–52.

Kitagawa, Hiroshi, and Bruce T. Tsuchida, trans. *The Tale of the Heike*. 2 vols. Tokyo: University of Tokyo Press, 1977.

Kitagawa, J. M. "Three Types of Pilgrimage in Japan." In *Studies in Mysticism and Religion*, 155–64. Jerusalem: Magnes Press, Hebrew University, 1967.

Kokumin Tosho, ed. *Shichinin bikuni*. In *Kindai Nihon bungaku taikei* 1, 171–226. Tokyo: Kokumin Tosho, 1928.

Komatsu Shigemi, ed. *Gaki sōshi, Jigoku sōshi, Yamai no sōshi, Kusōshi emaki.* *Nihon emaki taisei* 7. Tokyo: Chūō Kōronsha, 1977.

Kubota Jun, ed. *Senzai waka shū.* Tokyo: Kazama Shobō, 1970.

LaFleur, William R. *Mirror for the Moon.* New York: New Directions Books, 1977.

————. *The Karma of Words: Buddhism and the Literary Arts in Medieval Japan.* Berkeley: University of California Press, 1983.

Lane, Richard. "The Beginnings of the Modern Japanese Novel: *Kanazōshi,* 1600–1682." *Harvard Journal of Asiatic Studies* 20.3–4 (1957):644–701.

Lanser, Susan Sniader. *The Narrative Act: Point of View in Prose Fiction.* Princeton: Princeton University Press, 1981.

Matsumoto Ryūshin, ed. *Otogi sōshishū.* *Shinchō Nihon koten shūsei.* Tokyo: Shinchōsha, 1980.

Matsunaga, Daigan, and Alicia Matsunaga. *The Buddhist Concept of Hell.* New York: Philosophical Library, Inc., 1972.

————. *The Foundation of Japanese Buddhism.* 2 vols. Los Angeles, 1974, 1976.

Matsushita Daisaburō, ed. *Kokka taikan.* 2 vols. Tokyo: Kadokawa Shoten, 1968.

McCullough, Helen Craig, trans. *Tales of Ise: Lyrical Episodes from Tenth-Century Japan.* Tokyo: University of Tokyo Press, 1968.

————, trans. *Kokinwakashū: The First Imperial Anthology of Japanese Poetry.* Stanford: Stanford University Press, 1985.

————, trans. *The Tale of the Heike.* Stanford: Stanford University Press, 1988.

Mezaki Tokue. *Hyōhaku.* Tokyo: Kadokawa Shoten, 1975.

————. *Shukke tonsei.* Tokyo: Chūō Kōronsha, 1976.

Miki Sumito, ed. *Hōjōki.* In *Shinchō Nihon koten shūsei.* Tokyo: Shinchōsha, 1979.

Minamoto Takakuni (supposed author). *Konjaku monogatarishū.* In *NKBT* 20–26. Yamada Yoshio, et al. eds. Tokyo: Iwanami Shoten, 1959–63.

Miner, Earl. *Japanese Poetic Diaries.* Berkeley: University of California Press, 1976.

————. *Japanese Linked Poetry: An account with translations of renga and haikai sequences.* Princeton: Princeton University Press, 1979.

Miner, Earl, Odagiri Hiroko, and Robert E. Morrell. *The Princeton Companion to Classical Japanese Literature.* Princeton: Princeton University Press, 1985.

Mochizuki Shinkō, ed. *Mochizuki Bukkyō daijiten.* 10 vols. Tokyo: Sekai Seiten Kankō Kyōkai, 1957–60.

Monier-Williams, Sir Monier. *A Sanskrit-English Dictionary*. Oxford: Clarendon Press, 1970.

Morrell, Robert E., trans. *Sand and Pebbles (Shasekishū): The Tales of Mujū Ichien, A Voice for Pluralism in Kamakura Buddhism*. Albany: State University of New York Press, 1985.

———. *Early Kamakura Buddhism: A Minority Report*. Berkeley: Asian Humanities Press, 1987.

Morris, Ivan. *The World of the Shining Prince: Court Life in Ancient Japan*. Harmondsworth, England: Peregrine Books, 1969.

———. *The Nobility of Failure*. New York: Holt, Rinehart, and Winston, 1975.

Mulhern, Chieko. "*Otogi-zōshi*: Short Stories of the Muromachi Period." *Monumenta Nipponica* 29.2 (Summer 1974):181–98.

Murasaki Shikibu. *Genji monogatari*. Ikeda Kikan, ed. *Nihon koten zensho*. 7 vols. Tokyo: Asahi Shinbunsha, 1969.

Muroki Yatarō, ed. *Karukaya*. In *Sekkyōshū*. *Shinchō Nihon koten shūsei*. Tokyo: Shinchōsha, 1977.

Nakamura Hajime, ed. *Bukkyōgo daijiten*. Tokyo: Tokyo Shoseki, 1981.

Nara Ehon Kokusai Kenkyū Kaigi, ed. *Otogi zōshi no sekai*. Tokyo: Sanseidō, 1982.

Nihon Daijiten Kankōkai, ed. *Nihon kokugo daijiten*. 20 vols. Tokyo: Shōgakukan, 1972–76.

Nihon koten bungaku taikei. 100 vols. Tokyo: Iwanami Shoten, 1958–68.

Nihon Rekishi Daijiten Henshū Iinkai, ed. *Nihon rekishi daijiten*. 10 vols. Tokyo: Kawade Shobō, 1974.

Nishizawa Masaji. "*Genmu monogatari to Sangoku denki to no kankei*." *Kokubungaku: Kaishaku to kyōzai no kenkyū* 15 (December 1970):218–21.

———. "*Chūsei shōsetsu kō ichi—Sannin hōshi*." *Bunkyō ronsō* 10.1 (December 1974):17–36.

———. *Meihen otogizōshi*. Tokyo: Kasama Shoin, 1978.

———. *Chūsei shōsetsu no sekai*. Tokyo: Miyai Shoten, 1982.

Okada Keisuke. "Hiren tonsei monogatari no kōsō to tokushitsu." *Teikyō kokubun* (June 1970):24–28.

Pigeot, Jacqueline. *Michiyuki-bun: poetique de l'itineraire dans la litterature du Japon ancien*. Paris: Editions G.P. Maisonneuve et Larose, 1982.

Plutschow, Herbert Eugen. "Is Poetry a Sin? *Honji suijaku* and Buddhism versus Poetry." *Oriens Extremus* 25.2 (1978):206–18.

Putzar, Edward. "*Sarugenji sōshi* ('The Tale of Monkey Genji')." *Monumenta Nipponica* 18 (1963):297–312.

Reischauer, A. K. "Genshin's Ojo Yoshu: Collected Essays on Birth into

Paradise." *The Transactions of the Asiatic Society of Japan*, second series, 7 (1930):16–97.

Rodd, Laurel Rasplica, and Mary Catherine Henkenius, trans. *Kokinshū: A Collection of Poems Ancient and Modern*. Princeton, Princeton University Press, 1984.

Ruch, Barbara. "The Story of *Yokobue*: A Study of the Muromachi Period *Otogi zōshi*." Master's thesis, University of Pennsylvania, 1960.

——. "'*Otogi bunko*' and Short Stories of the Muromachi Period." Ph.D. dissertation, Columbia University, 1965.

——. "Medieval Jongleurs and the Making of a National Literature." In *Japan in the Muromachi Age*, 279–309. John Whitney Hall and Toyoda Takeshi, eds. Berkeley: University of California Press, 1977.

——. "Bijutsu—bunjutsu—majutsu." In *Zaigai Nara ehon*, 3–10. Nara Ehon Kokusai Kenkyū Kaigi, ed. Tokyo: Kadokawa Shoten, 1981.

Sakaguchi Genshō. "Kyōgen-kigo no bungaku kan." *Kokugo to kokubungaku* 8 (May 1931):57–73.

Sakakura Atsuyoshi, ed. *Yamato monogatari*. In NKBT 9, 229–366. Tokyo: Iwanami Shoten, 1957.

Sakakura Atsuyoshi et al., eds. *Ise monogatari*. In NKBT 9, 109–87. Tokyo: Iwanami Shoten, 1957.

Sanford, James H. *Zen-man Ikkyū*. Chico, California: Scholars Press, 1981.

Sasaki Nobutsuna, ed. *Shinkokin waka shū*. NKBT 28. Tokyo: Iwanami Shoten, 1969.

Seidensticker, Edward G., trans. *The Tale of Genji* by Murasaki Shikibu. New York: Alfred A. Knopf, 1978.

Sekine Kenji. "Ichidai ki—zange—monogatari." *Kokubungaku: Kaishaku to kanshō*, special edition, *Monogatari bungaku* 39.1 (January 1974):51–56.

——. "*Sannin hōshi*." *Kokubungaku: kaishaku to kanshō* 46.11 (November 1981):86–87.

——. "*Sannin hōshi* shiron." *Ryūkyū daigaku hōgakubu kiyō* (*Kokubungaku ronshū*) 26 (January 1982):55–67.

Sidney, Sir Philip. *An Apology for Poetry or The Defense of Poesy*. Geoffrey Shepherd, ed. London: Thomas Nelson and Sons, Ltd., 1965.

Skord, Virginia. "The Comic Consciousness in Medieval Japanese Narrative: *Otogi-zōshi* of Commoners." Ph.D. dissertation, Cornell University, 1987.

————. "*Monogusa Tarō*: From Rags to Riches and Beyond." *Monumenta Nipponica* 44.2 (Summer 1989):171–98.

Smith, Barbara Herrnstein. *On the Margins of Discourse: The Relation of Literature to Language*. Chicago: The University of Chicago Press, 1978.

Statler, Oliver. *Japanese Pilgrimage*. New York: William Morrow and Company, Inc. 1983.

Stevens, Chigusa. "*Hachikazuki*: A Muromachi Short Story." *Monumenta Nipponica* 32.3 (Fall 1977):303–31.

Suleiman, Susan Rubin. "Redundancy and the 'Readable' Text." *Poetics Today* 1.3 (1980):119–42.

Suzuki Tōzō, ed. *Koji kotowaza jiten*. Tokyo: Tōkyōdō Shuppan, 1956.

Takagi Ichinosuke et al., eds. *Heike monogatari*. In *NKBT* 32–33. Tokyo: Iwanami Shoten, 1959–60.

Takahashi Kōji. "Hōnen ni okeru zange to metsuzai—toku ni sono rinrisei o motomete." In *Hōnen shōnin kenkyū*, 185–205. Bukkyō Daigaku Hōnen Shōnin Kenkyūkai, ed. Tokyo: Ryūmonkan, 1975.

Takakusu Junjirō et al., eds. *Taishō shinshū daizōkyō*. 100 vols. Tokyo: Taishō Issaikyō Kankōkai, 1924–32.

Tanaka Hiroshi. "*Sannin hōshi* ni tsuite." *Bungaku kenkyū* 39 (July 1974):40–50.

Tashio Minoru, ed. *Tsurezuregusa*. In *NKBT* 30, 81–290. Tokyo: Iwanami Shoten, 1957.

Tsunoda, Ryusaku, et al., comps. *Sources of Japanese Tradition*. 2 vols. New York: Columbia University Press, 1958.

Ury, Marian, trans. *Tales of Times Now Past: Sixty-two Stories from a Medieval Japanese Collection*. Berkeley: University of California Press, 1979.

Varley, H. Paul. *Imperial Restoration in Medieval Japan*. New York: Columbia University Press, 1971.

Watanabe Tsunaya, ed. *Shasekishū*. *NKBT* 85. Tokyo: Iwanami Shoten, 1966.

Yamaguchi Yasushi. "Zange ni tsuite." *Bukkyōgaku seminā* 9 (May 1969): 1–14.

Yanai Shigeshi. "Kyōgen-kigo kan ni tsuite." *Kokugo to kokubungaku* 39 (April 1962):23–34.

Yokoyama Shigeru and Matsumoto Ryūshin, eds. *Muromachi jidai monogatari taisei*. 14 vols. Tokyo: Kadokawa Shoten, 1973–87.

Index

ABOUT THE AUTHOR

Margaret Helen Childs is Associate Professor of Japanese Language and Literature and Chair of the Department of East Asian Languages and Cultures at the University of Kansas, Lawrence, Kansas. Her research interest is medieval Japanese narrative literature, especially popular Buddhist didactic tales and homoerotic stories.